Praise for *Spinning Tea Cups*

"While the uncovering of a magician's trick often drains it of power, the revelations in Alexandra Teague's essays only increase the potency of their magic. *Spinning Tea Cups* is fantastic in both senses of the word. It is smart and compelling and gorgeously written. It also balances credulity in the other-worldly with clear-eyed reassessment of what's usually called 'the facts,' creating a complex, deeply human portrait of self and family."
—KATE LEBO, author of *The Book of Difficult Fruit*

"This memoir-in-essays recounts growing up in a family of 'feral Victorians' in the eccentric occult town of Eureka Springs, Arkansas. With essayistic ruminations on matters of faith, kitsch, mental health, gun violence, and memory, *Spinning Tea Cups* has all the page-turning pleasures of an engaging story, along with insight, wisdom, and exquisite prose."
—KATHRYN NUERNBERGER, author of *The Witch of Eye*

"Part *Portrait of the Artist*, part picaresque, Alexandra Teague's *Spinning Tea Cups* is a brilliant ride through the landscapes of an artist, starting with the author's unforgettable mother—a woman psychic, artistic, mercurial, maternal. Like one of the Disney rides that anchor the book, family, lovers, and grief pop in and out in a rollick that magically turns kitsch into wonder." —SUSANNE PAOLA ANTONETTA, author of *The Terrible Unlikelihood of Our Being Here*

"Alexandra Teague's *Spinning Tea Cups* narrates an extraordinary family's struggles with the realities and unrealities of mental illness. Is she the child of psychics who can see ghosts, spells, spirits, and foreknowledge as clear as a fire at night? Or is she collateral damage of people too lost in their own magical thinking to see her needs? Erudite, intellectual, literary, these essays explore puns, ghosts, tourism, but always at their heart is Teague's own relationship to her family, and by extension, to her understanding of self, a young woman moving through the definitions others have for her to take control of her own destiny."
—CRIS HARRIS, author of *I Have Not Loved You With My Whole Heart*

Spinning
Tea Cups

A Mythical
American
Memoir

Alexandra Teague

Oregon State University Press   Corvallis

Oregon State University Press in Corvallis, Oregon, is located within the traditional homelands of the Mary's River or Ampinefu Band of Kalapuya. Following the Willamette Valley Treaty of 1855, Kalapuya people were forcibly removed to reservations in Western Oregon. Today, living descendants of these people are a part of the Confederated Tribes of Grand Ronde Community of Oregon (grandronde.org) and the Confederated Tribes of the Siletz Indians (ctsi.nsn.us).

Cataloging-in-publication data is available from the Library of Congress

ISBN 978-0-87071-255-5 paperback; ISBN 978-0-87071-256-2 ebook

∞ This paper meets the requirements of ANSI/NISO Z39.48-1992 (Permanence of Paper).

First published in 2023 by Oregon State University Press
Printed in the United States of America

Oregon State University
OSU Press

Oregon State University Press
121 The Valley Library
Corvallis OR 97331-4501
541-737-3166 • fax 541-737-3170
www.osupress.oregonstate.edu

for my family, living and dead, with deep love,
and particularly for Nathan and Gabriel

"Truth is shrill as a fife, various as a panharmonicon."
RALPH WALDO EMERSON

Contents

Tea Cups

"It's a poor sort of memory that only works backwards."
LEWIS CARROLL, *Through the Looking Glass*

Sometimes, my mother saw visions. From across a living room while visiting friends in her twenties, my mother saw the woman poisoning her husband.

Overtly, the man had had a stroke. They were elderly; his wife was caring for him—trundling soup and water and pills from the kitchen. But my mother saw the real story, the way decades later, in those 1980s vision games, Single Image Random Dot Stereograms (SIRDS), you could attune your eyes to see the dots on the page as a 3D scene by staring down the bridge of your nose.

I could never see anything but a page of dots, though for a while, in high school, I used to try. "A lion!" my mother or my boyfriend would exclaim, or "What an amazing Tower of Babel," squint-crossing their eyes as I glared at the page that refused to reveal its other dimensions, as my childhood armoire had also refused to open to Narnia no matter how long I crouched by my skirts.

But seeing other people's motives or seeing the future wasn't just some magical dimension of sight for my mother. It was, she felt, heavy moral responsibility. It was, like so many things in her life, a burden, a martyrdom.

Like the Greek prophet Cassandra, cursed with true prophecies no one will believe, my mother felt alienated by her own knowledge. But unlike Cassandra, she often didn't trust herself enough to speak her visions. She had no curse or backing from the gods. She wasn't a king's daughter; she was, for years, a 1950s American housewife and high school dropout, a mother.

After she had read bedtime stories to her two young daughters (who, two decades later, when she remarried and I was born, would become my half sisters), cleaned the kitchen, and ironed her husband's work shirts, my mother lay awake worrying. She could see that man so clearly: the slack gape of his mouth as his wife spooned in soup, the poison circulating through his body.

Her knowledge had that too stark, slightly uncanny clarity of a nighttime street revealed by Southern sheet lightning. A flash so intense and sky-encompassing, there is no single point of illumination: just sepia daylight, then, as quickly, night again. How could she show that to anyone?

If she alone was charged with this knowledge, she had to go to the police. She had to tell her husband or a family friend. She had to say she had seen that old man trying to cry for help, saying, "She's killing me," while his mouth also, in concurrent physical reality, wordlessly crumbled bits of oyster crackers. She had to explain she saw these at once. But how? What could she point to? Not tarot cards on a coffee table. Not a china cup with tea leaves in the bottom, leaves everyone at least could agree existed there, to be scooped into the trash or read for fortunes.

Though, in my lifetime, my mother was the center of any conversation—the raconteur with a lengthy story for every occasion—she always described herself as an outsider. In the raucous Siggins family, with maternal aunts who danced a conga line through frozen New York streets to stave off loneliness, fear, and boredom with their husbands shipped off to World War II, my mother was the quiet, shy child, the observer, the one who would later tell these stories, tinged with awe and longing: if only instead of observing the fun, she could unselfconsciously enter it. And when her father died in World War II when she was ten, and the family was exiled, she felt, from New York to Arizona, she became yet a further observer, at a remove from the sandblasted, surreal reality of the desert.

"Had I been blessed with even limited access to my own mind there would have been no reason to write," Joan Didion wrote, and it seemed that if my mother had been blessed with even limited access to what she experienced, she would not have had to describe it again and again so vividly. Naturally self-conscious in social situations, she wanted nothing more than to be alone, or at least she always said so, even as she struck up conversations with strangers in line for movies and restaurants, sometimes even inviting them for dinner. Even as, finally out of her loveless marriage to my sisters' father, she did not live alone, but, after a series of intense relationships, married my father. Still, she used to say her dream job was long-distance truck driving: listening to Vivaldi and Rachmaninoff as she drove alone across the country, then reading in the cab's narrow bunk.

But being psychic wasn't being alone. It was isolation with invisible strings. If others didn't share her visions, yet her visions tied her to them intimately and morally, she was trapped in isolation within isolation, like the cube she taught me to draw as a child: diagonal lines making two simple squares into an apparently 3D object.

The man whose death she foresaw did die soon after, but his wife was never accused of poisoning. There was no autopsy. Until years later, my mother never told anyone what she had seen, nor about her deep, unfading guilt that she had not somehow saved him. She told no other stories about this couple. I don't know how she knew them, nor whether she went to the funeral. Presumably, immobilized by horror and disempowerment at what she'd seen and unable to figure out how to speak, she cut all ties. They exist only in that story: a lightning flash that taught me it is a terrible burden to see the world as it really is, and that how the world really is is not what most of us see.

Growing up with my mother's words that told me everyday things like, "Lift this lever on the water dispenser, and hold your cup steady" and visionary things like, "Once, an old woman's ghost was sitting on a porch swing in my sewing room," I didn't doubt her. If we usually saw the same things, and she was the one teaching me how to see the world, how could I?

And besides, why would she spend more than twenty years feeling guilty about that man's death if she did not deeply believe the truth of her vision? Wasn't her suffering its own proof?

And didn't she have other proof too?

Back in the 1950s, shortly after moving into the house in Fort Worth where I was eventually raised, my mother started working as a seamstress. Her husband was out of work on strike, and they lived near the Stockyards with its rodeo riders who needed costumes. My mother set up a small room at the front as a sewing room; she cut out gold netting, rickrack, satin for shirts and vests.

One morning, when she walked into the room, a porch swing was hanging from metal chains beside her pattern-cutting table. A woman, facing away from my mother, was rocking in it. From her slightly stooped shoulders and pinned white hair, she seemed elderly, maybe frail. She was so fully there that for a second, my mother didn't even think this was odd. And then she realized, and the woman and swing vanished.

Although she had never seen a ghost before, my mother had no doubt the woman had been there, and for some reason, she wasn't scared to say so. When she told the previous owner of the house, Irene answered, a little surprised, but also confident: "Oh, you saw my mother! That room used to be part of the porch before we closed it in, and there was a swing she loved to sit in."

My mother told this story so many times that I know Irene Root's name, though I never met her. I have what feels like my own memory of Irene's mother swinging. I also have a deep imprint of what this story made clear. My mother could see through both time and space.

Decades before I heard of Michel Foucault or a panopticon, or even the Greek giant Argus Panoptes with his hundred all-seeing eyes, I was aware of myself in, at least potentially, "a state of constant and permanent visibility." A visibility beyond visibility, toward which I could at best only squint. Toward which, if I hoped to avoid my mother's, and perhaps others', judgments, I must squint harder.

Unlike my friends, I never once snuck out at night; I seldom lied about where I was. If I did something wrong, I often preemptively confessed—convinced my mother already knew whatever I'd done or might do. And just like when I told her about a boy I liked or a fear I had, she'd always answer with, "I'm not surprised" or "I suspected as much." Of course she did: she had already seen all the dots of my life in their 3D truth. I was living a life that should have been newly mine, and yet existed before me.

As a teenager, of course, I did sometimes lie. I smoked cigarettes behind Basin Park with my friend Leslie, then claimed it had been smoky in the bar-restaurant where we were rehearsing for a play (this backfired: my mother pulled me from the play). I pretended to be studying with my boyfriend when we were really having sex, though I sobbed so loudly over a pregnancy scare that my mother guessed. I tried to deny it, but then confessed. "I suspected as much," she said.

If prophecy is "foreknowledge of future events, though it may sometimes apply to past events of which there is no memory, and to present hidden things which cannot be known by the light of reason," it is a vision that can go in all directions—looking back beyond our memory, looking forward, penetrating deeper into now. According to *The Catholic Encyclopedia* that offers this definition, it is a vision given by God. But for my mother, who had stopped believing in God after her father's death, it was a vision both somehow mystical and unsourceable. Her visions weren't planned or gifted by a benevolent deity; they were closer to Greek tragedy—in which prophecy can lead to punishment as much as safety, in which the path is strewn with dangers, in which too much sight is often the same as blindness. Think Oedipus. Or a burning house.

The summer I was ten, my father, who was a feature and travel journalist for the *Fort Worth Star-Telegram,* was assigned to visit historic sites related to the Texas Sesquicentennial (which, given Texas's obsessive state pride, was the subject of countless stories). Since this was 1985, decades before cell phones, we were out of touch with everyone for weeks as we checked into and out of sometimes flea-ridden small-town motels and drove scorching hours in our unairconditioned Oldsmobile to ruined forts, where my mother, as photographer, framed clouds and tall, dry grass through crumbling stone walls.

On August 8, we pulled into New Braunfels—a historic inn that my father was also writing about: a rare fixed mark on our itinerary. I remember the lobby's oriental carpet and large porcelain vases. A row of wooden cubbyholes holding room keys. With our key was a note: *Raymond, Jane says to call her immediately.*

My father dialed his editor on the rotary phone as my mother and I waited by the front desk. We were sweaty from the road, ready for baths in what would hopefully be a clawfoot tub like at home where I'd grown up taking bubble baths before climbing into the four-poster bed with a lace canopy my parents had built for me so I could be like the girls in old-fashioned storybooks.

But we never took that bath, and we never took another bath in our own clawfoot tub.

I don't remember what my father said, but I know that when he set down the phone and my mother called my sister, I began walking circles around the coffee table on that oriental rug. It was burgundy. Around me, even the dust motes seemed to have been polished. It was sickening: the carpet, the smell of lemony oil, being in that room, the dizziness of my circling, but I couldn't stop. If I stopped, I would stop existing. Or if I stopped, it would be true: our house would have burned to the ground.

That first time I experienced true, deep shock, I felt what I now know is disassociation after a line is crossed between the world as you know it and must come to know it. It was not possible. Not my bedroom's maple floor with its ink stain; not the stairs where I'd stretched my metal slinky; not my mother's sewing room where I'd played as her machine whirred; not my dolls, my stuffed animals, my twister-bead necklaces, my plastic seagull from Galveston that screeched believably when I pressed its soft rubber stomach. None of them could be gone any more than the entire city called Fort Worth, the entire state of Texas with its famous outline, which I had learned to draw in school.

During the interminable eight-hour drive back, we could not stop enumerating. All my Outdoor Girls books. The turquoise ring from the Arizona roadside stand. My father's childhood Mickey Mouse Club hat. The wood and velvet miniature high heel made by a Sing Sing prisoner and gifted to my mother's uncle, a guard. The Mother Goose china cup that had been my grandfather's as a child. The blue silk ribbons on my canopy bed posts. The wallpaper my mother had hung during her thirty years in the house: room by room, meticulously, by first nailing muslin to the old wooden shiplap walls.

I can't imagine how my father could drive through that rainstorm of everything we'd lost. Each item remembered into being only momentarily until, with a knifing, stomach-dropping pain, we remembered why we were remembering.

At some point in the never-ending drive, my mother told us something that made the fire more impossible and more real: "I saw months ago that the house was going to burn, but I didn't have a way to stop it." As my father and I sat in the sticky vinyl heat in our too-new-to-bandage grief, my mother had already grieved before us. For months, she had already seen this moment, or one like it. She had read the tea leaves of this future again and again in her mind in secret.

She had known as we packed the car, as we loaded the ice chest with wax-papered lentil burgers, as we closed every house window, sealing in the heat that would—when we opened the door (though she knew we would never open the door)—feel as suffocating as sticking our faces into pillows. She had grieved as she picked up the lantern-shaped tea pot, as she walked through the library, ceiling-high with books she'd accumulated from three decades of library sales and book-of-the-month clubs. She had looked for the last time at each of her paintings: the Apache scout on the cliff, the tall blue cathedral, the vase of daisies.

She had imagined packing away the paintings, hiding them in the garage or in our car. She had wanted to tell us so that we could suffer with her. She had wanted to do anything to stop the fire. But how could she? To whom can you report the future burning of a house?

"I was so scared the insurance company would think we'd set it if I removed any keepsakes," she told us that day, and for decades after. "It was so painful to know and not be able to tell you."

"The prophetic knowledge that for some might be a blessing only serves to enhance the pain of her existence," literary critic Seth Schein writes of Cassandra. Or, as Schein says, quoting Herodotus, "the most painful thing for mortals is 'to take thought for many things but to have power over nothing.'"

And now the future tense of my mother's premonition had been seared into past tense. Back down the corridor of time ricocheted the fact that her knowledge *could not* save us and *had not* saved us.

The fire had started two nights before on our back porch, and by the time neighbors saw, flames had spread to all thirteen rooms. According to the front-page story the *Star-Telegram* had published, it was a five-alarm fire. In the photo, firefighters are battling what looks like a heaving, flaming, smoking sky. Although they fought for hours, in the end, *2309 Market Avenue burned to the ground.*

It is one of two clippings I have about the house. The other— *October 23, 1974, Mr. and Mrs. Raymond Teague welcomed their first child, a daughter, to 2309 Market Avenue*—is my birth announcement. In 1970s style, the house is named as if I belong to it, as I would grow up feeling I did.

Finally, we pulled up in front of it—black and caution-taped, the front door boarded over. We had to climb in a window. We entered a space the size and location of our living room, but as unrecognizable as the surface of a detonated moon.

The once-red carpet was black and brittlely crisp underfoot, but also squishy, sodden from firehoses. The couch and coffee table had been charred into gnawed-looking spindles and strangely still-stuffed, black protrusions of cushions. On the floor, my stuffed Odie (Garfield's dumb dog friend) sat like an upright shadow with ash-glazed plastic eyes. And everywhere: the smell of ash condensed, ground down, aromatic as a spice stripped of all sweetness. A smell that, three decades later, from burned houses or extinguished camp-fires, still makes me sick. Like astronauts, or miners, we walked forward toward the impossible, toward our hall.

The beginning of the stairs, we discovered, were not gone. We could walk a few steps up, but where the stairs should have continued to our bedrooms and library and bathroom, there was a cliff. Air. On our melted kitchen linoleum below, between the sink and what had been the table, was our clawfoot tub, on its side like a shipwreck.

Or that's how I remember it. After that one day, my parents didn't let me go back. They left me at my older sister's house as they sifted rubble for dishes and the few photo albums that had survived, smoke-damaged, but somehow swerved-around by flames. Anne's house was supposed to be safer and less traumatic, though for hours each day I stood at her kitchen sink in the summer heat, obsessed with scouring our hexagonal Christmas dishes with steel wool. The ash had bonded solid black over every inch of china, so only after hours of scrubbing would a bit of the white, a branch of the Christmas tree pattern, the curl of one of the presents, begin to emerge.

My parents hadn't asked me to do this; it was my own obsession, my way of fighting against the fire. But of course, my soap-chafed hands and that acrid and unmistakable smell of ash proved over and over that the house was gone. At best, I could scrub back to my memories.

Because I have never seen visions beyond small premonitions, I cannot fully imagine what it felt like for my mother to sift through the ashes of a fire she had seen coming. And I can't imagine how it felt for her to not want these powers, and yet have them. Like the witch who doesn't mean to start tornadoes when she sweeps her kitchen with her magic broom, or the medieval French monk Émilion, who fled town to town trying to escape the fame from each of his miracles, and eventually hid in a cave in Bordeaux (only to have a cathedral built beside the cave in his honor), my mother was ostensibly on the run from her powers.

But what none of us ever said in my childhood, and I haven't fully articulated until now, was how much more powerful this made her. How could we doubt her if she didn't even want her powers? How could we blame her for not saving us when *she* was the victim—the one plagued with the memory that worked forward and backward?

If she was boxed within boxes of knowing too much, my sisters and nephews and father and I were triply or quadruply boxed in. We didn't know our own futures. We had to rely on her to tell us, though of course what she told us would not usually save us.

Years later, my nephew Nathan said it felt as if she "controlled the weather" in our family. When he first said this, I thought he meant she was moody, which she wasn't really. Sometimes strongly emotional and reactive, but not mercurial. But what I think he meant was something more like *mood setting*. She controlled the fogs and lightning storms and flames through which we saw the world, and it was easy to forget to check our own perceptions.

Is it lightning? Don't bother looking outside. Sylvia will tell you.

Are you heartbroken? Sylvia (or Nana or Mama or Mom) knew you were going to be.

Did you just find out you've lost everything you know? Yes, but even that shock existed invisibly before you ever felt it.

In one sense, my mother came by her powers naturally. Her mother had sometimes also seen ghosts. Decades after my grandfather died in World War II, my grandmother woke in Arizona to find him standing at the foot of her bed. The most striking thing, she said, was that he didn't look like she remembered. Instead, he looked as he actually had—as she had forgotten, and therefore could not have invented.

Years after, while visiting us in Fort Worth, my grandmother woke to the sound of someone playing the grand piano. When she went downstairs, she clearly saw a girl with long black braids who sat on the piano bench, then vanished.

My aunt Diane, my mother's youngest sister, was also psychic, as was her son Dustin, who died suddenly of an undiagnosed heart condition as a teenager. When the bills for his coffin and funeral arrived, they added up, to the penny, to the money in his savings account. Diane and my mother didn't doubt that Dustin, who had always been a planner, had foreseen his own death.

But while my mother wasn't truly alone in having visions, she was the only one in our immediate family—my father and sisters and nephews—with these powers. And she was the one who told us Diane's and my grandmother's stories and told and retold her own. The family matriarch, thirteen years older than my father, extraordinarily well-read despite once being a high school dropout, the only one of us with an advanced degree, a brilliant storyteller, my mother was the one who stood at the center of this Tesla coil of family electricity arcing between minds, unsettled and burned by its brilliance.

In some versions of Cassandra's story, she has twin sons who are killed before she can raise them. She is a prophet without a family, a country. But my mother had a family. And as her stories also reminded us, she alone had suffered us into being, and then seen us as we were.

In one of these stories, it was 1953, a month before she turned eighteen, and she was in labor with her first child in the hallway of an overcrowded Fort Worth hospital. She was alone, terrified—in 1950s style, her husband working. Eventually, the nurses drugged her into a twilight sleep. When she groggily woke, a nurse said, "I'll bring you your beautiful baby boy."

But when my mother saw the baby, she knew, she just *knew*: "That is not my child."

"Of course it is," the nurse said. But my mother insisted, "I know my own child, and that is *not* my child." Of course, until that moment, she had never before had a child to know, but even then, she must have been good at saying things as if they were "the gospel truth"—a great Southern expression that implicitly links truths to the divine and unverifiable but also unassailable, and which my father will use to describe her years later.

Finally the nurse huffed away and a few minutes later returned—Did she apologize? Did she explain?—carrying my mother's beautiful baby daughter, Elizabeth Rose. Or as I've always known her, my oldest half sister, Beth, who is clearly in looks and manners our mother's daughter.

This story says: your very existence in our family is predicated on my *seeing* you as others fail to. The story says: not all sight is equally powerful.

Although I have never had more than mortal vision, I have been fortunate, until very recently, to be the only member of my family who doesn't wear glasses. And when I finally went to an optometrist, I was shocked when she said some people don't want to see clearly: "One of my patients likes the blurriness," she told me. "She says it's like living in a Monet painting." Raised to love visual art, by a mother who had worked as a framer for a painter in exchange for paintings, I found this poetic and beautiful, and also utterly terrifying.

I have spent my life believing it should be my goal, everyone's goal, to see as clearly as possible with both our eyes and our minds: to try to know what's *really there.*

Though I have also spent my life believing that seeing what's really there might not save me. And of course I'm not sure if I know what I mean by *what's really there.*

Impressionists like Monet were, after all, trying to capture real subtleties of light and perception that had been made static or ignored by prior realism. And in addition to my relatives, I have perfectly rational friends who are confident they've seen what others usually can't. One, Joni, bought a flat in London and then discovered she and her husband were cohabiting with a spectral older woman who sometimes paced the hall. One night, Joni was cooking and Greg was showering; Joni had set water glasses on the table, but, a few minutes later, when she carried in silverware, the water glasses were gone. She second-guessed herself: she must have misremembered filling them.

But when she opened the cupboard, there were the glasses—full of water, and on the highest, barely reachable shelf.

Although Joni asked the ghost to please not make itself visible, people throughout history have also sought out, and claimed to hear and see, spirits—including, also in London, in the mid-1800s, a painter and spiritualist medium named Georgiana Houghton. A reviewer in her own time called her work "the most extraordinary and instructive example of artistic aberration"; now she's sometimes described as the world's first abstract artist. But she didn't think of her work as aberrations or abstractions. In her watercolors, which look like thread caught in a beautiful windstorm or psychedelic spirographs, she's showing what she herself called "the unknown beauties and unsuspected truths" of seeing beyond the world of the living. This is what it *really* looked like. One painting, like a sunset of red, orange, and gold peacock feathers, is called *The Eye of God*. I read people online discussing Houghton feeling watched, though growing up with my mother's powers, I can't help wondering if it's a sort of self-portrait. And when some people are seeing through the eye of God, where does that leave those of us with only ordinary sight?

A few years ago, my oldest sister Beth told me a story that happened when she was in her thirties and I was in my teens. By then, Beth and her son Logan, my oldest nephew, were living about twenty miles away from my parents and me in the Ozark Mountains of Arkansas.

The land next to ours had come up for sale, and my parents—worried about noise from a football field if the high school bought it, as rumor said they might—bought it as a buffer. They had reason to fear noise, since the land had been used in the seventies as a car racetrack (there was still a low concrete wall and a two-story concession stand), and then for horseback riding lessons (there was still a run-down tack room at the center). Beth wanted to live closer to us, and my parents offered to sell her the concession stand so she could convert it into a house.

The concession stand was nondescript—blocky and concrete—its one distinguishing feature, a plaster jockey statue that stood by the front door. Since Logan and I had first trespassed on that land as pre-teens—climbing barbwire fences or balancing on the concrete wall to walk as far as the overgrown brush allowed—the jockey had always seemed like the daemon of that land. Like old statues often are, he was somehow both icon and junk. One leg and arm (and the lantern it was uplifted to hold) were broken off, ending in rebar substructure. He had faded-red-paint jodhpurs and chipped-black boots. Beth also loved that statue, and one day after work, when she stopped to check on the construction, in the raining debris, she saw the jockey over-turned in the scrap pile. She didn't want to ask the workers to stop, so she made a mental note to come back and rescue it. But when she came back a few days later, the jockey was gone.

Next time she saw our mother, Beth mentioned this, and our mother said, "Oh, we moved the jockey from the concession stand before you bought the property."

Oh, Beth thought, *I wonder why I thought it was there the other day and I needed to move it.* Who was Beth—who would have been raised by strangers if not for our mother's vision—to question any of our mother's claims about the visible or invisible world?

A few months passed, and after Beth had moved in, she got a roll of film developed. As she later told me, "As I flipped through the photos, many of them of the construction, I stopped cold. There, in a pile of debris, stood the jockey. That feeling I'd had when Mom had said, 'Oh we moved that before you bought the property,' the flash of con-fusion, the immediate shucking of what *I* remembered, was all too fa-miliar. I'd felt it repeatedly throughout my life. Now that I knew, that I had photographic evidence, I understood why so many times I'd felt bewildered, why I didn't trust my sense of things and my perceptions. So many times Mom had rearranged reality for me."

When Beth tells me this, I'm in my mid-thirties and Beth is in her fifties, and I too stop cold. No one has ever suggested that our mother "rearranged reality." If so, how do I even begin to re-rearrange everything in my life that might have been rearranged without my knowing?

And why would our mother rearrange the truth about an inconsequential jockey, which for years after lived on a broken hunk of concrete outside the old tack room that Beth and my parents shared for storage?

Beth told me she chose not to confront our mother with the photo because just having this realization was so freeing, but I also wonder if Beth was avoiding the way our mother might bend that interaction too—not apologizing for being wrong, but saying something like, "Oh, I had a vision that the jockey was going to be damaged, so we moved it." I can imagine our mother sliding a new layer of vision on top of the other, still being the one with the clearest sight.

This past summer, about a decade after Beth told me about the jockey, my father told me another story. I was living in Cardiff, Wales, and he had flown to see me. We were at a coffee shop, looking out at the bay, and he said, "I have something to tell you. You probably already suspect this." And then he said, "I'm bisexual." He had come out to my stepmother; at age seventy, he was feeling whole for the first time in his life.

Then he told me that he'd actually tried to come out forty years ago, when I was a child.

He'd had a crush on a colleague at the *Star-Telegram* and had told my mother—not that he wanted to act on his feelings but that he blushed distractingly every time the man spoke to him. My father was in his twenties, and I imagine he thought he could, and should, confide in my older, wiser mother. In another version of reality, I could imagine her smiling in her wry way, saying, "I suspected as much."

It doesn't take psychic powers to see my Judy Garland–obsessed, theater-geek father may not be straight. The majority of my parents' close friends weren't—including my godfathers: Jay and his life partner, Richard, the professor of the community college class where my parents met; and Aunt Judy and her series of female partners. Judy wasn't really my aunt; she was my mother's first husband's niece. And the woman with whom my mother had had a lengthy, tempestuous love affair in the late 1950s, when my sisters were young.

But that day when my father confessed his feelings, my mother didn't say, "I suspected as much." And she didn't commiserate. Instead, according to my father, she looked at him in her "gospel truth," seeing-through-walls way, and said, "No, you're not. I can *see* that you're not gay just as clearly as the way you're holding that tea cup."

"And that was the end of that," my father says. He had no photograph of his sexuality. My mother had seen his life for him.

In William Butler Yeats' poem "Leda and the Swan," there's a line that has always haunted me. After the mortal Leda is raped by Zeus in the form of a swan, Yeats asks, "Did she put on his knowledge with his power...?" What does it possibly mean to gain knowledge and power only via violent disempowerment?

Overpowered by Zeus in the form of visions, my mother presented herself as Leda. She, who had lost her beloved father in childhood, who had lost her childhood world to move across the country, who had been raised by an unloving mother, who had been trapped in a loveless marriage, was now plagued by unwanted visions. Her life and knowledge had been *put on* her against her will.

But wasn't she also our Zeus?

Describing the prophet Cassandra, Seth Schein writes, "she evokes the same awe, horror and pity as do schizophrenics." "Awe," yes, "pity," yes, but in my mother's case, the "horror" was often buried because she was so good at eliciting the other two. It took my father almost fifty years to feel truly horrified that he'd spent most of his life overriding his own vision of himself.

Did my mother believe she saw a truth about my father that he was too young or confused to see? Was she threatened by the possibility of losing him after she'd agreed to have me at almost forty because he so much wanted a family?

Did she honestly just misremember when the jockey statue had been moved (my father would have been the one to move it; he did the yardwork, including mowing a walking path around the racetrack wall)? Was she covering for my father, who had a tendency to do what we called "neatening up," which sometimes involved throwing away things the rest of us still wanted?

Did she ever wonder if what she told us as the gospel truth was not the gospel truth?

Though no one in my family seems sure about the details, my mother had had a mental breakdown in her late twenties or early thirties. In the version I remember her telling, she went to a doctor who said she "felt too much" and prescribed some kind of shock therapy. Though she was always resistant to calling herself a feminist, she said the doctor didn't understand women's feelings, and so took hers from her. After the therapy, she felt cut off from her own emotions, never fully herself, the edges of her vision blunted.

Less a story about her unreliability or her diagnosis (was there one?) or the possibility of further therapy, this came to me as a cautionary tale—another way she had suffered. The story says: whatever senses you have, even if they plague you, you want to keep them. The story says: others will try to take your vision from you.

When I was a teenager, passionately furious about something, she'd say she was jealous of how much I felt. I know now that emotional peaks and troughs subside with age, though I also distrust her claims of numbness. I remember her screaming at me, crying violently over ways I had hurt her, driving away in the Oldsmobile in the midst of fights with my father or me—though, long-distance-trucking visions set aside, she always returned to us, chastened.

Years later I learn that Beth remembers her agreeing to the shock treatments because she was in awe of, and maybe a little in love with, her doctor. And my father remembers her saying she *wanted* the visions to stop; perhaps that was even what she went in asking for.

Because my father-in-law was schizophrenic (brilliant, deluded, unable to hold a job or act as a father), my husband, Dylan, and I were interested in articles a few years ago about a theory that schizophrenia may originate when the brain overprunes synapses. Ordinarily, synapses are pruned gradually in adolescence, leaving the ones essential to a person's environment. This is necessary: if synaptic pathways branch and branch, the brain is oversensitive to all experience; picture a sort of neural lightning storm. But if too many synapses are pruned, the usual, or more adaptive, routes of perception get short-circuited. Visions fill in for logic.

Although she may have had some delusional tendencies, I don't think my mother was schizophrenic any more than Schein means Cassandra was, but the line between prophecy and delusion seems sometimes more Monet than Mondrian. And I'm interested in the image of the brain with its pathways that can become overactive as lightning storms or overpruned as topiaries. It is true the topiaries at Disney World are just boxwood hedges; it is also true they are Mickey Mouse.

Raised by a mother who saw ghosts and felt that nothing "ever seemed real" after my grandfather died, it's of course possible, probable, that my mother carried lifelong shock and trauma. And it's possible these contributed to confusions about where reality began and ended. Maybe that's what the doctor meant when he said she "felt too much."

Or maybe she wanted reasons for her own and others' often inexplicable suffering so desperately that she saw reasons. That friend wasn't dying of simple old age or an arbitrary stroke; there was someone to blame. Poison in a bottle. It's true that she felt empathetically connected to others' suffering and taught all of us to be.

In shock from the house she'd lived in and carefully restored for more than thirty years burning to the ground, it's very possible *she felt as if* she'd known the loss was coming. Or felt that she *should have known* and, as the family matriarch, should have been able to stop it and save us. It's possible that guilt and grief and longing and other emotions filled in or blurred with sight, as they so often do for all of us.

In *Alice in Wonderland,* the March Hare chides Alice, "You should say what you mean," and Alice replies, "I do . . . at least—at least I mean what I say—that's the same thing, you know."

"Not the same thing a bit," says the Hatter, although of course it is common and human to confuse these layers of meaning.

Yet even as it's possible that my mother was well-intentioned or innocently confused or meant what she said without saying what she more deeply meant, there is another possibility that I don't like to consider: that she knew she was lying. Or at least that she distrusted her own mind and said everything as "gospel truth" as a coping mechanism to control the narrative, to control us, to make us doubt our own perceptions so we'd lean on hers. As she offered tea cups full of leaves we couldn't see, who was to say who was clear-sighted and who was delusional?

Though my parents were obsessed with old movies, and I grew up with black-and-white suspense—*Rear Window, Dial M for Murder*—I didn't hear of *Gaslight* or the concept until my forties. The closest I came was *Hush . . . Hush, Sweet Charlotte*, in which Bette Davis as a young woman discovers her lover axe-murdered, and is, I know now, gaslighted into believing he's haunting her. That movie, with its creepy music-box soundtrack and Davis alone in the house going mad, horrified me more than any other in my pre-teens and teens. Though I couldn't have put this language to it, I was terrified of being alone with my own mind and unable to trust it.

Or was I terrified of thinking I was alone with my own mind, when I never actually had been? How would I, or anyone in my family, even know what that would really feel like?

The summer I was twenty-five, I went on a trip to Europe with my new husband, Will, and his parents. Unbeknownst to me, just after I left, my mother told my father she'd had a vision I wouldn't be returning: I was going to die on that trip.

My father spent the next month and a half afraid of every email and phone call, as I whirled obliviously on fun-park rides in Spain, and visited the Van Gogh Museum, and toured the monolithic cathedral in St. Émilion. After we left Will's parents, I danced on Ecstasy for the first time at the aptly named Doctor Music Festival and felt as if I'd fallen inside the prophecies of another visionary, Walt Whitman, whom I had first loved in high school. I felt connected to everything: "the mate and companion of people, all just as immortal and fathomless as myself."

Though my mother's stories had documented a million ways the world could hurt me, and I had grown up trying to guard against all of them—to see clearly before the hurt came so I wouldn't be both hurt and at fault for not seeing it coming—on Ecstasy, for the first time in my life, I felt no fear or need to see more than I saw. And though the intensity of this utter safety was temporary, some new sense of self and security stayed.

A few days after I got back to Kansas City, my mother and I were doing dishes. I was already scared she knew about the Ecstasy—she, who did not need drugs for visions, was staunchly antidrug and prone to saying we could "never darken her door again" if any of us did them—so when she asked if I felt like the same person who had left on the trip, I turned away. I pretended to be rehanging a dishtowel so she wouldn't see me lying as I tried to sound nonchalant. "Hmm," I said. "I guess not really. I mean, going so many different places and relying on ourselves to backpack was really transformative."

"I suspected as much," she said. And then, "I knew you wouldn't be returning, and now I see what that meant."

My father tells it differently. When he told my mother that he was overjoyed with relief that she'd been wrong about my death, she said, "Oh, I saw weeks ago she'd be alright."

"What?" my father said. "And you didn't tell me? I've been worried sick for six weeks."

"I forgot to mention it," my mother said.

Forgot?

Among the possessions that strangely survived the fire, scorched but mostly intact, are a series of photo albums that my mother made for me when I was young. Not only did she take the pictures, she wrote the captions—in first person, from my perspective, to help me remember: *I love going to the zoo. My favorite are the peacocks, although I found the llamas a little boring. Aggle-gaggle* [my attempt to say "grandmother"] *came for a visit. I thought her hat was pretty funny!*

She has inked in exactly who I was before I could articulate it. It is she who knows what I will say, how I will feel. She has already seen and voiced all of me.

Yet in her voice as mine, which I have read and reread, and cherish, I also hear the curiosity and care for the world I learned from her. I hear her humor and attention to detail. I hear the imagination that helped me become a writer.

When I write, I rely on intuition—often "knowing" what should happen next in a story or poem from what feels beyond me or deeper inside me than ordinary sight. Unlike Vladimir Nabokov's famous claim that his characters were "galley slaves" he controlled, I feel far more akin to a Ouija board planchette that my characters or imagination nudges here and then there (not that I believe my characters *exist* outside me).

And at times, I've had strong intuition beyond my writing. Once, I cancelled a trip last-minute based on *knowing* I shouldn't go and was, therefore, home the next morning to receive an email that led to my first book's publication. But I have also wanted to cancel trips, suddenly sure the plane would crash, and I've gone and been perfectly safe.

And most of my "premonitions" have been inconsequential, like the time as an undergrad when I was about to buy dessert, and thought out of nowhere, with perfect certainty: "But Greg is going to bring cookies to workshop." Greg Pape, my professor, a somewhat aloof Western poet, had never seemed at all inclined to baking, but that day the cookies were delicious.

I am fascinated by intuition, but I don't trade on it as power in the real world. I try—or at least I think I try—to discern what are my own emotions or dreams and what is really here, though admittedly, some of that surely cannot be known or seen *by the light of reason,* as the definition of prophecy concludes.

Present hidden things which cannot be known by the light of reason seems to me, in addition to a definition of *prophecy,* a definition of so much of being human. Or at least who I once was: a girl who scrubbed literal pictures of presents up from Christmas plates' blackness because she knew from memory they existed there, and knew from emotion they needed to exist again.

And the woman I still am: arranging and rearranging words as I try to see through the lightning flashes and ghosts I have inherited from my mother, whom I am trying to see clearly, though my mother has not for two decades been alive to be seen.

For my mother's sixty-fifth birthday, a few years after she was diagnosed with chronic leukemia, she wanted to go to Chartres. Despite not being religious, she had always loved Gothic architecture, light, traveling. She wanted to walk the last twelve miles as a pilgrimage: watching the distant cathedral grow closer across the fields.

In her stories after the trip, she didn't focus on the cathedral, nor the pilgrimage (which must have been tiring; her energy was already unpredictable). What had impressed her most was a stranger. He walked up to her as she was standing by the cathedral doors. He laid his palm flat against her heart and said, "What is this hurt?"

He had the most piercing blue eyes. His name, he told her after, was Spencer.

My mother, after five decades of atheism, told us she thought he was an angel.

"What hurt?" I asked when she first told this. "Did he mean the leukemia?"

And she said, clearly disappointed I'd had to ask, "He was talking about all my pain—my whole life. His eyes looked right into the center of me."

At the time, I heard this as another vision: a story on the borderline between mythic and real—my sick mother touched by an angel in France.

But when I think now of Spencer, with his piercing eyes and his palm flat against her chest in that gesture that means "stop" and also "compassion," I see my mother finally being truly *seen*.

Did my mother see an angel and ghosts and a burning house? Maybe her visions were finally less about her looking out and more about her wishing that one of us would look inside her. Maybe story after story, vision after vision, what she really wanted most was for someone to lay a hand against her heart and say, "What is this hurt?"

Around that same time, shortly after her diagnosis, when she had the strength, my mother loved to walk the trail my father mowed outside the racetrack wall—past the shallow frog pond and Beth's house and the twin cedars and the steep ravine (or "holler," as she liked to remind us the locals said). At the top of that ravine, she began to hear a particular oak tree speaking to her.

Though trees had never talked to her before, this tree, like Spencer after, knew she was suffering. She and the tree would discuss her diminished hearing and eyesight, the ways the forest would continue without her, whatever was on both of their minds. Having been raised originally near the Adirondacks, with dense forests of white oaks, northern red oaks, black oaks, swamp white oaks, and bur oaks, maybe she had a particular connection to oak trees. "I had a conversation with my tree again today," she would tell me on the phone when I called from Florida. "It says I shouldn't be afraid."

On October 30, 2001, three days after my mother died, my father and Beth and I drove from Kansas City to our land in Arkansas.

In the late October dampening chill, we reached into the ordinary plastic bag and pulled out handfuls of the end of what she materially had been, devoid of her voice, her sight, her stories. As ashes do, they seemed not human at all and, simultaneously, horrifyingly human, some dust-like and slippery, some chunky with gristle and bone. They coated our hands, but when they fell, seemed to have always been part of the roots, the corroding red and yellow leaves, the sticks and mushrooms and dirt. They fulfilled the only prophecy all of our lives do.

My father and Beth and I closed our eyes and bowed our heads beneath that tree that had truly understood her. We knew this because she'd told us. Though only she could have heard, when we stood on its leaves and sobbed, what words, if any, its branches spoke.

Wings

"Thus should have been our travels: / serious, engravable."
ELIZABETH BISHOP

The Queen Anne Mansion in Eureka Springs, Arkansas, where I got married at nineteen, was next to another Victorian tour home called Wings. Wings had a year-round Christmas theme and was filled with cages of tropical birds.

What tropical birds had to do with Christmas or Victorian houses wasn't a question Wings was set up to answer. It was set up to contain over-the-top cheer and squawking and doilying and reindeering. Like Taco Bell menu items, the idea seemed to be *things people like, they will like even more together.* Dorito-crunch-enchilada-burritos. Candy-cane-bedazzled cages with Victorian filigree and finches chirping as Gene Autry's "Here Comes Santa Claus" blared from the speakers above, and dazed tourists looked everywhere and nowhere at once.

Room after room in Wings, it was Christmas, yet also the air-conditioned Ozark Mountain summer tropics. It was a Victorian parlor. It was a blizzard of snow globes and kitsch.

As a pre-teen and teenager living in a tourist town, I feared and loathed kitsch. Years before *The Unbearable Lightness of Being* taught me that kitsch is "the denial of shit," I felt this. Kitsch turned away from the real world's mess and pain. It installed fringed lampshades and wreaths. It replaced real people with Precious Moments figurines.

Those porcelain figures stared with blank black seed eyes from Eureka's gift shops: bulb-headed children with cartoon smiles; pointed-headed kids clasping hands on tree stumps or cradling kittens. The apogee of cloying, the figures wore floppy porcelain hair bows and dresses with hems that twined into flowers, and their faces were less child than cult member. They came from a factory two hours north, where a Precious Moments Chapel opened the year I turned fifteen, which I would not have been caught dead in. Or maybe dead: with by-then goth red lipstick and a witchy crystal and The Cure playing in the background as Precious Moments cherubs simpered from the altar, missing all my beautiful irony and pain.

Although its main tourist season was May to October—months that often drippily blazed above ninety—Eureka Springs boasted not only Wings but also a shop that sold only Christmas ornaments: a forest of fake trees hung with wooden snowmen and Jesuses and glittering balls. Ornaments make good souvenirs, and— as I'd come to understand later—holidays are inherently touristic: dates, rather than places, we arrive at with our suitcases packed with what to feel and see.

Play Lee Greenwood's *Christmas to Christmas*, and you feel nostalgia; hang tinsel, and you're amid the wonders of a winter wonderland. Have your picture taken in front of the ghostly Crescent Hotel, and you've stood inside the past the postcards promised.

As Hans Magnus Enzensberger wrote in his seminal early theory of tourism, "These postcards are the travel itself on which the tourists set out. . . . [Tourists] only consume the second-hand, confirming the advertisement poster that enticed them in the first place."

Although I also didn't understand this then, self-reflexivity is what makes both tourism and holidays often kitschy. As Roger Scruton writes in "The Strangely Enduring Power of Kitsch," kitsch "is not about the thing observed but about the observer. It does not invite you to feel moved by the doll you are dressing so tenderly, but by yourself dressing the doll." Or as Milan Kundera writes, "two tears flow in quick succession. The first tear says: How nice to see children running on the grass! The second tear says: How nice to be moved together . . . by children running on the grass!"

Even as tourists enjoy looking at a candy-striped bird cage, they're enjoying themselves enjoying the candy-striped bird cage: being the kind of people who come to see this quirky Victorian thing. "At Christmas," Scruton continues, "we are surrounded by kitsch— worn out clichés, which have lost their innocence without achieving wisdom."

And what did I want more as a teen than the opposite of this? Wisdom, loss-of-innocence, life's real shit. I wanted a serious, engravable life, as I'd later love Elizabeth Bishop saying. I had big ideas about what this would look like. But also, really, no idea.

This was the pre-Internet late eighties to early nineties. For grown-up context, I had only *Seventeen* magazine and my parents' books, like *East of Eden*. My older half sisters had moved out before I was born, no help in teaching me to be cool and wise. And, unlike friends' parents, mine weren't cool pot-smoking hippies or crystal-shop-owning Wiccan witches. My parents chaperoned field trips; they worked from home, writing, of all geeky things, high school English textbooks.

This job kept them in a perpetual double bind. Publishers hired them to create exercises that teenagers would think were "cool" and "be excited" to do, but Texas's conservative State Board of Education controlled the largest textbook market and would reject anything controversial. So my parents scrambled to find pop culture references that would excite teenagers yet offend no one. One year, Michael Jackson and his monkey, Bubbles, made a great appositive exercise. Before next year, they needed to be revised away. At dinner, my parents would ask, "Is Billy Joel controversial? Everyone still likes Tom Hanks, right?"

And I, with great situational irony, would answer. I'd just asked for Bon Jovi's new album for my thirteenth birthday without understanding *Slippery When Wet* referred to anything but a highway. When we'd moved to Eureka two years before, I'd still loved Barry Manilow. In our tan, boxy farmhouse eight miles from town (with many gift shops, one bookstore, and no mall or movie theater), I lacked all wisdom except book smarts.

While I had crush after crush—Whitney with his parachute pants, Ryan with his freckles—at best, boys called me "The Brain." At worst, they made fun of me as fat. I was. The adult height I'd already reached made me tower over many of my classmates at five feet four but hadn't been enough to stretch out several years of cake therapy. By cake therapy, I mean that after our house burned when I was ten, instead of real therapy, my parents and I moved to Arkansas and watched double features on our first-ever TV and its laser disk player, while eating, nightly on the weekends, an entire homemade layer cake.

But what I *did* have, what I shared with my classmates and we could always bond over, was that none of us were tourists. Compared to nouveau riche honeymooners from Dallas and busloads of Tulsa retirees gawking at prescribed sights, *we* were wise and non-naïve. We didn't rent mopeds and sputter around pointing at limestone buildings. We didn't turtle through the winding streets on the made-to-look-old-fashioned trolleys. Except when out-of-town relatives visited, we never entered Wings or Frog Fantasy (a museum with over seven thousand frog statues and other frog-themed pieces). We knew it all already. We sort of *were* it.

To live in a twelve-hundred-person town to which over five hundred thousand strangers flock annually is to feel like a cast member or stage crew for a play. *Eureka Springs! The Victorian town! Little Switzerland!* (Nicknamed for winding, forested hills, and played up by gingerbread-trim motels). As teens, we dipped ice cream for tourists or worked in parents' restaurants, or wandered as de facto backdrop or extras, purposefully giving tourists wrong directions because we were bored. Because we were desperate to match our lives to a postcard view of somewhere more real and exciting than here. (Though, as a teen, I would have denied trying to match a post-card at all.)

Eureka Springs exists, or at least really grew up in the late 1800s, because of tourism. As legend goes, white settlers "discovered" the curative cold-water springs, and one cried out "Eureka! Springs!" and soon carriages of visitors began arriving to take the waters and stay in quickly built hotels. From its origins, the town is premised on being a place worth visiting. On an exclamation.

Following a post–World War II economic collapse, in the 1960s, hippie artists started moving in and restoring Eureka's by-then-decaying Victorians. This explains the art galleries and crystal shops and our mayor posing naked for a newspaper article (sort of behind a rock).

Eureka is often likened to San Francisco for its Victorian mansions and Arkansas's largest per capita gay population. A former-brothel spa hotel still blazes with a penis-shaped sign trimmed with florid neon scrollwork. But there's also a popular outdoor Passion Play, started by an anti-Semitic white supremacist in the 1960s, who also constructed the United States' largest Jesus statue and the adjacent Holy Land attraction. As the poet Frank Stanford, who lived in Eureka two decades before me, wrote: "The streets wound back and forth, up and down; the buildings were an odd mixture of gothic, Victorian, Swiss, and hillbilly design. They weren't built by sane men."

If Christ of the Ozarks looms over one side of town, the other icon directly across the steep valley is the huge, notoriously haunted Crescent Hotel, which has been a hotel, a girls' school, and in the 1930s, a sanitarium run by "Dr." Norman Baker: a con man on the run from the feds, who'd shut down his Iowa radio show, Know the Naked Truth (KTNT), because the cancer cure he invented and advertised kept killing people. Baker bought the Crescent and hired "model patients" to sketch and read on its balconies. He built a huge octagonal desk surrounded by bulletproof glass. He built an air calliope on the roof, which he played loudly as his real patients drank watermelon seed mixed with brown corn silk, alcohol, and carbolic acid, and died. In the lobby, tour guides point out what remains of his desk, describe his famous purple suits, and scare tourists with stories of ghost nurses still seen pushing gurneys down the red-carpeted and anciently slanting hallways.

As a local, of course I didn't take these tours, but friends and I would cut through the furniture-polish-redolent lobby looking, as always, for "something to do." We'd eavesdrop on tourists, whom we always referred to as "terrorists." We'd snicker as they exclaimed (identically, though they were too naïve to know this): "Doesn't it look just like you imagined?! Did you hear the guide say? This is where we look for the ghost!"

I never admitted to my friends, but much as I disdained the tourists, I also wanted to be a tour guide. A reader who dreamed of being a writer, I liked the idea of cranking the music box of history until Eureka's strangest stories spilled out. Or maybe I liked the idea of having an exciting story to tell, even if it didn't exactly belong to me.

Guides match the world to itself. They forestall what Dean MacCannell, in *The Tourist: A New Theory of the Leisure Class*, calls "touristic shame": the feeling of failing to adequately see the prescribed sights you came to see. Long before social media intensified FOMO, people feared that they were missing even what they were looking at.

Is this really the quirkiest and most haunted hotel!? tourists worry.

Of course, the guide implicitly reassures. "Just keeping looking toward that mirror; that's where some groups are lucky enough to see an old man in a top hat!"

Finally seeing the Northern Lights in Iceland in my forties, I found myself doing it too: pointing at the streaking, pulsing sky, repeatedly exclaiming to my husband, "Look! It's really them! They're really green! They're doing that column thing! That wave thing!"

The more that people read guidebooks and set time aside from work, the more pressure they feel to see and do what they should. As Enzensberger wrote in the 1950s (about a century after the term *sightseeing* first appeared), "A sight is something that one is expected to see. Fulfilling this duty delivers the tourist from the guilt that is implicitly recognized in taking flight from society" (which, in America, involves shirking capitalistic and Protestant work duties).

Maybe touristic shame in part explains why a mixed-up place like Wings exists: if you miss a finch, at least you saw a giant wreath. If you miss the wreath, there's always a sliding pocket door.

As a teenager, I didn't, of course, think of my entire life as filled with touristic shame. But that might be a good way to describe it. I'd arrived at my teens—years in which dramatic and romantic things were supposed to happen. But where were they? What did I have but the minor role of Smart Girl in a tourist town, a lot of road trips, a burned house, and, by fifteen, one boyfriend I'd dated for a few months before he broke up with me?

In contrast, by fifteen, my mother had met her first great love and almost already lost him. I knew this because she was an amazing storyteller. She could have been a tour guide if she weren't busy writing grammar questions. She knew how to make the past so present you're standing in it.

Although I'd never seen a picture of Rex, I saw him perfectly: his dark hair and slightly shy smile. He was leaning against the porch post of an abandoned house in Arizona, his legs stretched out. He had on worn jeans and cowboy boots. He was reading a Zane Grey paperback to my fifteen-year-old mother.

It was the summer of 1950, and since her father died in World War II, my mother had spent most of her preteens and teens here in near-ghost-town Congress Junction. She'd just spent her freshman year, even more miserably, away at Catholic boarding school where her mother had sent her after she complained that her older stepbrother was coming on to her. Her family wasn't even Catholic. My mother didn't believe in God. She didn't belong at St. Joseph's Academy, or anywhere.

But then Rex appeared in Congress. A few years older, he was traveling for the summer, picking up work, like a lot of young men did then. He and my mother both loved reading. After lugging rocks up-hill for a shrine he'd been hired to build on Yarnall Hill, he'd drive to see her. They'd read aloud Western love stories in which, when the avalanche comes, you're trapped inside a wild desert canyon together. They read for so many hours my mother's mother yelled, "You're go-ing to end up pregnant by that drifter," to which my mother yelled back, "You can't get pregnant from reading."

When my mother returned to St. Joseph's, Rex wrote weekly in his beautiful handwriting. He called her *Cousin Sylvia* because the nuns only allowed mail from boys who were family. Once, he sent her a teddy bear with eyes made of crooked crosses of black thread. He pinned a note to its fur, naming it "Gladly My Cross-Eyed Bear." With a single, perfect pun, he spoke to my mother's wry sense of humor, her feeling she was carrying crosses she should never have been asked to. She'd cry against Gladly about missing Rex and how wonderful it would be to run away—plans they were already making via coded Zane Grey references. When he sent her one of his rings—a rectangle of dark red agate, veined with green—she kept it hidden, or some-times slipped it on her finger.

That Christmas, Rex drove back to Congress, but my mother hadn't arrived yet on the bus. So he stood on the porch with his hat in his hands, like a gentleman, to talk to my grandmother. Or without a hat, like a dashing 1950s rebel. What matters is what my grandmother said: "Sylvia has fallen in love with someone else; she's spending Christmas with his family. Didn't she tell you?"

Why would my grandmother do this? The woman who, in my lifetime, seemed innocent and soft as her toy poodles. Maybe she thought Rex wasn't good enough. Maybe she hoped my mother would marry Don, the slightly older airplane mechanic who was also courting her. (My mother used to say that she was so uninterested in Don that if she heard his car, she'd run out the back door and hide in the desert until he drove away). Maybe my grandmother, having lost her first great love, my grandfather, didn't want to see my mother happy. Maybe she was cruel.

That was, of course, how it felt to my mother when she found out—weeks, or maybe months later, after Rex's letters stopped arriving—what had happened. But by then it was too late. By the time she heard from Rex again, he was in jail. In desperate poverty (but also, in my mother's story, desperate grief), he had used his beautiful handwriting to forge checks from his boss.

Instead of her fated life with Rex, my mother became a stifled 1950s housewife. First, she'd threatened to run away from boarding school and wait for Rex, but her mother had threatened back: she'd call an uncle in the FBI to track her down. So my mother ran the legal, trapped way. She stopped escaping out the back door when Don came to visit, and accepted his proposal. She got as far as Fort Worth, Texas, and promised herself as soon as she turned eighteen, she'd leave Don. But the month before her eighteenth birthday, she gave birth to my half sister, Beth.

A brilliant high school dropout with a controlling, nonreading husband and one baby, and then a second, my mother washed so many slacks and little dresses, she accumulated whole sets of carnival glass that came free in boxes of laundry soap. She woke early to fix Don his insisted-upon eggs drizzled with disgusting Southern bacon grease. She read and reread *Raintree County, East of Eden,* Zane Grey's *Riders of the Purple Sage.* Each Christmas, she baked gingerbread men with perfect dollops of icing buttons; she unwrapped the same griefs.

With his red thread mouth and black crossed-thread eyes, Gladly watched all of this, with that patient, martyrly look of old stuffed animals. Decades later, in my childhood, he still lived in a keepsake box—an icon of my mother's whole other life before she'd finally divorced Don and gone to college in her thirties, met my father, and had me at almost forty. Gladly and that agate ring were all she had left of Rex, whom she had seen only once in those years, when she visited him in jail.

Because my mother was such a good guide, who knew exactly where to direct attention and sympathy, I didn't think of obvious questions until years later. If Don wouldn't let her get a driver's license, as she always said, how did she get to a jail in Arizona that one time to see Rex? And why was Rex's forgery excusable, while I "should have known better" for all simple mistakes? And was Rex in jail or prison or both? The only online reference to Rex I've ever found says he was admitted to prison in February 1954, when my sister Beth was one.

All I heard as a child and teenager was what my mother's story made clearest: Rex Haslam was the only possible appositive for *my mother's first and greatest love.*

I knew if I found a love like that, I should hold on as tight as I could. I knew this story marked my mother—despite her adult heaviness and blunt-cut bangs—as having once been more desirable and loved than I'd ever been. At fifteen, she had two men driving miles to the middle of nowhere just to see her—like *she* was the shrine.

I had none of this, though by fifteen, I'd finally lost weight and was growing out my begged-for but frizzy perm. My sophomore year (I'd skipped eighth grade), my friends and I had figured out that beyond being locals, we were *alternative,* which meant indiscriminately mixing goth, hippie, New Wave, and punk clothes and music, and making wordy inside jokes. For a while my favorite jean-jacket pin read, *Do not disturb, I'm disturbed enough already.* Though more than disturbed, I was insecure, waiting to be discovered, exclaimed over. *Eureka! I have found her! With her Thoreau quotes and stacks of journals and love of watching Jeopardy! and crystal-on-a-shoelace necklace and thrift-store-vests and cloth buckle-over Chinese shoes and dreams of being a French teacher and novelist!*

Growing up in Eureka, I probably had a heightened sense of myself and the world needing to be sights. Though maybe I was just a teenage romantic who could have been anywhere, and happened to be here, with thirty students in my class, and boys who were friends, but *just* friends.

The boy I most wanted to "discover" me was Christian-Slater-Matthew-Broderick-Rex- Haslam plus Derrick, with his heavy-metal, curly blond ponytail, who sat in front of me in algebra, plus Drew, with his punk, curly black ponytail who sat behind. (I had to turn back and forward a lot.) Recently, Drew had been teasing me in ways that made us both laugh as if something were incredibly funny, but I couldn't tell if he was really flirting. Drew was hard to read like that. And often purposefully weird. When he didn't know a Quiz Bowl answer, he'd say, "Fred MacMurray."

"What country, until this year, was called Kampuchea?"

Fred MacMurray.

Sometimes he said that, or other random things, to ordinary questions.

At sixteen, he was six feet six, and rather than being one of those slumping, trying-to-not-seem-tall, extremely tall people, he dyed his jean shorts bright yellow and webbed them with safety pins and sometimes sprayed his hair straight up in the air. Even in summer, he wore black steel-toed boots and a black trench coat, which earned him our friend-group nickname: "Reaper." For Grim.

One day, after Quiz Bowl practice, friends ended up at a friend's house watching the 1950s sci-fi movie *The Blob*. Drew and I sat close. And—wonder of wonders—he gradually put his arm around me. And then, pushing his black bangs from his dark brown eyes, he leaned closer and kissed me. And then, maybe even better, he looked into my eyes, like I was really worth looking at.

If kitsch meant safe and sanitized, Drew was the antithesis. Although he was in Gifted, he just made okay grades, and he sometimes skipped classes to hang out in the art room. He believed in abstraction, like the early Modernists, who'd first decried ornamental art as *kitsch*. Cool art had crisscrossing masking-taped lines; you couldn't say what it was or wasn't.

His young, single mother rented a trailer on the Passion Play road, almost in the shadow of the seven-story Christ of the Ozarks. Because the original height would have necessitated blinking lights to warn airplanes, Christ's blocky head sits on his two-million-pounds-of-white-mortar-and-steel body without a neck. He looks like a milk carton with outstretched arms. Friends and I once doubled over reading a tourist's comment-book praise: *Worthy of Michelangelo!*

In reality, the statue was predominately the work of one of the men who'd constructed Dinosaur World: a rundown 1960s concrete-dinosaur roadside park, where Drew had worked the summer before we started dating.

Drew would have been punk anywhere, but with giant kitsch Jesus and highway gift shops selling duck-and-pond scenes painted on sawblades, he was Salvador Dali in a world of Precious Moments. Together, we were sights on a better, stranger map than anywhere I'd ever been.

In an iconic picture of our first year, I'm fifteen and a half and he's almost seventeen, and we're outside Kansas City's Nelson Atkins Museum, where my parents have invited him to see big-city art with us. He's wearing his trench coat, and his hair is floofed up dramatically à la Robert Smith in The Cure. I'm wearing my requisite crystal and look not-quite alternative, but not entirely the straight-brown-haired, freckled, ordinary girl I fear being. A little edgy. Much more edgy with him.

My mother didn't have pictures of Rex because it was the less-camera-ubiquitous 1950s, and besides, she and Rex were going to be together forever. But from the start, I feel as if the pictures of Drew and me exist to reinforce our permanence. Maybe they're even replacements for pictures of Rex. Because doesn't my mother say how much Drew reminds her of Rex? She doesn't explain exactly how, but I know. Like Rex, Drew is misunderstood yet understands me; he's deserving of a better life than he's been given. We're imperfectly perfect for each other.

In that picture at the Nelson Atkins, we're tourists, confirming *we've found the best museum*, but, also, I'm a girl confirming I've found my first true love. My mother's lost love reincarnated (though Rex is not, so far as we know, actually dead). My mother's new son-in-law.

This is 1990, not 1950, so of course we're not getting married. But isn't Drew becoming part of the family? In addition to our inside jokes, doesn't he have jokes with my parents? Doesn't he help with grammar exercises, even if Robert Heinlein, his favorite sci-fi author, might be controversial, and Pink Floyd, his favorite band, definitely is, and *Fred MacMurray* isn't serious? Doesn't he start coming to our house for dinner several nights a week?

Drew loves my mother's cooking. He can devour most of a margarita pizza, plus pesto pizza, plus cake. He's a bone-thin 180 pounds, always hungry. His mother makes minimum wage and is bad with money, so the power is always being shut off, or they don't have groceries beyond some cereal or a two-liter Mountain Dew. His mother calls him "Little Shit." He's never met his father.

My mother makes it clear that she, the older, wiser mother, needs to save him. Didn't this work for my father? Twenty-one to her thirty-four when they met, now, by being a responsible, doting father, he's making up for his childhood spent partly in foster care. (He also tends to go along with my mother's more domineering opinions, which we all call his being "the nice one.")

With Drew around, in addition to Christmas gingerbread, my mother suddenly makes a *bûche de noël*, an elaborate French yule log cake: chocolate angel food rolled around whipped cream and cherries. On Christmas morning, Drew comes over, and my parents give him turtlenecks, art books.

Sometimes, after school, Drew and I lie about doing homework and really make out. Or, at an older friend's house, we watch Pink Floyd's *The Wall*, the most rebellious movie I've ever seen: not just violence and drugs, but the truth about the smothering brick walls of parents and schooling. I understand when Pink shaves off his eyebrows and stares blankly at a TV as a song plays about wanting to fly but having nowhere to go. Don't Drew and I have that same strong urge? And isn't being together the first step toward flying?

By Drew's birthday in April, we pretend we're reading in an old tack room on my parents' land and actually have sex. The condom breaks, and I get so scared I confess to my mother. Over the years, she's yelled at me for eating Cheetos (we don't eat junk) or coming home fifteen minutes late (I have to be responsible), but she strangely doesn't get mad. She just asks if I really love Drew.

Of course I do.

I do. And already, though I don't say this, I'm confused. Some days, he won't speak. Or he snaps if I ask what's wrong.

I ask, "Do you still love me?" and he says he doesn't know; he doesn't even know who he is.

Once, he says there's darkness swirling inside him, and it terrifies him, like he's falling somewhere deep and dark inside. That time, we cry and hold each other like life rafts. Aren't we saving each other? And didn't my mother's stories warn me that love feels painful?

And doesn't Drew, at the best moments, make me feel loved and special: when he looks into my eyes and smiles or paints me an abstract Georgia O'Keeffe-esque heart?

Doesn't he distract me from my insecurities? Though—I don't see—some of my insecurities are worsening. I fear with my mother's copious cooking, I'm gaining weight. I fear Drew wants a girlfriend with big breasts and a tiny waist, like the women he says are sexy in Heinlein novels. I fear Drew can't get into the liberal arts colleges across the country I've dreamed of and ordered glossy brochures for.

But what are these fears compared to my luck? My first love isn't being taken from me. In fact, my mother is doing everything she can to help us be together.

Because my parents have been hired to revise a whole series of textbooks, after a lifetime of road trips and lentil burgers cooked on hot plates in our car, we suddenly have enough money to travel to Greece and Italy the summer after my sophomore year. We're going to see the sights of Rome and Athens and Florence and take a ferry across the Aegean. My parents are too busy writing textbook exercises to figure out how to navigate countries where they don't speak the language, and they're the sort of nonconformists who never work to conform or not conform, so they've booked a package tour.

I'm excited about the trip, despite the embarrassing tour. But I'm also sad to leave Drew for three whole weeks. I'm sure I say this. What I remember is my parents calling the archeology camp that Drew and

I are attending in southern Arkansas. They've had an idea. Would Drew like to come?

I can't imagine Drew had a passport. Born in Texas, he'd never traveled farther than California. So I must have the timing wrong, but within what I remember as a week, we're in St. Louis, then Rome. With one overnight flight, we've replaced Christ of the Ozarks with the real *David* and *Pietà*. I'm holding my punk boyfriend's hand in the hallowed marble Uffizi Gallery. He's lifting me off my feet, as he often does, to spin me around at Delphi.

Isn't this—the ruins, the heat on the rocks, even the days he won't speak—*serious and engravable*?

In the poem beginning "Thus should have been our travels: / serious, engravable," Elizabeth Bishop contrasts her travels with idealizations in a book with "Over 2,000 Illustrations and a Complete Concordance." She admits the messy gap between reality and touristic expectations, including the holy grave that doesn't look "particularly holy." But at fifteen that summer, I'm an idealistic teenager. I've never been anywhere as exotic; never had a serious boyfriend. When expectations and reality gap, I just need to try harder. When Drew withdraws or says something snappish or strange at the Colosseum, I just need to try harder. When it's confusing to be my parents' perfect daughter and his perfect partner, I just need to try harder.

I don't think then, nor for years, how hard Drew must also be trying to fit the role of happy middle-class tourist and member of my family. I don't know—none of us do—that his mood swings are signs of being bipolar.

I believe my parents that he just needs more opportunities and love. And, having taken flight from our ordinary lives, it's easy to believe that for every lack there's an answer: a real Italian pizza, a scoop of gelato, Mykonos' pretty, whitewashed houses.

The family we become on that trip will continue for the next six and a half years. Maybe Drew's mother is resentful he's in Europe, or it's all she can afford, but while we're gone, she moves into a trailer with just one bedroom. It's in a different town, closer to her new job.

Drew will have to transfer schools and scrunch his six-foot, six-inch-body onto a five-foot couch. It's like a simple math equation or one of my parents' reading comprehension exercises: the context sets up the only right answer.

So I begin my junior year with my boyfriend living with me in the bedroom directly above my parents', where, a few years before, I was a heavy, gawky, dreaming-of-her-first-kiss twelve-year-old. Pale blue wallpaper, stuffed animals under posters now for R.E.M. and The Cure. Drew and I drive to school in my VW Bug; we go to parties in the woods (though now my parents set both our curfews); we take family trips to Texas, New York, Disney World.

Sometimes, my mother reaches from the front seat back to hold Drew's hand. He's basically her son now. Strange as it may look (my friends are definitely amazed my parents are letting him *live* with me), we all belong together.

Now, all December, my mother serves dinner on Christmas-tree-pattern plates, and when we eat far enough to see whose tree is upright, that person wins a Christmas cracker: one of those shiny foil-wrapped tubes that my mother remembers from her childhood. With a cheerful pop, they break to reveal small toys or paper crowns that we unfold and wear as we eat. Drew has never had family rituals; my mother has never seemed so happy at Christmas.

For Christmas or his birthday, my mother gives Drew the agate ring Rex gave her. Drew loves it and regularly wears it. Doesn't it, somehow, rightfully belong to him?

But despite good nutrition and love, Drew's moods keep being unpredictable. He skips his senior finals and fails all his classes. First he tells me he forgot he had finals. Then he says he felt sick. Then he says he just didn't feel like going. Eventually he says he has no idea why he skipped.

I feel confused and betrayed. But doesn't it all work out? Now he'll repeat his senior year and graduate with me. We'll go away to college together!

Sometimes, we fight until we chase each other screaming, grabbing each other. Once, I trip on the couch and break my toe. At school, Drew tells everyone I kicked the couch, and they all laugh with him. Of course he gets to tell the story: he was there; he's always there.

But don't I want him to be? Doesn't he make me laugh when he teases me? Don't we love the same art and music? And haven't my mother and I always yelled when we fought? Hasn't she occasionally slapped me? And don't we sit down to dinner after, laughing at a silly wordy joke? Isn't this all what love is?

One of my mother's favorite expressions is "Don't throw away happiness while reaching for the moon." She never had this choice, but I do. When I cry over a fight with Drew, she comforts me but also reminds me that he's funny, special, and kind at heart. I know this. I know how lucky I am to get to live both my own teen life and the better version of my mother's long-gone teens: where the first and greatest love stayed and stays.

Despite having run from kitsch, I am also, like probably all teenagers, in awe of the new, beautiful drama of my own pain. When I cry over a fight, or the fear of losing Drew, I'm also aware of being such a seriously in-love girl who could feel this. A girl who, straining toward the moon, could drop the armfuls of happiness she's been given.

Just look at the poster-sized photo in our bedroom. Taken by my mother when the First Gulf War plummeted flight prices and we visited Mont-Saint-Michel's famous tidal flats, Drew is spinning me in his arms so my feet are off the sand. He's in long, ripped jean shorts and Converse; I'm in my requisite black leggings and skirt. And between us and the ancient, walled island drifting distantly against the pale sky, Drew has carved with driftwood in huge capital letters on the rippled sand: *I LOVE ALEX*.

What more proof or advertisement do I need? There is our love, not only engravable but already engraved by Drew and then my mother's camera.

But of course there are pictures my parents don't get blown up for us. Like our high school graduation, where Drew has a purple-black eye and I've been sobbing.

My mother had invited Drew's mother for a family dinner before the ceremony, but Drew freaked out about his mother's visit before she even arrived. Increasingly irrational and shouting, he punched himself in the eye. When my father tried to calm him, Drew almost punched him too until, finally, my soft-spoken writer father wrestled Drew, still raving, to the ground beside our house.

Drew couldn't explain what had happened. We were all shaken and crying, but we carried on and ate homemade pesto pizza (Drew's favorite) with his mother before Drew and I put on our black and red nylon gowns and caps, and we all drove to the city auditorium. With Drew's eye swelling purple in one of the rows behind me, I gave my valedictorian speech. I quoted Khalil Gibran and tried to sound grown-up and wise.

I remember my favorite teacher once saying, "You'll outgrow him," but no one really questioning the black eye. No conversation about counseling, or us moving away alone. No suggestion there might be a diagnosis.

In retrospect, the age of a parent now, I want to blame my parents for not seeing what was happening more clearly than I did. But I also know they'd never gone to therapy for their own hard childhoods, and we lived, and live, in a country where mental health often goes undiscussed. And many bipolar teens aren't diagnosed precisely because it's so often hard to tell teen mood swings and rebellions from the start of real mental health issues.

Was Drew the cool kind of strange? The *do not disturb, I'm disturbed enough already* kind? Was he the kind of artsy *not sane* man who built Eureka? Or was he strange because he couldn't help it? Was he dangerous to himself or me?

I wonder if these were questions my grandmother *did* somehow know to ask herself. Though Rex was unfailingly kind and honest in my mother's stories, does it defy coincidence that my grandmother drove him away and he just happened to be a criminal? Did my grandmother hear something that made her call him a "drifter"? Or would his life—as my mother suggested—really have turned out differently if she'd been at home that fateful day? If she could have thrown her arms around him and they could have run away together?

Instead of the liberal arts colleges I've dreamed of, I apply only to Southwest Missouri State—which has offered me a full ride. Drew can easily get in. It's in Springfield, an hour and a half away. We can—and do—drive home each weekend.

In our first apartment (my parents cosign), I wake before 8 a.m. honors classes to cook us homemade biscuits and daffodil eggs, my mother's recipes. At my insistence, we don't go to parties because drinking makes Drew's moods more confusing. With our few friends, we watch movies in the Honors Dorms, where my scholarship would have paid for me to live if I didn't have a live-in boyfriend. Though I don't have the language for this, I know it's my responsibility, in our first home alone, by force of will, love, and nutrition, to hold us together—to keep Drew happy and stable, to keep him in love with me.

Still, sometimes we fight late into the night, and Drew storms away, and by morning I've cried so hard I feel as if fishing nets have been pulled through my skin, terrible long ropes tangled through both of us.

But then I meet him at the painting studio where he's working on a fragmented self-portrait, or we go to the one decent Mexican restaurant and laugh at our own inside jokes. Almost every single weekend, we drive the hour and a half back to Arkansas.

Though, strangely, I remember no details of where or how, when I'm eighteen and Drew is twenty, he proposes. It's a question, but also not a real question.

Since fifteen, the only time I've spent away from him was a month during the summer before my senior year of high school when I was accepted, via a letter from Governor Bill Clinton, to study creative writing at Arkansas Governor's School, on a real college campus. I quickly became friends with my violist roommate's musician friends, including a long-haired cello player I developed a crush on.

I began to walk laps obsessively; I refused meals until my collar bones jutted. Though I didn't understand this at the time, I wasn't actually trying to become more desirable for Jon; I was trying to become less capable of feeling. Or to erase myself from feelings that didn't fit.

Enzensberger writes, "The true effort demanded of the tourist lies in confirming the make-believe as the authentic," which is "no small accomplishment," and I recognize this effort. I don't mean Drew and I weren't in love, but the longer I, and all of us, invested in our love story and family, the more we had to keep confirming it.

In college, I distanced myself from our high school friends, telling myself it was "time to move on." This also meant I didn't have to answer real questions. A few months before our wedding, when Drew kissed my best friend from college, I didn't have to tell anyone.

Angie had come to see Eureka, and because I had a stomachache, she and Drew went hiking alone to see the land my parents had given us. When they didn't return after dark, my mother went looking for them. She found them, in our little overhang of a cave, making out. Of course, Drew couldn't explain why he was kissing Angie. Of course, I cried and screamed and felt heartbroken.

But leaving him was as impossible as reaching the moon with my hands. Where would I go? Where would he go? And by the next weekend, with Angie not there, weren't we a family again as always?

On weekends in college, I remember the relief of pulling up my parents' rocky drive—how desperately I wanted someone to take care of us. Unlike my mother who'd looked womanly as a teenager, I was often still mistaken for fourteen. I'd lost weight and had a girlish build, but I also suspect I'd regressed. Despite being a straight-A university student, I also was very much still, or again, a child.

On our drive home, I loved stopping at Table Rock Lake to see the Christmas lights: elves, candy canes, and wreaths sparkling on the docks and water. On the Roger Whitaker Christmas album, my favorite song was "Darcy the Dragon," about a dragon who wants to buy presents for his forest friends but keeps burning down shops when he speaks. Finally, he cries out in sadness, and snow goes down his throat and extinguishes "the fire inside." The song ends with a cheery Merry Christmas.

How could I, antikitsch teen and still die-hard fan of The Cure and Pink Floyd, unabashedly love such schmaltz? I know that older teenagers often regressively idealize childhood as adult responsibilities feel more real and frightening, but another motivation strikes me as truer and harder to admit. The more confusing my own life became, the more I wanted sanitized answers. *Of course, fire will be put out by snow at just the right moment. Poor dragon! He never meant to hurt anyone.*

What I hadn't understood, and still didn't consciously, is that kitsch is often underlain with desperation. If you could face the shit, you probably would.

The Queen Anne Mansion where Drew and I got married two months before my twentieth birthday is restrained compared to its next-door neighbor, Wings. The rooms hold only polished furniture and woodworking: inlaid mahogany and cherry pocket doors, intricately carved newel-posts, bay windows.

The twelve-thousand-square-foot, three-story mansion was built in 1891 in Carthage, Missouri, (later home to Precious Moments), but in 1984, the owners of Wings bought it, had it cut into numbered pieces and driven the almost-hundred miles to Eureka on forty flatbed trailers. Its reassembled grandeur is not quite a replica, but not quite real either.

By the huge triptych window in the men's parlor, even Drew seemed small: a punk groom cake topper in an off-white linen suit. His ring, self-designed, and made by a hippie jeweler friend, looked medieval-Modernist, silver like Rex's ring, which he still wore too. I wore a new but antique-style off-white lace dress with no train or veil (I was still alternative) and a white gold ring set, melted down from one of my paternal grandmother's failed marriages. I felt a little superstitious about this, but the diamond floated beautifully above the small curved waves.

As we were pronounced husband and wife, I cried with joy. I cried with genuine happiness and love. I cried with fear. I cried with the beauty of my own beautiful tears.

After a short honeymoon, we moved across the country for the National Student Exchange program in Montana—a state I'd always dreamed of living in. But a few days after we arrived, Drew told me it had been a mistake to get married. Why? He had no idea. It just was.

There, on the other side of the Rockies from everything I'd known, I was suddenly alone yet married. I spent a lot of time crying in the bathtub in our dark-paneled apartment or staring at my computer with writer's block. When Drew was assigned to paint a portrait, I stood naked and cold for hours on the shag carpet as he turned me into an abstracted, yellow, mouthless woman.

I remember my aching arms, my fears that I wasn't beautiful enough and that my hips and stomach were too round. How could I trust Drew even if he reassured me I was pretty, since he was obsessed with sex and thought a lot of women were? How could I trust myself? When had I ever known my grown-up body without him? For days, posing uncomfortable and self-conscious, I used Drew's skewed abstraction as my mirror.

The next months in Missoula passed in a blur of inversion-layer-grey skies, walking back and forth to class over bridges, fights, days of silences, weeks of Drew disappearing to the painting studio, intense seasonal depression I didn't know was seasonal depression. Drew's worsening bipolar we still didn't know was bipolar.

At Christmas break, we broke our lease and moved home. We needed stability, a familiar context. But the next semester back in Missouri, our fights grew worse. In one, I was in an armchair, and Drew ran toward me, and instead of just grabbing me, punched my stomach several times.

I felt more devastated and angry than ever, but told myself, *We need to try harder. We need to find a better apartment, a new better us.*

It was getting more difficult to see what this would look like. My mother had finally admitted that she and my father were having marital problems. And they'd just discovered that termites had eaten through two walls of their house.

None of us could afford it, but for spring break, we decided to drive to Disney World. What we needed was sun and topiaries shaped like cartoon mice. Though we all agreed that the animatronic Enchanted Tiki Room was stupid, we sat through the show with its singing birds and flowers. It was a space where no one had to talk. Where Disney magic could chirp and twitter and tell us how to feel.

"Through obedience [to seeing the pre-advertised sights] the tourist discloses the inability to endure the freedom that s/he ostensibly desires," Enzensberger wrote in 1958, a little over a decade before Disney World opened. But maybe real freedom is rarer than we pretend. Privileged though I was, educated, with loving parents, at twenty, I didn't experience a free choice between *Escape a codependent increasingly abusive marriage to the man you've been with for almost a quarter of your life by going to Disney World* or *Actually fly into the life you really want—strong and independent.*

Where would such a self or life appear from? There was no version of myself that was not part of us. There was no version of my life that involved saving myself and not saving Drew.

Instead, our senior year of college, I suggest we try the Unity Church I've seen in a strip mall. Unity is New Age—less mainstream Christianity than akin to the crystal I wore on a leather cord during high school. The teachings say to believe your life into alignment with what you want. *Eureka! I have found it because I believe I've found it!*

I love the feisty woman minister. I make a spiritual counseling appointment and confess that Drew occasionally punches me. I ask for advice.

The minister says that when she's upset, she hits a pillow with a tennis racket or screams into the pillow. She suggests that I try this.

In a new nicer apartment—rented during a Unity prosperity seminar that tells us to go into debt and believe the money will come (it doesn't)—I try to kill myself with herbal sleeping pills. Surely I know they wouldn't work, that I'll just wake groggy. But it's a cry for help, part of the days and weeks that I now spend crying.

Where are my parents? We talk on the phone almost nightly; Drew and I still drive home. But I'm too embarrassed to tell them everything. Don't I sometimes hit Drew back? Aren't I often now also irrational?

When I cry over money, Drew insists we're about to win the sweepstakes. He says I should get ready: there will be news crews suddenly one morning, flashbulbs on our concrete landing. Doesn't someone have to win? Every week, he pastes stamps onto the sheets that arrive in the mail. He asks me if I want a white or silver Lamborghini.

No one says *bipolar, domestic abuse, depression, delusions, grandiosity.*

Instead of the sweepstakes, I get a call from William Logan: I've been accepted to University of Florida's MFA program in poetry. Drew applies for late admission in digital art. My parents help us move to Gainesville. We pick the safest, prettiest apartment we can barely afford. Pale pink stucco. Balconies, swimming pools, weeping willows, ponds, and lawns that look like golf courses. There is not a bit of shit or real life to be seen.

I tell the other poets in the MFA I'm so glad to have escaped Missouri winters. I'm married to my high school sweetheart. Obviously, we're artsy, alternative. What else is there?

It's November when I tell my new friend Erin there's more. Erin and I often stay after workshop commiserating over feedback on our poems. One professor likes to refer to the *Poor reader* who must face our flawed writing, and Erin and I now begin our emails to each other, *Dear poor reader.* Erin has, like my mother and me, a dry sense of humor. She's a few years older and has been working at a bird sanctuary near Sarasota from which she's adopted an African Grey, which is beautiful and talkative, and very unhappy when she's in class. Beyond zoos and a few times at Wings, I've never been around caged birds, and Erin—responsible for this exotic, talking bird and living alone—seems worldly. Her apartment, scuffed-up, with hardwood floors, seems like a place where real, grown-up life happens. When I go back to mine, I'm aware there's something swaddled and artificial about my beautiful white couch I could barely afford, the off-white carpet. Erin teases me if I try to say she's more grown-up. Aren't I the married one?

One night, Erin and I see a teepee set up for some festival on the UF campus lawn and decide to sit inside. Maybe because it seems so sheltered, part of some different reality, I'm unusually honest. Erin knows that Drew dropped out of his MFA after only two months because he didn't like his classes, and has had a hard time finding a job. Now I admit we've been having screaming fights about credit card debt. He's been vanishing all evening and can't, or won't, explain where he's been.

A few months ago, I found a stack of pornography hidden on top of our cabinets. Having taken one class in feminism in Montana, I understand that pornography often degrades women. I'm nowhere near sex positive (nor do I know the term). I'm a product of hippie Eureka and then the Bible Belt. Of self-criticism and insecurity. And Florida is full of billboards for places like *Diamond Dolls* and *Sinsations*: double-D, violin-waisted women sexily posed in lingerie. They're impossible to miss, though the strip clubs they belong to—boxy, windowless buildings on the highway turnouts—look nondescript. Every time we pass, I fear that whatever is inside is confident and beautiful in ways I could never be. I fear Drew's repeated comments about how sexy the women are, which are jokes, but maybe not. I've been running punishing laps in the heat around our complex trying to try to make myself thinner, more beautiful.

I don't tell Erin all of this, but I do tell her I found a card in Drew's pocket for *Café Risqué*. With a handwritten phone number.

When I confronted Drew, we had the kind of fight we often do where questions and answers don't line up. Like a surrealist word game. *Whose number is this? I don't know. Did you get it at a strip club? No. How did you get it then? Yes, I got it at a strip club. Why? I don't know. Is it a stripper's? No. Then whose is it? It's a stripper's. Did something happen with her? No. Did you talk to her? Yes. Did you kiss her? No. Why do you have her number? I did kiss her, but only once.*

Erin says she's so sorry; maybe she tells me something about one of her own relationships, says this must be so hard and confusing after so many years together. And at some point, with perfect dark humor, she adds, "You know how people sometimes have kids to save marriages? I don't think that'd be a good idea. But maybe you should get a Christmas tree." I swear she says this. I must have told her it's a holiday we both love.

I know Erin's joking, but a little tree sounds cheerful. I suggest to Drew that we buy one. It's crispy from sitting in a parking lot's heat, and immediately loses needles on our plush carpet. We hang ornaments. We drown the silences by vacuuming. We count down days until my parents arrive for Christmas and Disney World.

In *Vinyl Leaves: Walt Disney World and America,* Stephen M. Fjellman writes that one appeal of the Disney parks is that you don't have to feel touristic shame because there is no real, missable experience. Because the parks are a carefully constructed "simulacra of the touristic world," whatever you're experiencing *is* the experience. If the timetable says that Tigger will be outside the Peter Pan ride at 4 p.m. for photos, he will really be there. If the sign says *Adventureland,* there will be adventures. The Magic Kingdom is all its own reference points.

Yet that trip, as we sat through the Tiki Room and ate ice cream in scooped-out orange halves, I remember feeling as if I wasn't quite there. Or too much there—not connected by rides and laughter and pretty photos but by my own unraveling viscera. I remember the cable cars stalling over 20,000 Leagues—Drew and me swaying in one basket, my parents in the basket behind—and feeling stark terror. Below was the too-blue lagoon, and around me, the pale blue sky, and though I was sitting on a fiberglass seat across from my husband, I was in all that blue free fall.

Because there's something I have not told anyone. Another fight. I don't remember why, but Drew and I were yelling on our outdoor stairway landing. We were about to unlock our apartment, though neither of us did. I remember our raised voices, the tops of the willows at eye level. The pink stucco wall, treefrogs suctioned, as always, to its nubs.

Then Drew lifting me up. But not in the romantic, sweep-me-off-my-feet way. In anger, he held me out over the railing—as if he were going to throw me or drop me. Three stories above that perfect lawn.

Something happened then. Something turned over inside me. How can I tell my parents, Drew, even myself, that I am going to leave? That there is the good kind of painful love, the tragic alive kind. And then there is whatever this is.

Those first months of 1997, I swung between taking the first steps away and desperate romantic gestures. I told Drew I was moving out when the semester ended, but for his April birthday, I made an elaborate trifle. I bought a schmaltzy tropical-beach-sunset card we would have ridiculed as teenagers. I wrote a note neither of us believed. For days, in place of speaking, we ate too-sweet, whipped-cream-drenched trifle from Tupperware.

Some days, he begged me not to go. Some days, I cried and held him. Some days, with that kitschy card announcing my love on the kitchen counter, I stepped right over him when he cried in a fetal position on the carpet, while playing Pink Floyd's "Comfortably Numb" on repeat.

My first month on my own, I lived in an apartment a friend had moved out of with time still on her lease, so I had two floors of rooms with absolutely no furniture. I slept on the carpet. I swam laps in the courtyard. I made the simplest decisions for only myself—what did *I* want for dinner? I was twenty-two and asking for the first time. I felt as if I was living without skin. Like I was made of air. Like I was that apartment itself: all bare walls, with nothing, suddenly, to match my life against.

In my recurring nightmares, Drew chased me through high, empty barns—the light swirling with dust, too dim yet too bright. I had to leap splintery, high rafters to escape him. I was terrified he'd catch me. Terrified I'd fall.

My mother called and said Drew couldn't understand why I wouldn't speak to him. "He's so upset," she said. "He just wants to see you and talk. After all these years."

"I can't," I kept saying. I didn't know how to explain this, but if I spoke to him, how would *now* be different from *all these years*?

It was late summer, the day we signed no-fault divorce papers at the Alachua County courthouse, when we spoke again. We said something bland and impossible like "hello," then talked stiffly about what we'd done with our wedding rings. He'd thrown his in a retaining pond. I'd sold mine. As a grad student, about to rent her first apartment alone, I'd been hoping for a few hundred dollars, but the jeweler had said the diamond was chipped underneath and nearly worthless.

"So the diamond wasn't so perfect after all," Drew said snidely. At the time, I thought he meant this as a metaphor for my imperfections. Though maybe he meant that I'd wanted him to be perfect and he'd failed. Or that we'd both failed to be our own great love story.

I wonder if Rex ever told his children, if he had them, stories about his first, greatest love, Sylvia Berry. Did he think of my mother that way? Did he wonder what happened to her? Would he have been shocked to learn that as she was dying in 2001, fifty years after she last saw him, she asked my sister Beth to try to find him? Or that a boy named Drew wore his agate ring even after he'd thrown his own wedding ring into a Florida retaining pond?

In those first months single, I remember meeting Erin at bars, learning what beer to order (Harp or Bass), floatingly kissing a guy I'd just met at a student union meeting, having no idea what to do after. Soon, I'll take shelter in a relationship with an older, infantalizing PhD student. I won't know what to do with my freedom. But I'll have the repeated, dizzying realization that my life, which had only one possible future and framing, can have others.

When Drew first tries to kill himself, a month after we divorce, my parents tell me. Unlike my college attempt with herbal pills, it's almost deadly. He drives his mother's car into a brick wall in Arkansas. Something in the car catches fire, and he's severely burned all down both legs. In the hospital, finally, he's diagnosed as bipolar.

In the years after, he'll go in and out of institutions, group homes, rehab, on and off different meds. He'll try to commit suicide, afterwards stabilize at least enough each time. As terrible as bipolar is, he'll be glad to have a diagnosis: an explanation after all those years alone in his mind.

He'll stay in touch with my parents, and after my mother dies, my father. They will also always be, in part, his parents.

I'll get married again codependently in my mid-twenties. Move to San Francisco—"big Eureka Springs," which I've resisted for that reason: it seems so predictable. I'll still love The Cure, Pink Floyd, then techno. I'll "make up for lost time" by partying too much; I'll struggle with depression, insecurity, my mother's death. I'll get divorced again. Marry, finally, a truly stable partner. Go to therapy. After a decade and a half, Drew and I will talk on the phone.

He won't remember some of our worst times. There aren't pictures to confirm him holding me off the balcony, but he'll believe me. He'll say he must have been out of his mind; he didn't mean to hurt me. I'll say I didn't mean to hurt him either. There was so much I didn't see. I'll say, "we were kids." It'll take me years to realize how true this is.

These days, we message each other on Facebook every week or so. *Howz the weather? Raining more here.* Or he sends pictures of new paintings, abstract still, but often with crosses since AA. Or we reminisce about my mother's cooking: *Those pesto pizzas! Yum!* Occasionally, he'll post for Throw-Back Thursday: me in a black satin prom dress my mother sewed me, bright red goth lipstick; him with his hair straight up—the year he shaved *Fuck You* into the back at a friend's house and got in trouble for it at prom.

Did my parents know? How could they not have? But I don't remember them saying anything. In retrospect, it's hard to untangle what we knew and didn't mention, what we really didn't see, and what we wanted to see.

There are, of course, no pictures of the day we divorced, and I don't know exactly how he remembers it. Besides the imperfect diamond, what I remember most is arriving at the courthouse in a straight summer skirt and heeled sandals. I'm trying to look professional but not too dressed up. I'm twenty-two and do not know how to get divorced, and am about to.

The waiting room has dark wood and high ceilings, and the chairs along the wall—wood with upholstery—look stiff and old-fashioned. Most are full. I glance over. I'm dreading, have been dreading for two months, seeing Drew.

But then something worse happens. I don't see him. I look again at the rows of strangers. Their arms on the chair arms. Their faces. The high, closed windows, the pale blue Florida sky. I begin to panic. I think, *Of course he didn't even come. Can I get divorced alone?*

But then I realize I've looked right at him. My love for a third of my life. The only man I've had sex with. My six-foot, six-inch foster brother. He's right there. In a linen shirt, partly unbuttoned, like a Victorian rake or an escaped lunatic. He's the man I have not recognized without hair or eyebrows.

Haven't I wanted a love who would do something this extreme, this serious, this engraved-on-his-own-body? Just like Pink in that iconic scene, where blood drips into shaving cream, and his face, with his wild eyes, becomes alien?

But isn't copying a movie also cheap? Isn't it a premade postcard from the edge of society, which might not even be addressed to me?

Though maybe that's what I most fear: it *is* addressed to me. No one copies a scene like that by choice. Drew's behavior is *too* real, *too* desperate.

Before I cross the room, before we say "hello," all of this—*love and teens in the Ozark hills and punk madmen and confusion and hurt and this courthouse of strangers, and one stranger who is not a stranger, and myself about to walk toward him*—swirls inside me. Or I swirl inside it. Here is a shaken snow globe. Here is my real life.

Frontierland

"A man's style is his Mind's voice."
RALPH WALDO EMERSON

A century before Walt Disney constructed Frontierland's fake rock canyons and Big Thunder Mountain, Buffalo Bill was galloping across the American West. Summers, he'd work as an Indian scout, and off season, he'd reenact his exploits. In 1876, he shot, then scalped, the Cheyenne warrior Yellow Hair near Warbonnet Creek, then promptly began "scalping" a headdressed actor onstage to thunderous applause. He called his show *Buffalo Bill's Wild West*, as if the real place and his version weren't conflated enough.

Across the Rivers of America from Frontierland, The Hall of Presidents' audio-animatronic presidents are Buffalo Bill's heirs. They're reenactments of themselves, made grander by a stage. Life-sized yet larger than life, they're men enough to speak in baritones, no matter the presidents' original voices. Lincoln, the first president Imagineered into being, commandingly recites a pastiche of speeches: "To the humblest and poorest among us are held out the highest privileges and positions. . . . At what point shall we expect the approach of danger? By what means shall we fortify against it? . . . As a nation of freemen, we must live through all time, or die by suicide. . . . No, no, man was made for immortality."

In 1993, after a revised Lincoln premiered wearing reading glasses and glancing down at his notes, one review complained that this "dumbed down the depiction of Lincoln as a prominent and iconic figure." Prominent, iconic American men have perfect sight. Before they speak, they've memorized themselves. Showing weakness means becoming prey or comedy. When the animatronic bears in the Country Bear Jamboree play banjos in ear-holed straw hats like country bumpkins over in Frontierland, they plummet from apex predators to beary funny jokes.

Although my mother partly grew up in Arizona and loved Zane Grey novels and *High Noon,* my sisters and I weren't Western girls. We were born in Fort Worth, Texas, "Where the West Begins," but, by our lives, a dull, glassy city. Aside from a few trips to Arizona, I saw much of "the West" first on our trips to Disney World, which led to confusing experiences as an adult of first seeing the Idaho Sawtooths' glass-green waterfalls or the iconic boulders of Lone Pine, California, and being reminded of somewhere, only to realize it was a place made from concrete to look like them.

My family, dominated by my mother, felt matriarchal. Though my sisters had only sons. My oldest sister Beth's son, Logan, had been born two years before me, always more cousin or brother than nephew. Anne's sons, Nathan and Gabriel, were born thirteen and sixteen years after me, in 1987 and 1990, making them perfect for me to babysit each Thanksgiving when they visited Arkansas where my parents and I had moved by then.

Nathan was gregarious, with blonde curls like Anne's in childhood. Gabriel was shyer, quieter. He loved animals and science. He'd spend hours in the yard inspecting butterflies and ladybugs and the spring-feet of frogs. He had a pet rabbit. With straight brown hair snipped at home into the same floppy bowl cut Logan and I have in childhood pictures, Gabriel looked like an updated Victorian urchin: Oliver Twist with a science-museum-shop magnifying glass.

He wasn't the kind of sensitive child who cried a lot, but the kind who felt everything deeply. There was something almost ethereal about him. He was "too sensitive for this world," as my mother once said. She meant it as a compliment, and a concern about this world.

Anne, a case worker at a battered women's shelter, and Michael, the decade-older contractor she'd married after a string of musician boyfriends, lived in a run-down Fort Worth neighborhood: a few sturdy old houses, but also graffiti, break-ins. In one, Anne lost most of our great-grandmother's costume jewelry, not valuable, but irreplaceable. She and Michael increasingly talked of moving. They'd buy a house Michael could restore—in the country with space for the boys to explore on their own. In Arizona or New Mexico. The real West.

The summer of 1995, Michael went scouting near Santa Fe, but land was too expensive, so he worked his way south. In Lincoln County—made famous in the late 1800s by a mine boom and Billy the Kid, and then sparsely inhabited for almost a century—he saw a sign for *White Oaks: Ghost Town and Artists' Community*. He continued down the highway, stopped for eggs at a diner, kept thinking about that sign. He turned around, crossed a train track, rumbled down a hard-packed dirt road, followed a more rutted road uphill. He passed a deserted red-brick 1800s schoolhouse, but hardly noticed. What he was driving to—what commanded the scrubland—was a white Victorian: two tall stories plus a tower.

Most people would have stayed in their car and imagined life there. But not Michael. Quintessentially strong and silent in some ways, but also prone to educated, opinionated speeches about politics or history or science, he was the rare kind of man who could have lectured in a humanities library or built the library. "I love this house," he told the man who answered the door when he knocked. And the man, a caretaker, said, "Well, it's for sale."

So, within a year, Anne, Michael, six-year-old Gabriel, and nine-year-old Nathan—i.e., half my immediate family—had moved to a weathered Victorian mansion in a New Mexico ghost town.

The Gumm House, one of White Oaks's two mansions from its boom days, was built in 1895 by a woodworker and sawmill owner. As apocryphal local legend has it, Gumm was going to sell Pat Garrett the wood to build gallows to hang Billy the Kid. But then Garret ran into Billy in a saloon and shot him. That was during White Oaks's brief prosperity, when gold discovered in the Jicarilla Mountains had bloomed it into the second largest city in the New Mexico Territory. At its height, White Oaks had over two thousand residents.

And then, as happened across the West, the gold dried up, litigation over competing claims drained the fortunes, and the White Oak city fathers failed to court the railroad men, who chose a different route. By the time Anne, Michael, and the boys arrived, White Oaks had been a ghost town for half a century. Technically, the area has about forty residents, and the town has never been fully deserted, so Anne prefers to call it not a "ghost town" but a "diminished mining town."

Town consists of the red-brick Hoyle Mansion and the white-wood Gumm House, the historic 1890s schoolhouse, the Brown Store (with dusty antiques and sometimes paintings for sale), the nondenominational White Oaks Community Church, a few scattered artists including a ceramicist, and, in a brick building where the town's early newspaper was printed, The No Scum Allowed Saloon, named one of *American Cowboy*'s Best Cowboy Bars in the West. The summer of 1996, I first saw all this, when my parents and I drove two days from Arkansas.

My sisters had been raised, and I'd been raised until it burned, in a hundred-year-old house in Fort Worth. We felt at home in houses that needed fixing up, houses with history and character. And here was the ultimate feral Victorian house: vast, slantingly hardwood-floored, dusty-windowed, drafty, its paint flaking faster than my sister and Michael could repaint.

The water was so mineral-thick it stopped up the pipes, stained the tub, and wore everyone's skin sandpapery. Since water was scarce and the family lived on what Michael could make doing carpentry, they had to conserve water and gas: washing dishes in a trickle, reusing paper plates they could burn later in the woodstove. The lace curtains Anne hung were always spider-webbed, dust-blown; quilts faded on the clothesline in the desert sun; floors shifted and creaked anciently.

But the space. The light. The possibilities for reconstruction. The frontier freedom of having slipped into this other world. Here there were no sounds of neighbors; nothing but wind and the house's set-tling, and sometimes desert silence, which always feels bigger than other silences.

As Michael and Anne had dreamed, my nephews could roam freely through the scrublands. They could conduct explosive science experiments without noise complaints (though as Gabriel got older, he was more likely to practice yoga or read about Buddhism). They could watch for cottontail rabbits in the brush.

When my parents and I visited for Thanksgiving, we'd cook beans on the woodstove, or hike into the fields, or feed apples to Anne's burros. Once it opened as a museum, we'd go to the schoolhouse, where one room had been restored to look as it had in the 1890s, the desks still carved with names of bored, long-dead students. The hall held a display of barbed wire: Kelly "Diamond Point" Right Twist, Merrill Four Point Twirl, Bronson Single Strand Double Loop, Hunt's Link—more twists than I'd ever imagined existed.

At night, we played board games at the long plank table Michael had made, the electric lights above seeming, against all the darkness, like new miraculous inventions, barely wired through desert.

Or I'd sit on the dusty oriental rug looking at books with Nathan and Gabriel. Nathan was obsessed with movies. Gabriel still favored books about science. Both had good senses of humor—wordy like all my family—typified by Monty Python and Far Side cartoons mag-neted beside their report cards with all As from the Carrizozo school, twelve miles away.

Sometimes, we'd walk to the Cedarvale Cemetery, which Gabriel particularly loved. He'd narrate its famous graves: John Winters, who had helped start the gold rush in 1879; William C. McDonald, first

New Mexico governor; Charles H. McVeagh, Congressional Medal of Honor Recipient for his *Bravery in scouts and actions against Indians*; deputy sheriff James Bell, killed by Billy the Kid in his escape from the Lincoln County jail. Even the famous graves were little more than worn stones or statues of lambs: marble-fleeced relatives of the bleached bones we'd see in the desert.

Being in the cemetery felt like wandering the bed of a long-dry river that had washed the town away. Yet the town also felt most full here: thickly, invisibly inhabited by the frontier dead. Legend had it, Billy the Kid had once walked here on his way to White Oaks's saloons. Or been secretly buried here.

Gabriel was fascinated by Billy the Kid, and maybe felt a kinship to the boy bandit, described in his 1881 obituary as "quiet-mannered," and in several sources as a lover of animals, particularly his racing mare and butterflies.

Although Billy was orphaned at fourteen and died at twenty-one, he's not usually described so gently. Instead, his manly reputation is epitomized by the biography Pat Garrett wrote after killing him: *The Authentic Life of Billy, The Kid: The Noted Desperado of the Southwest, Whose Deeds of Daring and Blood Made His Name a Terror in New Mexico, Arizona and Northern Mexico.* If Billy's real youth or gentleness is mentioned at all in most stories, it's like chiaroscuro: the flicker of light that makes the *deeds of daring and blood* seem even darker.

Rather than moving to the true middle of nowhere, Anne, Michael, and the boys had moved to a place that used to be somewhere. A place dominated by Western legends. By men who were so much someone that they echoed on in the scrublands a century after themselves.

By the time Nathan and Gabriel were preteens, film and TV crews looking for a quintessential, affordable Western landscape had also found White Oaks. Sometimes, they'd lodge at the Gumm House, where my sister had made a sign about the house's history, which she propped on an easel by the grand staircase the family seldom used, coming and going instead through the mud room, kitchen, and narrow servants' stairs. The house wasn't museumlike, but it unquestionably belonged to the West and its history more than to our family.

To our pride, Nathan and Gabriel got hired as extras. They spent winter nights huddled by the pellet stove watching VCR tapes, and Nathan dreamed of being a director, so acting seemed natural. They'd appear as shoulders or profiles in jostled crowds, with a rare line or close-up. By now, growing toward Michael's over six-foot height, they looked like believable 1800s boys: rangy, pale, a little hungry-looking. Their characters wore cowboy hats and leather vests they never would have worn to school or at the Gumm House, where they helped Michael and my sister with house projects, and also spent hours reading, doing homework, playing board games, like the children of liberal readers and NPR-listeners they were.

I imagined them able to slip in and out of their Western roles, like Frontierland's "gingham and denim clad Cast Members" roaming "clapboard buildings . . . [with] animal heads on the wall . . . turquoise jewelry, Native American or cowboy toys," as one Disney ad says. But White Oaks wasn't an amusement park. The land, long before the gold rush, had been Mescalero Apache hunting grounds. By the 1990s and early 2000s, many neighbors were white or Latino ranchers. This was the new Old West where men were expected to have deep voices and shoot things. Where trucks sported bumper stickers like *The Earth is Not Your Mother. It's the Creation of Your Father.*

I laughed and cringed at these slogans, but I didn't really consider that the dominant culture in nine-hundred-person Carrizozo's school wasn't pet bunnies and burros, but animal heads on walls. Not arty movies or old literature, but real fist fights and guns. And my nephews weren't just actors passing through to recreate the West. They lived there.

During these years, I moved from Missouri to Florida to Missouri to Hawaii to California. Logan lived in New York, Texas, California, got a master's in architecture, married. My mother had died in 2001, and without her to bring the family together, communication became sporadic. Since Anne and I had never been close, I got most family news from Beth, who still lived in the hippie tourist town in Arkansas where Logan and I had gone to high school.

Beth said Gabriel had started practicing yoga in his room. He was staunchly vegetarian, like Beth, my parents, and me. As my classmates had made fun of me for eating "rabbit food" or hid pepperoni under my pizza's cheese (a joke they never tired of), PETA's envelopes had arrived, stuffed with glossy photos of white test bunnies excoriated by Gillette razors: horrifying but also a lifeline to likeminded people somewhere.

Although Anne tells me later that Gabriel read every PETA flyer, too, he and I didn't discuss this at the time. I was wrapped up in the barbed-wire twists of my twenties. At best, for "the boys'" (as I still called them) birthdays, I'd send checks for twenty dollars. Once, Gabriel's—cashed six months later—overdrew my account, which made me unreasonably mad. I'd long forgotten it and respent the money on yoga (which I'd predictably fallen in love with in San Francisco), or Ecstasy, which I'd fallen in love with as a self-critical, depressive twenty-something who loved to dance. When I came to New Mexico in those years, I was not quite a tourist, but close: glancing at the sign about the Gumm House beneath its stained-glass window, laughing with my partner about the name *No Scum Allowed Saloon*.

By now, Anne and Michael had divorced, and Michael had moved to even more isolated land thirty miles away. The boys continued to live in the Gumm House, though in the summers, sometimes traveled with Michael, who now worked as a storm insurance adjuster.

Nathan was still the more outgoing one, who, in a few years, when he went to The University of New Mexico, would start DJing parties. Who, with his striking blonde looks and charm, would date aspiring actresses. Gabriel was still quieter—destined, as Anne once predicted, to grow up to be "a scientist or monk." He loved writing and, as a teen, started posting stories to a blog. He didn't share the links with me until later, but when I read them, I'm reminded of my own writing at that age: observant, overly descriptive, the product of reading too many old books and not talking to enough living people.

"Grace," which he's categorized as a "gloomy masterpiece," is set in a graveyard and includes lines like "We just existed, hanging from the stars and the moon."

Another, "Habits," reads:

> There was something about being withdrawn from her environment that helped her to see it, as a deep sea explorer could better observe the depths of the ocean from the inside of a submarine. . . . In this way she reflected on the fish that passed through her scope, and the sharks that pursued the fish, without having to defend herself from them. It was about eight in the morning.

The stories often include that kind of staccato sentence in which the quotidian jars against internal reverie. The protagonist is a misfit, isolated, sensitive in some way others don't see or care to see.

Even if I'd read Gabriel's stories then, I wouldn't have worried. Everyone in our family felt sensitive and slightly isolated. Or at least my mother, sisters, and I always had. And I was wrapped up in depression over my mother's death, desire to be the writer I'd studied to be in graduate school, avoidance of that same writing, antiwar rallies after September 11, and disillusionment. I didn't think about Gabriel and Nathan having my same too-artsy-to-be-mainstream, too-self-critical-and-proper-to-be-truly-bohemian family and genetics, and growing up in a less forgiving place. Because I loved them, I imagined everyone loving them.

I didn't think about Gabriel having trouble finding other fifteen-year-olds who wanted to talk about Flannery O'Connor. I didn't know I'd gotten off easy with kids hiding pepperoni on my pizza. Until Nathan told me years later, I had no idea Gabriel was being repeatedly teased and beaten up for being gentle. For being weird. For caring about other living creatures and feeling too much—the way a Western boy, or man, is not allowed to.

The *New York Times* obituary of Billy the Kid also describes him as "one of the most dangerous characters which this country has produced." And *produced* seems honest.

Gabriel didn't become an outlaw or killer of other people. And he didn't become a scientist or monk. He followed Nathan to UNM, three hours away in Albuquerque, on a full ride. It's the only place he applied. No one in my family had college savings of the kind I've learned my middle-class friends consider part of raising children, and it was a luxury to attend college at all.

In one email, he told me he was volunteering on Democratic campaigns and had written a paper on Pakistani-Kurdish politics and another on aviation technology and international relations, which he thought would make his grandfather (my sisters' father, an airplane mechanic) proud. He also started sending me stories. It was clear he also wanted me, in my new job as a visiting poetry professor in Arkansas, to be proud.

Maybe inspired by Nathan, who'd gotten a turntable, he'd also started writing hip-hop lyrics. Unlike the political hip-hop I listened to, his tended toward boasting—which strikes me now as in line with much of the genre, as well as a far older tradition of Western bravado. It's not a stretch to imagine *Noted Desperado Whose Deeds of Daring and Blood Made His Name a Terror* to a beat.

Anne wrote to me years later that "around the time he left for college, he started eating meat on a regular basis. That didn't surprise me as much as that he offered no explanation into what appeared to be a sudden and drastic shift away from his closely held ethical principles." He also traveled to Mexico with friends and became, after me, the second person in our family to get a tattoo.

Since Anne and I seldom talked on the phone, the tattoo came up in passing one Thanksgiving as if I somehow knew. "It's not like yours," Anne said. "It's not what you'd expect." She grimaced, as she does, as if she were both making fun of herself for being critical and really grimacing. "He'll have to show you."

Despite Anne's warning, when Gabriel pulled up his shirt, I was startled. On his abdomen—on clearly weight-trained muscles—a bare-breasted Mexican woman swayed amid flowers. Below her, cursive said *El que no habla, Dios no lo oye.*

My Spanish was decent, but he translated: "If you don't speak, God won't hear you."

"That's beautiful," I said. After my double take, I thought it was, in a sailor-style way. And since moving to Idaho the year before, I'd gotten more familiar with masculinity appearing in surprising places—like my creative writing grad students who joked about "getting pumped," as if it were a stereotypical masculine desire they couldn't possibly share, then spent hours spotting each other in the weight pit after poetry workshops.

I didn't ask Gabriel what *El que no hablo, Dios no lo oye* meant to him, but I imagined I knew. Even if our family didn't believe in God with a capital G, we believed in stories to make sense of a confusing world—to connect us across enforced and self-inflicted isolation. Even if no one might be listening, even in a ghost town, or maybe especially then, we believed in the power of voices.

And that same year he'd gotten the tattoo, Gabriel had changed his voice. I don't mean the natural lowering that had happened in his teens. I mean a purposeful, cultivated, throat-hurting lowering. He was suddenly speaking in a bass that strained his throat ragged, gravelly. With his over six feet of height and somewhat fine features, the voice descended toward whomever he was speaking to like steps blasted in a granite mountainside. Like the heaviest-gauge wallet chain that says *thug* with each link. Like, in that famous picture, the gun Billy the Kid leans on.

The quintessential American male voice that's carved from rock—or concrete or audio tape and wiring that convincingly resembles it. Though Lincoln's real-life voice was "high pitched and reedy" (as Michelle Krowl writes for the Library of Congress) or "rather falsetto" (as one contemporary described it), the three men who have voiced Lincoln in The Hall of Presidents over the decades have all spoken in a stentorian baritone. Of course they have.

Gabriel's voice sounded, though it came from him, almost like ventriloquism. Its gravitas and unnaturalness made it hard to question him or have ordinary conversations.

Maybe that's partly why I didn't ask more about the tattoo, nor the business card he handed me for White Rabbit, Inc: his name as CEO above the outline of a rabbit. He explained that White Rabbit, Inc. was his "umbrella for future business ventures."

"Oh, cool," I said, or something innocuous. With its heavy paper and stylized jackrabbit, the card seemed, like his new voice, both fantastical and authoritative. You could follow either of them to Wonderland. Or Frontierland.

"Gabriel doesn't usually sound like this," I told my new boyfriend that Thanksgiving, as if this needed saying. And Beth referred to "what Gabriel has done to his voice," but we didn't otherwise talk about it, and never with him. Instead, the whole family zipped up coats for a walk between dinner and pies. We crunched down the dirt road, which was frost-crisp that time of year, so the rocky landscape seemed frozen into being. We walked across the fields and down into a ravine, where we stood inside a huge cylinder of aluminum drainage pipe. In its cavern of dusky ripples, we sang whatever Christmas carols we could all remember.

I'm sure Gabriel couldn't maintain that voice when he sang, but you couldn't tell with all of us as one harmoniously off-key instrument attempting "Angels We Have Heard on High"—my favorite for "Glor-or-or-or-ia in excelsis Deo," those elongated syllables comforting even if none of us believed in Glory to God in the highest.

Or if we did, we meant this: stark desert light at both ends of the cylinder, and us together as a family, joined loosely but powerfully by shared blood. Laughing and starting a new carol when we forgot the lyrics, as if our voices came easily to us.

Though that tenuous, solid moment is what I return to now, that's not when I last saw Gabriel. That was three years later, at the plank table in the Gumm House, when we played the Victorian parlor game Exquisite Corpse, in which one person draws a head, then folds the paper so you can't see the neck as you're drawing the shoulders, etc. In this variation, which my boyfriend and I had learned in a Mexican hostel, someone starts by writing a sentence, the next person draws it, the next person writes what the drawing is, the next person draws that. Since the writer or artist only responds to what's immediately before, the simplest statement—*Mary couldn't believe she won the sweepstakes*—inevitably transforms by the end, through misinterpretations, to something like *The girl climbed inside the giant donut and set off for Tahiti.*

"That was supposed to be money?" someone will say, unfolding the accordioned paper and doubling over laughing. "I thought her hands were on fire!"

Gabriel went outside to smoke after playing only a few rounds in which his drawings and sentences were strange but not funny. It's only years later that I'll wonder if the game was too close to the way his mind was working by then: the out-of-synchness frightening instead of humorous. The paper again and again unfolding to what should have, but didn't, make sense.

By then I knew he'd failed out of college and was living with Michael. On the day we visited, he joined the rest of us for a snowball fight, then retreated to his room, messy in a way no one in our family had ever lived: crumpled with papers and cigarette butts. When he spoke, it was still in that strained, deep voice.

We all knew by then that he'd had a series of mental breakdowns, though we didn't generally talk about them. In the first, he'd driven his car into a field outside Albuquerque and walked away, talking irrationally. He'd spent two weeks in a public mental institution where the staff had sedated him so much he didn't even know who he was. After, he'd thrown away the prescribed medication and refused to get more.

A few months later, he'd been evicted from his apartment for flooding it by leaving the shower running for days. Repeatedly, my sister and Michael and Nathan had to find him or take him to safety, though the safety never lasted. He was a legal adult, and he insisted he did not need help.

I learned this in pieces from Beth, the confusion compounded by getting the stories third-hand. Later I learned that Anne had stopped inviting us for Thanksgiving because she never knew if Gabriel would be well enough. No one knew when Gabriel would be well, or what was wrong.

As a community college adjunct in California, I was the only family member with health insurance. No one could afford specialists, and Gabriel wouldn't have gone anyway. Public health doctors said probably bipolar. But they admitted this diagnosis might be incomplete. There were delusions, irrational decisions, the way he, or the version of him we'd known, had retreated somewhere inside strained bravado.

Was this inherited? Some trauma we didn't know about? Had his brain chemistry been altered by drugs? Later Nathan will tell me that at parties at UNM Gabriel often took three pills of whatever his friends were taking one of.

Had he been trying to hurt himself? Had he been trying to reach some more meaningful frontier inside himself? Had he been trying to escape from some frontier he already felt lost in?

At the time, I kept telling myself he'd grow out of whatever was happening. Maybe he'd move to a bigger city as I had, figure out who he really was. But first, he'd need a reason to move, and the money to, and to admit he needed help. And what I knew from my first husband wasn't hopeful. Since Drew had been diagnosed as bipolar in his twenties, he'd gotten by with frequently changing meds—sometimes working, sometimes on disability, sometimes institutionalized, always in and out of AA. When I called Drew for advice, he said, "He needs to be taking meds. He needs to admit there's something wrong." But I was scared to confront Gabriel and drive him away by saying this. And how could I, across the country, outside his mind, know what he really needed?

The fall of 2011, Gabriel started calling me in Idaho, where I'd just moved as an assistant professor, to tell me how much he admired my being an academic and writer. He was enrolled at UNM again, but on the verge of failing out for good. He once referred to his "break" from the university, but never once mentioned his breakdowns. When I asked how school was, he told me at length about concepts. He talked as if he were writing an essay. "Knowledge can ultimately confuse you if you have too much of it or not quite enough," he said.

He told me he'd been reading Machiavelli and believed that human nature was vain and self-centered and competitive. He wondered if anyone did anything from real generosity. He said he didn't believe that humans were bad per se: they just wanted to pursue reward and avoid pain.

"I go into my study in the evening, and I take off my boots and peasant clothes and I put on my regal imperial clothes, and I enter into the studies of the great men of history, and I ask them the reason for their actions, and they answer me, and for three or four hours, I do not tremble at the thought of death," Gabriel read me from a parody of Machiavelli he'd written. His voice on the phone was somewhere between his real voice and the affected one, though what he was saying was becoming so outsized, he didn't need added bravado.

He told me he was looking into small business loans for White Rabbit, Inc. to go into "Agrobusiness USA" with an angora clothing business. A vendor was offering two thousand pounds of rabbit fur for five dollars per ounce. He would buy it in bulk, find investors. He'd develop a winter line plus casual business apparel. He'd make up for growing up poor. His goal, he told me, was to make millions.

His voice spooled from subject to subject, convincingly, articulately, if I didn't think too much about outside logic, about reality, about the ways in which all the words sounded both live and pre-recorded. A pastiche of mismatching speeches.

Cue the young eccentric entrepreneur speaking in a strained but now-familiar macho baritone about making millions, though he's living in a trailer on land Michael found him near Albuquerque. At least to my knowledge, he doesn't know how to sew, or have any rabbits or fur.

Cue a more reasonable-seeming twenty-two-year-old talking about his new seasonal job: stringing Christmas lights for rich people in Santa Fe.

Cue him as a tough Albuquerque dude on Facebook posting hip-hop lyrics or new lengthy rants that call women *bitches*. (I wasn't on Facebook yet, but Beth and my boyfriend told me.)

Cue him quoting his favorite author, Flannery O'Connor, from his favorite story, "The River," in which a boy drowns himself to find God. Saying he doesn't believe in God exactly, but in having faith in something. Paraphrasing O'Connor, a lifelong Catholic: "You can live without faith, but life has no meaning that way."

If you don't speak, God won't hear you. You can live without faith, but life has no meaning that way. Put together, maybe meaning *is* speaking and being heard. Or having faith you will be heard: that what you cast out into the world, one angora fiber at a time, one line of writing at a time, might be met by someone listening at the other end of all that emptiness.

When he talked about making millions, I wanted to tell him this was delusional. And no one in our family cared about getting rich. But it was hard to interrupt his speeches. And I didn't want to hurt him, or drive him away, or further inside. And what if I was wrong? Maybe angora clothing could actually lead out of the frontier of self he'd gotten lost in. Tough bandits might make millions and want all the bitches to love them, but they don't usually call their business White Rabbit, Inc. and plan to sew—themselves—women's sweaters from bunny fur.

And what other solution did I have? Anne, Michael, and Nathan were doing everything they could to give him a safe place and time to hopefully get better. And my own experience with depression—in college, and worse after my second divorce—had been a series of bad therapists, then a good one, time, a new relationship. And I only had depression-prone brain chemistry, worsened by raising and tanking my serotonin with Ecstasy in my twenties, but mostly kept stable with Vitamin B, therapy, exercise. I'd gotten lucky. And, at the time, I lacked the language to talk about any of this. I was too close to it, or too far from him.

Knowledge can ultimately confuse you if you have too much of it or not quite enough. And how often do we have exactly the right amount of knowledge about anything?

It's only years later that I imagine that Gabriel—less outgoing than Nathan, less self-confidently given to authoritative speeches than his father—was trying to find, or adopt, a swaggering, sailor-tattooed self that would be heard in the gun-toting ranch culture and thuggy-Western-city parties. Or maybe just trying to find a voice that made sense in his own mentally ill mind.

During one phone call, in which he talked for several hours, I started taking notes, scrawled in light blue pen like doodles. At the bottom, I circled *Design?* Was it a question for him, for myself? Were those notes a way to try to make sense of what he was saying? Or to archive what was too painful to fully listen to? Or to try to listen, through the scrawls, for either of our true voices?

"You're writing better than most of my students," I remember telling him, which was true. "I love you too," I'd say, also true. But I still often wanted those phone calls to end: to not have to know this other nephew who my gentle, brilliant nephew had become.

In an art exhibit I saw in Spain during these years, the video artist overlaid voices just barely out of synch with bodies, as a reckoning with his father's schizophrenia. His statement explained that *The Exorcist* is terrifying precisely because we want the voice and the lips to match.

When they don't, we're in the *uncanny valley*: that term in robotics for the frightening, liminal point at which a figure sounds or looks human but is somehow just off. Human voices coming from stiff presidential mouths. Mechanical hands doffing top hats.

But if too-human mechanical figures can be slightly frightening, it's infinitely more frightening to hear a beloved, fully human person speak in a voice that seems prerecorded or off. To hear them slip in and out of synch with reality.

That was supposed to be money? I thought her hands were on fire!

I can't imagine how terrified Gabriel must have felt when, after being a straight-A student, he lost his scholarship, left college, moved in with Nathan, then with his father, then to that trailer in the high desert, then back in with Nathan, then to a shared house in Santa Fe. Unable to say he needed help but relying again and again on his brother and parents to save him.

One weekend, Nathan didn't hear from him when they were supposed to get together. The next day, Nathan tried calling, but the phone rang and rang. He drove to Gabriel's apartment, where a housemate answered. Nathan said he'd come to see Gabriel, and the housemate—a Spanish speaker, with slightly awkward English—said, "Gabriel? No, he die yesterday."

There is, on one fold of paper I cannot stop writing and reading, that sentence. A man standing in a doorway, saying—nonchalantly as if he's stepped out for pizza—that Nathan's brother is dead.

On the next fold of paper: blankness. The suicide note Gabriel didn't leave, although his computer was filled with other writing.

Then Anne is calling Beth. Beth is calling me. I know, even before she says it, from her voice, what she's about to say, although I have not known until this moment that this is a call I've been fearing.

Fold again, and I'm picturing Gabriel alone in his room. He holds a gun, gotten somewhere.

Fold again, and my sister, Michael, and Nathan are IDing the body. They dress Gabriel in his best suit but can't find his nicer shoes, so they buy a pair, which are black and shiny, like he's going to a wedding, or of course a funeral.

Then my sisters and I are crying inside the Gumm House with its too many rooms. One of them, with a balcony, is where Gabriel used to do yoga and read about Buddhism. One of them is the library where he showed me his tattoo. One of them is the kitchen where we all stood by the stove as one of us rolled out pie crust. One of them is the living room where we all watched movies. All of them are late-March cold and empty, empty.

Fold again, and Michael is pulling up the rattling rock road in a pickup carrying a casket. As it comes closer, Anne clutches her heart, and her body folds backwards as if the pickup is towing a wind so strong she cannot stand in it.

The casket is heavy, planed, natural wood, beautiful like everything Michael makes. He has, in the past days, worked and worked on it. Michael, his brother, Anne, Beth, and I cannot, with its thick rope handles, lift the weight of it and the grown man's body inside it.

Then Michael is saying, "We're going to have to take the lid off."

There is my baby nephew a week before what would have been his twenty-sixth birthday. His face held firm with embalming fluid. He looks exactly and not at all like himself.

There is a spell against evil, carried down perhaps from Celtic mythology: *rabbit rabbit,* or *white rabbits.* In the UK, it's said at the first of the month for good luck. During war, the Royal Air Force bombers said it when they woke to ensure they'd live through the day. I don't know this yet.

There is a snapshot in my memory. Gabriel as a late teenager: barely muscled, shaggy-haired, his eyes somewhere between gentle and vacant. He has one hand raised in a gesture that looks like a benediction. His red muscle tee says *New Mexico Boys State.*

There is a voicemail on my cell phone from a month or so before his death. I've told myself I'll call back *after the semester slows down, after I finish this grading, after, after.* I'm phobic of phones and uncomfortable calls. At best, I've sent an email, saying *I'll call soon.* His message says, as he always does, "This is Gabriel New," as if I might not recognize his voice, his voices, as if he is not in my contacts, as if he is not my baby nephew. "Call me if you have time sometime." But I have not called. I have not called.

There is the back doorway the family always uses. The mudroom door, which, when we reach it, is impossibly narrow for the casket. We all stand there, the casket on the ground, and look at that doorway. None of us can understand how one space ever led to another.

Then there is Michael, haggard but practical. He unscrews the hinges from the east porch door, below Gabriel's old room.

On that porch the next morning, Nathan and I clean up broken glass from a vase knocked over as the casket was carried through. As we kneel to pick up shards with our bare hands, Nathan tells me that Gabriel told him more than once that he believed in some kind of afterlife and that he would be better off in it. He said he was tired of being inside his own mind. Tired of what he was doing to all of us.

White rabbit, white rabbit, white rabbit, white rabbit, white rabbit, white rabbit.

There is bright desert light that seems to define each shard of glass, but is really defining the emptiness between them.

There is March 27, 2016, which also exists in a time centuries ago on the frontier when families still buried their own dead. Gabriel is in a casket on sawhorses, next to the plank table where we used to play games. We try to eat dinner at that table. Then Anne and Beth and a family friend and I sit for hours at the woodstove and drink red wine and smoke clove cigarettes, which some of us used to smoke, and none of us smokes anymore, but we all do, right there in the kitchen.

There is a friend reading aloud one of Gabriel's stories called "Paradise":

> In the beginning, there was a desolate grey plain. Within it slept the crocus of life. Time and space were one stream. . . . In the stream of time and space there were pebbles which traveled at the whim of the current. . . . The seeds grew into a garden that was watered by the stream. Some trees killed, and some protected, but all wanted simply to live. . . . Some beasts killed, and some protected, but all wanted simply to live. In the bones of the plants and the beast there were spirits, and all of this was God.

There is what I imagine Gabriel meant by God. Not a conventional father God, but a force that wants to simply live. Or maybe someone listening to that wish.

In the Cedarvale Cemetery, a mile from the Gumm House, amid centuries of gravestones that maybe Billy the Kid once walked among, there is a new rectangle backhoed in the dirt. Later, there will be a white stone headstone. In relief across the top: a running white rabbit.

Then words: *Gabriel Scott New. April 3, 1990. March 25, 2016. Beloved Son and Brother We Miss You So.*

There are my family's lives that are never again going to match up with themselves.

There is no ghost town or cemetery in Frontierland. Just, in Liberty Square, near The Hall of Presidents, the Haunted Mansion, which houses nine hundred and ninety-nine ahistorical "happy haunts." Unlike the dead presidents, resurrected by robotics, the mansion's ghosts know they're dead and revel in it. They spookily remind visitors that there's room in the house for one thousand. Walt Disney created the Haunted Mansion after visiting the Winchester Mystery House in California, where, legend claims, Sarah Winchester kept building the sprawling, disconnected, or oddly connected rooms to confuse or house or appease the ghosts of everyone killed with Winchester rifles. It's the perfect fantasy story for westward expansion: all the violence and guilt contained neatly in a single, strange house we can pay to visit but do not have to live in.

America likes its ghosts housed tidily away from living bodies; we like our bandits bad, our heroes male and good. We don't want to look down history's long, winding tunnels. To do so is gothic, or feral, or too sensitive. Or to do so is to be in certain kinds of minds. Or certain kinds of families. Or both.

I cannot pretend to know what Gabriel was really thinking when he killed himself. I cannot speak for him.

I know some of the statistics: 25 to 60 percent of people with bipolar disorder will attempt suicide. Between 4 and 19 percent will succeed. Attempts often begin in the twenties, when bipolar develops or worsens.

I know there is still so much I do not know about those years, or him. So much I didn't think to ask, or was frightened to.

I know the night after the funeral, Nathan and a friend and I sat in the kitchen and drank wine from juice glasses, and Nathan told us about a tradition that Gabriel had started in high school. He'd proclaimed Flannery O'Connor's birthday as Flannery O'Connor Day, and each year would invite a few friends, misfits (not in O'Connor's sense) to Cedarvale Cemetery to read aloud from her work: a birthday party for ghosts and the living. In its Gothic Victorianism and literary geekiness, it seems like something only a member of my family would do. Or only Gabriel.

The way Nathan explained it, the other kids didn't know or care who Flannery O'Connor was, but a few were willing to humor Gabriel by hanging out in a graveyard, probably drunk or stoned, as they took turns reading by flashlight to the high desert emptiness. I have to imagine that one of those years they read "The River," the story Gabriel summarized for me on the phone.

I imagine Gabriel reading it, in either of his voices. Or one I never got to hear.

"You can't leave your pain in the river," a preacher tells a boy in the story.

But then the preacher goes on to say, you *can* leave your pain, but only if you accept everything else the river stands for: in the preacher's cosmology, the blood of Jesus, the suffering, the salvation. What you *can't* do is just casually set your pain down.

The story ends with the boy returning to the river alone:

> He intended not to fool with preachers anymore but to
> Baptize himself and to keep on going this time until he
> found the Kingdom of Christ in the river.... In a second
> he began to gasp and sputter and his head reappeared on
> the surface; he started under again and the same thing
> happened. The river wouldn't have him. He tried again and
> came up, choking. This was the way it had been when the
> preacher held him under—he had had to fight with some-
> thing that pushed him back... He plunged under once and
> this time, the waiting current caught him....

In the kitchen of the Gumm House that night, sitting on stools near the wood cookstove, I asked Nathan when Flannery O'Connor Day was. "I don't know," Nathan said. "I think her birthday's in spring; it's probably coming up." Then he said, "We should each read something by her aloud that day in Gabe's honor."

"Yes," I said. Of course I'd been thinking the same thing.

Cell signal is rare in the Gumm House, but I got my phone to work in the bathroom when I went upstairs for bed. I almost dropped it when I saw the date.

I'll never know for sure if Gabriel was speaking to O'Connor for her birthday, March 25, the night he killed himself. Of course it comforts me to think he chose his script at the end, that he was, in some way, celebrating one of his heroes, a woman, a dark believer in meaning.

Reading "The River" helps me remember how human it is to want to baptize ourselves in what we feel is holy, or could still be holy. How often we don't fully know motives. How human it is to do anything we can to set the pain down.

Some of us are lucky enough to come back to the surface, sputtering from therapy or luck or time or place. Some of us figure out the voice that fits us, or we're born with it. Some of us say what we think a god wants to hear, or the only thing we know that's left to say.

Some of us have to take the whole river, or the whole desert, into our mouths to say it.

Space Mountain

What I wanted, living in Orlando the summer I was thirteen, was the wild, rushing, cosmic sense of plunging through star-punctured darkness toward growing up. I wanted to take the corners fast until I found my edges by being flung almost beyond them. I wanted to roller-coaster rush Space Mountain's galactic night again and again, then lie by the sun-needled pool listening to George Michael's "Faith." Pressing the Walkman's big, stiff repeat button as if the repetitions weren't already enough.

Oh let me have *faith faith faith* because I don't know what grown-up really looks like, and, like one travel guide to Disney World says, "not knowing where the car will go next" is "half the fun."

Or I can imagine the future, but only as an eternity of this summer: standing in line with my best friend, Sarah; deciding which boys are cutest; seeking fear in a roller coaster's safe plummets and turns.

Were we really brave enough to talk to the boys we giggled at? With our baby fat and bad perms were we the type of girls they'd notice? No, but we had *faith, faith, faith* we were riding on the star-lit track where that would change, just around the corner, the next galaxy: womanhood.

"Life Safety? Life Safety: Go." That's what the blast-off instructions for Space Mountain said. They also said, "You have a clear to launch space shuttles." I wanted to launch space shuttles. Was this what one looked like?

My parents had been hired at Harcourt Brace Jovanovich's Orlando headquarters for the summer, and HBJ was paying for us to live at Sonesta Village, which had two swimming pools, tropical landscaping, and extraneous tiki-hut thatching on whatever could be thatched. As my parents spent all day editing textbooks in a boxy, tan downtown building, I read by the pools, microwaved mac and cheese, and went to Sea World and a short-lived park called Boardwalk and Baseball (both owned by HBJ, so passes were cheap), or the Disney parks, which my parents had splurged on. This was nothing like my ordinary parent-surveilled rural Arkansas life—as if I'd suddenly lifted off into my real teens, which were day-glo and oddly vacant like Florida light.

Orlando was perfect for a thirteen-year-old in pre-Internet 1988— i.e., for girls like my friends (Becca, who visited from Texas) and Sarah (from Arkansas) and me, who were endlessly self-reflexive and not at all self-aware. Becca and I were "Italian sisters" because we spoke in bad Italian accents. The Magic Kingdom's *Tomorrowland* was the future because it said so. As ads reminded us, Space Mountain was "Florida's tallest mountain." Across the inland city, Sea World was the sea. It was an entire world of sea, in fact!

Sarah and I genuinely loved the Sea World band called (oh, wave-pool pun) Mocean. The singer looked like our utopian future selves: tanned, skinny, with white Keds like Jennifer Grey in *Dirty Dancing*, which would come out that fall. Mocean sang "Rhythm is Gonna Get You" and other dancey pop under colored lights, though the show was midday—aimed at people passing on their way to see the polar bears underwater.

But Sarah and I were actual fans. We'd get our favorite jumbo chocolate chip cookies and frozen lemonade and wait in the sparse palm shade for the show to start, crumbs flecking our matching sea-foam green tank tops, my perm fuzzing in the heat.

These days felt tinged with a wild freedom, but were also safe, even a little old-fashioned. As Stephen M. Fjellman writes in *Vinyl Leaves: Walt Disney World and America,* "Although much of WDW is named for the future . . . much of the activity at the parks is wrapped up in the trappings of the past." But I didn't notice, or it didn't bother me, that the Carousel of Progress showcased innovations that had stopped being futuristic in the 1970s or that all of Tomorrowland's space technology couldn't blast me as far as Adventureland. This was all mine to experience unsupervised: this Florida midday thunderstorm was mine to feel drenched by; Space Mountain was mine to be mildly dizzied by. I was both the most and least myself I'd ever been.

According to a Frommer's guide, Space Mountain is the Magic Kingdom's "fastest and wildest" ride. It's an update on the 1950s "wild mouse" style rollercoaster, but plunged into darkness, which "does indeed make the Mouse seem wilder." With its shell-like, futuristic spiraling and spired dome, it's iconic.

Raised by danger-fearing parents to fear danger, I'd never been skiing, or even sped down a steep hill on a bike, but I loved roller coasters. I loved the ratcheting, ominous, exhilarating clack as we approached the top; the whooshing down-rush and teetering knife-edge of turns. I loved the feeling of my own fear as the line inched closer. At Boardwalk and Baseball, I loved when the Shuttle Loop glided its loop, then casually shot straight up a vertical rail, then plunged the loop backward. I loved feeling like a brave, danger-seeking grown-up—not my folk-music-loving, bifocal-wearing mother (who I otherwise idealized for her strength and feared for her judgments), but a wild woman George Michael might sing to. This is what it would feel like, right? To be swept up by passion? To rush beyond the limits of the self I'd known?

That summer, if I could have looked down the tracks of my real future, I would have recognized this dizzying rush in a night almost two decades later. The galactic and ordinary has happened: I'm a thirty-year-old woman. I'm at a restored Victorian concert space in San Francisco, dancing to Subtle, a strange, glitchy electronic hip-hop band I love.

In the starry darkness of the dance floor, I'm being lifted by their spiraling synths; I'm riding back down on gravity-heavy downbeats. The lead singer, Doseone, is talk-rapping, "eating one's own shell is so depressing," his words pixilated through effects, but also so human. Doseone, who has named himself for the first ratcheting clank up to the chemical stars.

I'm with my second husband, Will, who I married spontaneously five years ago, and with whom I'm in love. His shoulder-length hair is ponytailed, and his very blue eyes are very blue even in the dark, and his T-shirt is softly sweated against his body as he dances. Sometimes I put my hands on his back, and the cloth is so soft, so him, so stardust and music, I feel steadied and dissolving.

Dancing beside us is our best friend, Ian, with whom I'm also falling in something like love. He has his Iranian father's height and nose, pouting lips, a good sense of humor. Like me, he likes to talk, which we do when Will, a loner, a Space Cadet (an old nickname), drifts to silence. And right now, Ian has leaned down to whisper-shout, "We should go off the rails." He's truly said this.

What does he mean? I don't know exactly. Or I don't want to know because it's *half the fun*. Or I can only imagine an eternity of this: dancing near midnight in San Francisco, spinning to star-shattering, synthesized cymbals, closing my eyes until I'm floating in pure space, then tumbling out to walk the pulsing, empty city night to the EndUp to dance till dawn.

This, this is where I belong. And if to go off the rails means to rush deeper into this starlit darkness with nothing to even hold me. Then yes. "Yes!" I shout to Ian.

Right now, in black knee-high boots, a short black skirt, and tank top, I'm on the music's rails but also maybe already off them. I'm not a socially anxious community college adjunct with a three-year-dead mother, eating my own shell in front of classrooms of students. I haven't almost died from an intestinal rupture. Will and I don't fight terribly. I'm not worried about the country being Code Orange since September 11 three years ago. I'm not depressed about how little has changed since we marched and marched in antiwar protests across San Francisco.

Or I am all of these, but also I am what Doseone promises: a shell cracking open until everyone can see—can't they? or does it blind them?—the starlight inside me.

As is probably obvious, I am, all three of us are, incredibly high. We've each taken two pills of Ecstasy, a new dose. Before this, we've spent the day at Ian's, listening to music, stoned on a giant pot muffin. This is before legalization, so pot comes from medical marijuana shops if someone can get a card, or friends of friends. This muffin was baked by an older gay man in the Mission. Like many San Francisco apartments, his is up a scuffed Victorian's steep stairs. But, also, it's in another galaxy because he's mosaicked floor to ceiling with mirror shards. It's a portal through a broken looking glass: a place you could enter and never exit.

In my rational mind, the record needle of my dead mother's warnings runs its grooves: drugs lead to ruin, madness. No, I don't want to end up like this man (always seemingly cheerfully, bumblingly stoned) or the man back in Arkansas who sat in his lawn for decades waving at passing cars, having never returned from an acid trip.

But that is not *my* life. That is not what going off the rails will mean for me. What my mother didn't understand—and conventional society doesn't understand, having never danced all night on Ecstasy—is that humans can be starlight. It's taken me most of my life to really feel this.

Let's loop backward to what happened after my exotic thirteen-year-old summer. Returned to Arkansas and Earth, I proudly showed off my Florida tan with long white Walmart shorts and boxy shirts my mother still sewed me. I grew out my perm and waited for boys to want to date me. It was a year and a half before my first kiss. The second boy I kissed, at fifteen, became my first husband four years later.

Instead of Space Mountain, my life looked like Spaceship Earth, that AT&T-sponsored Epcot ride: a story of linear, predictable progress from papyrus scrolls to fiber optic.

On the track to become the teacher and writer I dreamed of, I skipped eighth grade, graduated as valedictorian at seventeen, summa cum laude from Southwest Missouri State with a BA in English at twenty-one. I went straight to my MFA in Florida, where I won a teaching award and an AWP Intro Award in Poetry. Unless I was up late writing, I didn't burn any candles at both ends. Instead of backpacking Europe, I took family vacations (sometimes still to Disney World). I worried about my mother's opinions, like Baby does her father's at the start of *Dirty Dancing*. But I didn't meet Patrick Swayze and realize I could mambo flawlessly in eyeshadow and heels. Beyond twice smoking pot at parties in high school, I didn't experiment with drugs, or girls, or other things I'll later learn people "get out of their systems." Not knowing where I was going wasn't *half the fun* if I'd be held responsible by my judgmental mother or my anxious perfectionist self. And from fifteen to twenty-two, with a bipolar boyfriend, then husband, I worked doubly hard to keep us both stable.

Just after I got divorced at twenty-two, when I finally found myself in a scene from *Dirty Dancing*—Jennifer Grey and Patrick Swayze slow dancing and peeling off clothes in his cabin during a rainstorm—I swayed (in just my bra, to the drumming of real Florida rain!) with a guy who'd just picked me up at a graduate-union party, but I was too scared to do more than curl to sleep beside him.

Almost immediately, I took shelter with a smotheringly doting, decade-older PhD student. With his help, I got a job as a full-time instructor at University of Miami, and we moved to a condo on the not-cool end of the beach.

Down in South Beach, where we went on runs, Miami was a grown-up amusement park: mannequin-angular rollerbladers and Art Deco architecture and glamorous clubs with women in tiny dresses waiting between red velvet ropes, or spilling out to the sidewalk afterwards, tipsy, glittering like crushed ice. Across the bridge in wealthy, stylish Coral Gables, even my eighteen-year-old students wore strapless dresses to 8 a.m. classes, lips plumped with collagen injections.

By Miami standards, my just-above-the-knee "mini-skirts" looked like I was on *Little House on the Prairie*. I had never been clubbing. My boyfriend's idea of a date was watching a sci-fi movie for his endlessly unfinished dissertation. I ate popcorn while other people flew through space.

Or I lay in the bathtub wrenched by abdominal cramps. The pills that doctors had prescribed me for Crohn's disease (a misdiagnosis) only made me nauseated; food allergy tests came back inconclusive. To cheer me up, my boyfriend bought bubble bath in cartoon-character bottles. A large stuffed tiger. He started calling me *Teaguer*. He made me feel simultaneously young and old and doted-on and stuck.

My mother, dying of chronic leukemia back in Arkansas, loved him. When he asked me to marry him, I stalled, but finally said yes. He was so devoted, it seemed ungrateful not to. Someday, in the future he envisioned, I'd drive our SUV of kids to the Magic Kingdom. I'd tell them, "I used to come here when I was thirteen. Now *that* was a fun summer!"

How did I escape that future? Let's roll back again.

Yes, I'd been a straight-A high-school student who wanted to please teachers and parents, but I also believed passionately in art and social questioning. My boyfriend/first-husband had been our school's biggest punk, hair sprayed up like Robert Smith's, with, for prom, *Fuck You* shaved in. Rebellion and (I didn't know the term yet) performance art.

Long before I studied feminism, I knew my fourteen-year-old friends shouldn't be used for sex by the "cool" older boys, or left alone to get abortions. As people waved flags to "God Bless the U.S.A." during the first Gulf War, I Sharpied my T-shirt with peace signs and lyrics from Natalie Merchant's "Gun Shy."

I believed what music said was possible. When "Push It" came on at high school dances, I'd rush into the school cafeteria or hotel conference room and *pump hard*. Though I usually scrutinized myself in every mirror and window, sure I was *not* one of the sexy people, when Salt-N-Pepa said it to that beat, amid strawberry-scented smoke-machine clouds, I believed.

Or I played Pink Floyd's "Learning to Fly" on repeat as I got ready for school in the morning: the first time I clearly understood myself as an *earthbound misfit*. Someday, I'd fly from small-town Arkansas, study in Paris, write novels, teach French—find the world's and my limits, or limitlessness. Where were they? Who knew, but I was headed there!

In his book *Escapism*, which I eventually read in my twenties, humanist geographer Yi-Fu Tuan writes that while we often use "the real" to mean what impacts us—e.g., rain, cold, nature—people also speak of "the real" as the exact opposite:

> In this usage, it is daily life, with its messy details and
> frustrating lack of definition and completion—its many
> inconclusive moves and projects twisting and turning as in
> a fitful dream—that is unreal. Real, by contrast, is the well-
> told story, the clear image, the well-defined architectural
> space, the sacred ritual, all of which give a heightened sense
> of self—a feeling of aliveness.

And, though I hadn't always had the language for it, I'd always been looking for this. Artistic realness that was more real than daily life. *A heightened sense of self. A feeling of aliveness.*

Notably, Tuan doesn't judge escapism as bad; he argues that *all* human culture is an escape from our animal natures.

Though *Escapism* was published in 1998, I didn't read it until later. But in my first year in Miami, I did read and teach Antonin Artaud, who, in *The Theater and its Double*, makes a similar point. In his groundbreaking 1938 theory of theater, Artaud calls for ordinary reality ("empty as it is sugarcoated") to be swept away by the ritual of theater. Instead of being passive spectators, the audience should be "seized . . . as by a whirlwind of higher forces," into "a passionate and convulsive conception of life."

Although Artaud's theories were partly enacted in 1960s "happenings" and, later, Burning Man, if the ritual ever fully succeeded, audience and actors would be annihilated. But this didn't worry me. I just desperately wanted to transform my boring, lonely, full-of-grading-and-physical-pain, grieving-my-dying-mother life with the wrong partner into something more *real*. (Though of course I didn't quite consciously admit all this to my students or self.)

Some students in my honors class loved Artaud's ideas. Some were confused. One, looking at Artaud's mental-institution portrait on the back of the book, candidly asked, "Why is everyone you're teaching us crazy?"

I'm sure I said a lot of geniuses have been considered crazy. And a lot of what we consider sane (e.g., collagen lip injections for teenagers) is normalized insanity. If we're going to make our own realities, why not make them far better?

But how? At twenty-four, I kept trying to leave my fiancé, but he kept pressuring me to get back together. I had no real friends in Miami. I was insecure and not much more worldly than I'd been in line for Space Mountain at thirteen. I still dreamed of a future full of "constant magic" or "the magic freedom of daydreams": both terms Artaud uses, which, in retrospect, could be advertisements for Disney World.

But then one small thing happened that—like the potential energy that's created when a roller coaster is pulled up its first big hill—led to everything after. Or carried me back to where I'd always been going.

After fall orientation of my second year of teaching, a pretty, blonde PhD student invited a group of us out dancing. She knew the bouncers at one of Miami Beach's coolest clubs. She could flirt us in. The only "club" I'd ever been to was a Gainesville gay bar, but I raced to buy a silver sparkly minidress. I waited with Kara and the others in the velvet-roped line—feeling somewhere between intense self-consciousness and starlight.

And it seems too simple to say, but in the floating, thumping music of that club, my body remembered my future. Dancing for one of the first times in years, I felt like a girl—or a twenty-four-year-old woman—going somewhere. While my fiancé, huffy that I'd ridden in the cab with Kara not him, sulked by the wall, I sparkled in those ricocheting lights. In place of the indie music and radio pop I knew, here was something called *house music.* The name sounded like a structure, a *well-defined architectural space,* a place I could live.

And by dawn, it was me, a little tipsy, spilled out onto the sidewalk laughing with new friends, including a just-arrived-from-California, blue-eyed, long-haired PhD student named Will.

In the true roller coaster of a month that followed, I finally really left my fiancé, moved in with Kara in the heart of South Beach, went dancing every weekend, had my first one-night stand (in an Art Deco hotel owned by Madonna), discovered that large numbers of cocktails muffled my abdominal cramps, and found myself sitting in Will's lap at a hurricane-evacuation party as a real whirlwind whipped the palms.

Will was perfect for me. Exotically raised in California and Samoa, he was idealistic and hedonistic. We lay in bed reading books I'd never heard of: Howard Zinn, Leonard Cohen, erotica. Will believed in fighting the system and also in escaping it. In one fantasy, we'd escape Miami (which he hated already) for California, where he'd gotten his MA, or Hawaii, where his parents lived. When he could get pot, we smoked joints, which made me feel like I was floating both inside and outside myself. I'd thought I was against drugs, but now I was staying up all night, writing poems that felt urgently like my own voice I'd never quite heard before.

Did I say Will was perfect for me? He was, and terrible. Our tempers clashed; we drank too much and screamed at each other. He was often in his head and didn't answer me. His brother had died painfully of AIDS a few years before. My mother's leukemia was worsening. We were both depressed. Though I didn't want to go back to the Midwest, I was thinking of moving to Kansas City to be near her. I resented her martyrly reports ("I might be really dying this time, but don't worry") and couldn't face a future in which she wasn't alive.

And, despite amaretto sours and Seven and Sevens, my abdomen often still cramped unbearably, as it had done for three years, for reasons no doctors could explain. Often by evening, I'd lie on my kitchen floor crying from what felt like lightning zigzagging and gouging the soft flesh inside me.

One night, in the midst of all this, probably stoned, Will and I decided to get married. Who cared if we'd just met two months ago? Who cared if I'd already been divorced? We were madly in love, which was *real* in that more real-than-ordinary-reality way.

Forget *the fitful dream* of conformity! We'd get married this weekend at the courthouse. (A month before I'd planned to marry my ex-fiancé, who still taught in our department, which meant the three of us sometimes awkwardly ended up in the copy room together.)

A month later, for Christmas break, I flew with my new husband to meet my new in-laws in Hawaii. Our first night on O'ahu—before I'd even seen the island in the daylight—I woke in the most wrenching, nauseating pain I'd ever felt. When I went to the bathroom, I saw the scary kind of stars, and everything went brown, then black.

Where does it hurt? the doctors kept saying in the emergency room where Will's father raced me, but I couldn't explain. The pain in my abdomen was a galaxy exploding: body-crushing, mind-erasing. I remember soft, cold gel as the ultrasound wand circled my abdomen; then I blacked out.

I woke hours later being wheeled from surgery, with Will walking beside me.

Even the surgeon, Dr. Au, couldn't explain why my intestine—at the ileocecal valve, joining the large and small intestines—had ruptured. I'd been on the verge of going septic when he saved my life.

For a week, Will slept by my hospital bed, where tubes snaked green stomach fluids from my nose, and doctors changed the gauze in my deep, five-inch-long incision. The nurses made me walk daily, dragging my IV pole slowly through the hallways as I relearned to steady myself in my cut-apart-like-a-magician's-assistant body.

When I was released on Christmas Eve, I still felt weak, but also filled with adrenaline and joy. I'd been in an Artaudian ritual that had turned me inside out. I'd inadvertently ridden the world's most terri-fying roller coaster and survived. If life was this dangerous and inexpli-cable, who wouldn't choose intensity and as much real life as possible?

Life Safety? Maybe don't bother to come in, Life Safety.

At the end of the spring semester, Will quit his PhD program, and I quit my job, and we moved to Kansas City by way of Europe. Will's parents had planned the trip before he met me and were mostly pay-ing. After they flew home, Will and I used the rest of our savings to backpack with no itinerary. We took a train down the Spanish coast and ended up at Hogueras de Alicante, a fire festival; the hotels were all booked so we slept on a beach as wood sculptures burned around us. We wandered Amsterdam museums, took shrooms in Vondelpark; I bought a black vinyl motorcycle jacket from a London flea market, became the kind of wild, young traveler who wore it. Near the end of the month, we read about Doctor Music Festival. Beck was playing, plus a weekend's worth of bands. We got on a train back to Spain.

On the train, we met Bea, a Filipina American in her early twenties, also going to the festival. She said she couldn't wait for the DJs. She was going to buy Ecstasy. We admitted we'd never tried it. "It's amaz-ing," Bea said. "We can all do it together. I'll talk you through the trip."

So later that night, I found myself in a huge circus tent in Spain floating up up up through the dark on the rising-higher-and-higher beats of the most incredible DJ—not the repetitive house of Miami, but trance that swooshed us into the circus-striped sky until we shat-tered down—star dust, meteors—until the whole dance floor moved in one euphoric swirling galaxy. I felt dangerously far from ordinary society, yet completely safe. Everything was possible, though not just possible: it was perfect, already, right now.

Still awake at dawn, Will and Bea and I walked to the edge of the campsites—we floated; we flew—and drifted back and forth on a small, paved runway. Will's hand, sweaty in mine, the air velvet, our bodies glowing from inside out. I was both the most and least myself I'd ever been.

When we got to Kansas City to live near my dying mother, Will's newly pierced eyebrow and my newly pierced nose meant Midwest retail wouldn't hire us. We weren't sure we'd stay long enough for teaching, so we found jobs at a sports bar, him cooking, me waitressing. Our coworkers couldn't believe I was old enough to have taught at a university. Was I? Maybe that was my future. Maybe I'd rolled backward to a better past.

I cut my hair boy-short and dyed it black and wore my vinyl jacket and smoked clove cigarettes and drank too many free vodkas. In a self-portrait for a black-and-white photography class, I proudly showed off my long, white, bunched-at-the-edges abdominal scar with unzipped pants and a half shirt—more brazenly confident than I'd ever been.

One night in our boss's hot tub, I drunkenly kissed my coworker Cecilia. Will had encouraged my new fantasies about women, though he got jealous anyway, and we fought.

When I wasn't working, I read Ondaatje in our rundown apartment, or wrote, or met my parents for dinner. When they drove from the suburbs, I felt a swirl of gladness to see my mother, resentment I'd moved back to the Midwest, terror she was about die, resentment at myself for not being more attentive, guilt for feeling tired of worrying about her even as I worried.

On rare nights, a bartender sold Will and me E, and we went to Kansas City's one good club. I learned the trick of hiding E in my shoe so I could take it in a bathroom stall. Rolling on E is all about timing: the sometimes jittery ride up; the teetering intensity of those moments of floating but also almost free-falling when you have to tell yourself not to panic—to walk from the dance floor to breathe, smoke a cigarette, drink a bottle of water: the plastic sweaty in your hand, your hand against your partner's all that keeps you from swirling away; and then the rolling waves as the DJ's set builds: being suspended by that high that is music that is also your body.

It is, like all good roller coasters, partly predictable, partly newly full-body immersive each time. Will and I have never been so in love; he's never known how much he also loves dancing. Once, a queer Asian man we've seen before dances over to tell me, "I love your moves." Not a come-on, a celebration. I belong here in the underground of Kansas City, while a different, less real world continues elsewhere with its lunch specials and TV football and dying mothers.

"A human being is an animal who is congenitally indisposed to accept reality as it is," Tuan says—pointing out that, among animals, only humans *can* fully dream or imagine alternatives, rather than facing threats as they are. Escapism is a natural function of the human capacity to imagine.

Or, as psychological researcher Frode Stenseng writes, escapism has two dimensions or motivations: "self-suppression" and "self-expansion." Human behavior often includes both. Like the 1967 Summer of Love, which was both hippie hedonism and an enactment of genuine social changes. Or the early 2000s dance scene, which—as the dominant culture was creating deepening inequalities, war, and fear about terrorism and "the other"—was creating an inclusive, queer-friendly space where societal others could celebrate music, their bodies, unabashed joy, and self-acceptance.

And, in the spring of 2001, at age twenty-six, I landed in one of its epicenters accidentally. In Kansas City, Will heard that his cousin in San Francisco was looking for a house sitter. Would we want to stay in her apartment and feed her cat? With my mother's health on an upswing, and San Francisco a step closer to our current dream (go to Japan to teach English), we said yes.

I arrived sure I'd think San Francisco was overhyped and I'd stay just those two weeks. But I instantly fell in love with it. The city was so grittily real, with its metal-grated shops, foggy, homeless-filled streets, and slow busses that fell from their wires, creating delays to anywhere. But it was also real in the other sense of tirelessly making its own better realities. There were festivals, protests, street murals, Victorian apartments with DIY art: bicycles and retro parasols dangling from ceilings.

It was permissive, hedonistic, strange, grown-up. Like Tomorrowland, it was the past—Victorian plus Grateful Dead sixties—but also the techy future. And City College was hiring adjunct lecturers for summer classes (me) and AmeriCorps in Oakland was hiring and re-paying student loans (Will).

Blocks from the real Janis Joplin's old apartment, we found a one-room studio with a closet-sized kitchen. But it had a small claw-foot tub and bay window, and outside, an Ethiopian restaurant and a grungy beer bar with one hundred beers from around the world. The dot-com bubble had just burst, so we'd arrived as the people willing to write checks for the full year's rent had dissipated into people with rental resumes (what? we quickly made one). We could barely afford our tiny studio, but it was worth it. Already we'd met friends of Will's cousin's friends: bookstore workers, gay sex workers, students, servers at high-end restaurants—all with shared apartments and no savings, living the *real whatever-you-want-it-to-be* San Francisco life. Twenty-to-forty-somethings figuring out who they were or wanted to turn into.

We didn't talk about Artaud, but life-as-transformative-theater was everywhere. Our landlady (forties, thin and exotic in retro robes, and I'll later realize, strung out) was hammering a Burning Man sand-ship in the narrow garage. As a birthday party, a friend (brilliant, hand-some, a high-price gay sex worker in a committed relationship with a trained mime) created an all-day play. He told us to dress in Victorian funeral wear (black lace thrift-store dresses and suits) and meet at the Columbarium, the city's above-ground graveyard. With its dome, it looked from outside like a marble Victorian Space Mountain, though inside, in place of the darkness of the galaxies were urns with ashes. He handed us "aged" scrolls with the backstories of the imaginary relatives we were grieving. We read our melodramatic lines. We wiped our eyes on lace handkerchiefs as real twentieth-century mourners passed. We campily reckoned with mortality, took fabulous photos.

For "Unvalentines," a February holiday we invented between Will's and his new friend from AmeriCorps, Ian's, birthdays we wore retro sleepwear: feather-trimmed robes, heeled slippers. One Halloween, my new best friend Thoa—born in Vietnam, raised outside LA— and Will and another friend and I dressed as the sevenites porno *The Opening of Misty Beethoven*. (We'd just learned it was a classic.) Thrift-store go-go boots and sixties paisley short-suits or dresses for Thoa and me, big-collared shirts and sunglasses for the guys. It was dress-up, but also a new reality.

Thoa and I also worked the gates of the Folsom Street Fair, the city's leather/fetish/bondage fair, not exactly our scene, but we were sex-positive, and it was a fundraiser for LGBTQ charities: racy yet politically righteous, our favorite combo. We marched in every post-September-11 antiwar rally; we helped almost stop traffic to the Bay Bridge (until cops in riot gear stopped us). A couple times, we drunkenly kissed. Thoa was getting her BA in women's studies and was beautiful and tough, and I loved watching her pool-shark guys in bars.

And then there was the dancing: 1015 Folsom, The Warfield, The Filmore, Great American, Ruby Skye. There was house, hard house, trance, drum and bass. So many DJs I'd never heard of or imagined seeing: FC Kahuna, Underworld, The Crystal Method rattling the Warfield's Victorian windows, Miss Kittin, John Digweed, Fatboy Slim himself.

On the best weekends, when we could find E, Will and I and some- times friends would ride the bus downtown, me in a nylon slip I was pretending was a dress and thrift-store black knee-high Camper boots (flat, essential for dancing). We'd dance all night—the DJ building tracks up and up into the dark, plunging us all at once, slowly rebuild- ing, ratcheting down and around when we least expected, starting to drop new beats, swerving.

At 1015 Folsom, Fatboy Slim controlled a packed dance floor with just his hands. His fingers fidgeting turntable dials, he toyed with us, grinning, lifting his own arms as we rose. We gave ourselves over, a whole room collectively in love—waiting for launch instructions, moving only where he sent us. I loved this letting go of control. Each breath, each beat, the damp cotton of Will's shirt, even the simplest things: a strand of hair curling against a stranger's neck in line for the bathroom, beautiful, distinct. The *heightened sense of self, of being alive.* The chemical, alchemical potency of being here, here. Together, we floated in outer space: the queer, freakish, grungy all equally starlit and freed from the gravity of inhibitions. Strangers smiled, caught each other's eyes: *this is it, right? the best song yet! can you believe what he just did?*

We rode until we sweated—Will and I, or sometimes Will and Thoa and I, or later Will and Ian and I. After the club closed, we'd walk to the EndUp, where at dawn we'd still be dancing, then sharing clove cigarettes in the walled-in patio with its real-fake waterfall that spilled beneath the freeway's looming billboards. We talked rushingly, our arms casually draping each other.

Ecstasy: *elation, rapture, an exalted state of good feeling . . .* originally from the Greek: *a displacement or removal from the proper place.*

In the 1970s, when 3,4-methylenedioxymethamphetamine—MDMA, Ecstasy, or in the early 2000s, usually E, or X, (now Molly)—first more widely appeared in the United States, it was used therapeutically. Therapists gave an estimated five hundred thousand doses to help patients get better in touch with their feelings, openly communicate, and recover from trauma. Recent research on MDMA to treat PTSD shows a "49.9% average reduction in scores on the Clinically Administered PTSD scale," in contrast to the placebo's 12.8 percent. These statistics are, ironically, published by American Addiction Centers, in an online article that goes on to say that in rare genetic cases, E can be lethal, and thousands of people each year are hospitalized from it, though, in almost all cases, from dehydrating while dancing for hours. The other main risks come from E being illegal and therefore an unregulated street drug that's often cut with other drugs, usually speed, sometimes heroin.

Because of E's effectiveness at creating a sense of happiness and empathy—the Addiction Centers' article states that "a distributor in Los Angeles coined the name Ecstasy in 1981 . . . He felt that *empathy* was a better word to describe the drug's effects but that *Ecstasy* would help it sell more"—it also became popular recreationally, spreading through the eighties dance scene. Because of this, despite testimony by therapists and patients, the US government classified it as illegal, Schedule 1, in 1985.

I questioned, and question, this classification—given the number of deaths from E versus alcohol or guns. I can't help thinking that while drunk frat guys date-raping women is classic Americana, a dance floor packed with smiling who-cares-what-gender people in feather boas, telling each other they're beautiful, with glowsticks bobbing like phosphorescent plankton, is outside the status quo. It's a *removal from the proper place* of regulated, daylight identities.

What if those people are *so* empathetic and happy they don't watch TV or get plastic surgery? What if they don't *Keep America Open for Business* as the post–September 11 ad campaign soon urged?

Despite its illegality, E spread from the eighties dance scene to the nineties rave scene. Before we arrived, San Francisco had been famous for all-night Full Moon raves which morphed, after police crackdowns, into more mainstream but still-open-till-dawn clubs. By the early 2000s, old-school ravers lamented the scene going mainstream, but 1015 Folsom and Ruby Skye were installing new lighting and sound systems and starting to attract bigger crowds and the world's top DJs. If this wasn't the wilder, truer earlier rave scene, it was still a renaissance.

After dancing till dawn, we'd float home from the EndUp past an iconic San Francisco building where furniture spilled down the facade: chairs, tables, lamps seemingly in free fall. The perfect art for this city where the laws of gravity didn't exist, or existed only to power a roller coaster rolling toward the farthest, most beautiful reaches of ourselves.

But, of course, the tracks also surfaced to ordinary daylight: to teaching, to our mildewy apartment, to bills on an adjunct salary, to grief. Shortly after we'd moved to San Francisco, my mother had been diagnosed with a brain tumor. By fall, she was on hospice. Then gone.

How was this possible? How could the woman in whose body I'd floated in almost weightless space as my cells formed, never again smile at me, or judge me, or love me?

This was a month after September 11, and the world felt on fire. There was a new Department of Homeland Security, Code Orange warnings, anti-Muslim hate crimes. At City College, where Will now also taught, students were homeless or living in Bayview-Hunters Point projects amid drive-by shootings. Some still read at the grade-school level; they described being expected to share ripped-in-half textbooks in high school. One, with severe learning disabilities from a crack-addicted mother, always charmingly called me just "Teacher." He revised almost indecipherable papers semester after semester, determined to transfer to San Francisco State. I cheered for him, for all of them, terrified of how few safety nets our country had, and how much worse everything seemed to be getting.

Even being privileged, educated, white (or white-passing: Will's mother was Chicana), Will and I were struggling. If we'd wanted a house or children, we could never have afforded them. We lived paycheck to paycheck. We rode BART around the same loops. At twenty-seven, then twenty-eight, twenty-nine, thirty, I was only sporadically writing and still had no finished book. We taught about inequality and social justice as inequalities and violence deepened. I grieved my mother, as Will still grieved his brother. How was anyone supposed to live in a real world that looked like this? Hadn't we been heading to a better future?

Sometimes Will and I fought dramatically—abandoning each other in screaming fights on street corners. I shouted that he should listen to my feelings more. He shouted that I always wanted too much. We gave ourselves ultimatums. *If we're still this unhappy in two months, we'll separate.* "But we'll stay friends," I'd say. "No," Will would say. "If we split up, I don't want to be friends." He was like that: idealistically in love or cynically closed off.

And weren't we the whirlwind marriage that had beat the odds? In some ways, weren't we doing well? I was considered one of the best adjuncts at City College, likely to get a coveted tenure-track job. Several poems got published by good journals. I discovered yoga. Will became a ceramics lab tech and threw beautiful dishes. Our friends were still the closest, most inseparable we'd ever had. Thoa graduated. Ian got a tech job.

Since Doctor Music Festival, we'd joked we were too old for the dance scene. Will was thirty-five now; I was almost thirty. The rave scene's peak was a decade ago. But San Francisco was, in this way, too, perfect: a lot of the dancers were older gay men (particularly at the EndUp's Fag Fridays and Sunday morning T-Dance), and the city was famous for its Peter Pan syndrome, a term often used disparagingly, but which includes the possibility of transformation at any age.

And though Thoa and other friends had finally gotten tired of the crowds or E's comedown—the sometimes tooth-grinding, wiped-out day after—Will and I had become expert. We knew how to sleep a few hours, roll a joint, go to a thrift store, spend hours driftily trying on new old versions of ourselves. This was all part of the ride: the slow, flat stretch at the bottom.

Though, increasingly, as the world disappointed and frightened us, the ride back up—finding E, going out—felt more and more urgent.

The summer of 2004, we drove seven hours to our first Coachella. All-night dance tents. Electronica all afternoon. A joyous club-kid going campsite to campsite shouting "Merry Coachella!" Everything was the bigger, more beautiful, intense version of itself. Burning Man sculptures. The wind harp's long silver strings. A giant celestial chandelier called *Cleavage in Space*, which looked fallen from an H. G. Wells story, with filigreed metal arms that branched more than thirty feet high. It had red fabric globe lights, a huge rusted metal chain. As the artist describes it: "A chandelier from god's Pleasure Palace has fallen through the clouds."

One night, just after we took E, Will went to get water, and I waited beneath this chandelier. In every direction, music pulsed, and the distant mountains were just purpling, and suddenly, the lights came on above me. Magically, impossibly, the chandelier's globes glowed in the middle of this field, as if it and I were both wired to some invisible, celestial power source.

Back in San Francisco, Will and I told our friends about Coachella. Ian was most excited. Once like the goofy younger brother in our group, he was twenty-six now, more mature, but still boyishly excited. He was newly obsessed with electronica, thanks to a DJ roommate, and whenever Will and I went dancing, he started coming. Even on the nights that Will wasn't talking much or it felt like a lot of other nights (as it often did now), Ian made me laugh. When he leaned down to talk to me in the chill-out room, I could tell he was listening. I liked when he looked at me as if I were the kind of woman who sat under magic chandeliers from outer space.

The next summer, the three of us went to Coachella. The chandelier was gone. The DJs weren't as good. Will and I had been fighting for weeks and had almost cancelled. Ian suggested taking a double dose of E. If one was rapturous, wouldn't two be transcendent?

Or maybe one pill didn't feel as strong anymore, though this E, which we'd gotten in bulk from a friend of a friend, was jittery, mostly speed. We quit dancing early and Will went to the tent, depressed and moody. Ian and I drifted around a field and talked intensely until dawn.

In one way, what happened next is predictable. In another, it was and is hard to explain. It's mixed up with what the NIH calls E's "increased energy, pleasure, emotional warmth, and distorted sensory and time perception." It's mixed up with my inability to imagine leaving Will or being attracted to Ian. It's mixed up, and was summed up, a few months later at a Subtle concert, when Ian leaned down on the dance floor and said to me, "We should go off the rails," and I said, "Yes."

"Without a universal law there is no gravity. / Without no gravity there is no atmosphere," Doseone monotone sing-raps on "Soft Atlas." This sounds, from the distance of now, like a warning. (Or confused double negatives.) But at the time, it sounded like freedom. The most wonderful roller coaster without the rail to hold it. Letting go, at last, of all control.

What happened was that that night, or one soon, after the EndUp, Will and Ian and I ended up in bed. Despite E's notorious sensuality—the desire to stroke a friend's soft arm or gush about how wonderful they are—this had never happened with any friend, and Ian and Will were, while queer in the sense of non-normative, also straight. Weren't they? But what did that even mean? Maybe boundaries between bodies were just rails, and we were off those too. Maybe they'd flirted and I hadn't seen. Or we all wanted the pure intensity of giving in to what made no sense. Maybe we were all being pulled by the heedlessness of disappearing beyond limits and selves we recognized. This, more than the sex, is what I loved. Vanishing into outer space.

"It is upon this idea of extreme action, pushed beyond all limits, that theater [life] must be rebuilt," Artaud says.

"These are days of anyone being gone," Doseone says.

These are the days of coming down off double doses of E at dawn while smoking joints, the three of us under the velvet quilt as the neighbors' corridos drift up the airshaft. Or staying awake all night at the EndUp: three best friends letting our lives be played like a DJ set. Wasn't this the ultimate devotion to the dance scene? Weren't we rushing toward something higher and higher and *more* alive? They are both in love with me! I am in love with both of them! "I'm hurting no one, hurting no one," Karl Hyde of Underworld, my favorite group, chants.

But also, sometimes we *are* hurting. One of us is jealous. Tired. Confused.

Will yells that he never agreed to this: Ian and I pressured him.

Ian yells he doesn't know why we're even at his house, this is our problem, the fight is between us. (In retrospect, it probably was. We were probably escaping our relationship the only mixed-up way we really could.)

I'm crying. *Did* we agree to this? Is there enough E?

Is whatever we're doing not real, not serious? (They both say so.)

But it feels real. At the best moments, I've never felt more invisible yet brightly shining. Look at how they both look at me at dawn. Look at how the dawn fills the city, like it's just catching up to the light already inside us.

But other mornings, I've never felt so exhausted, spiked and dropped. During one fight, we all agree to take a break. But then we remember it's Love Parade weekend. On Saturday, the bouncer at Ruby Skye says "gross" when she sees Friday's stamp not washed off my wrist, and I feel as if she's seeing everything about the men on either side of me, sweaty, amped after almost twenty-four hours awake, and I care and don't. I think, *it's your club stamp; you're helping make this happen.* The theater is red-skyed and burning.

"The contemporary theater is decadent," Artaud says, "because it has broken away from gravity, from effects that are immediate and painful—in a word, from Danger."

Do I want safety or danger? Yes.

One morning, I teach without having slept, still clammily coming down—something I would never ever have imagined, and am terrified of, and am at the chalkboard doing.

Even though we tell none of them what's really going on, our other friends are worried. Why do we hardly hang out with them? Why are the three of us always together and fighting? Why are Will and I talking about separating? Why are we looking for our own apartments?

But now why are all three of us renting an apartment together?

We say we're doing it *just as friends.* (I keep ignoring those words.) It's a three-bedroom in the Mission, with lots of space. It's an impulsive decision, and one that requires many daylight steps: we sign a lease, pack up dishes and furniture, rent U-Hauls, find a friend to keep Will's and my beloved cat. But it's worth it: huge bay windows, a gas fireplace, my own room where I drape a red velvet cloth over a futon, like a Victorian chaise lounge. Maybe *this* is what going off the rails means: bringing *the magic freedom of daydreams* into daily life: moving into a chandelier that's fallen from space!

A month later, for New Year's Eve, Will invites a friend out clubbing with us. She's ten years younger than me and works at the ceramics lab. At midnight, she and Will kiss. (Of course he can date other people; there are no rules.) But with Ian gone to the dance floor, I'm alone.

In the weeks after, Ian is out with other women: new-generation club girls who wear too much makeup and impractical boots and say *X* instead of *Ecstasy*. Will and that woman are at the ceramics lab. Didn't I say I wanted to be alone? (Did I? I'm crying in my bedroom.) Ian is drinking too much (he always has, but now I'm living with it). He's passed out in the bathroom. He's not speaking in the kitchen. On nights without club girls, he's coming to my room drunk for sex, then not speaking in the kitchen.

"These are days of anyone being gone," Doseone chants again. But I'm not gone. I'm in an apartment above a shoe store in the Mission. I'm walking to the Twenty-fourth Street BART station, passing couples in ironic sweatshirts walking arm-in-arm (why does everyone seem to be a couple?). I'm waiting for the ordinary train beneath pigeon netting. On weekends, I'm waking to homeless people rummaging the trash cans below my window for glass to recycle: a concatenated clinking like some twentieth-century reverb-y remix of the music of the spheres. I'm waking to drunk people calling to each other. I'm waking lonely and crying.

I've never once gone dancing without Will or Ian. I can't imagine going alone. If I did, strangers would doubtlessly smile in that *you're-beautiful-this-is-all-beautiful* way, but don't I have to feel beautiful first? Maybe at some level, I'm also not sure even E can get me high enough.

For weeks it rains. Will and his new girlfriend eat at our kitchen table. Sometimes I yell at her, at him. I play, on repeat, not electronica but The Smiths' "There Is a Light that Never Goes Out," which imagines dying romantically by being hit by a ten-ton truck. Maybe this is what going off the rails means. Maybe the most primal escape is wanting to stop the pain at any cost.

Despite mild depression, and more than mild anxiety, I've been lucky the serotonin lows of coming down off E have never been bad enough to spin me, or they've been too mixed with other mid-twenties highs and lows and anxieties and griefs to notice. But now my mind is crashing. I've lost my husband and best friend and dancing not because of one explicable moment but because of some mixed-up free fall away from each other, which started by a free fall toward each other. I'm free-falling within free-falling and have no idea which way is up.

The one therapist I see during those months says snidely: "How's that working out for you: being a diva?" (Diva, from *dyeu*—*to shine, sky, heaven, god*.)

(Later I find out he was dying of cancer, which maybe explains his lack of patience.)

Friends who I finally really talk to give me obvious advice: stop living with Will and Ian. But all the apartments I tour are too expensive or rundown or both. Finally I admit to my friend Alisa that I don't want another apartment. All I think about now is wanting to die.

We're sitting outside the City College Diego Rivera mural with its women in bathing caps diving off bridges. I'm sobbing. Alisa says lovingly but sternly—like a big sister, which is how she's been since we became friends our second year of teaching together—that I have to tell her three reasons to live. She pulls a green index card from her overstuffed binder.

I can't think of one, but she keeps insisting. Finally I come up with *To teach good classes. To work on poems. To travel.* She writes them in her loopy handwriting, makes me promise to carry and re-read them.

For months, I go to work. I smoke joints before bed. I read that card's little list of *faith faith faith*. I cry. Some days, I still wake thinking of jumping off the Golden Gate Bridge. I know it's predictable, but it's true. If I'm in free fall, why not get it over with?

One day, sobbing in the shower, I remember it's two days before Stegner Fellowship applications are due. Because my life feels so out of control, I make the desperate decision to apply: to do one small thing that makes me feel like a writer—no matter how unlikely the odds. Will actually helps me choose poems. A few months later, also desperately, and at Ian's urging, I set up a profile on SF Gate's online

dating site. I answer the site's questions, saying I love poetry, dancing, traveling. Underworld is my favorite music. I'm separated (never
mind that my soon-ex-husband and ex-lover both still live in other
rooms of my apartment).

I wait for a hot club guy (or woman) to sweep me back up into the
stars. Instead, a dorky-looking guy in khaki shorts messages me. His
profile shows him posing by a dolphin statue with the caption "Does
this dolphin make my butt look big?" A guy in his late forties, who's
overbearing and bitter about his ex-wife, takes me on a stilted picnic
in the park. Even the better dates involve no dancing, or Ecstasy, or
anything resembling lowercase ecstasy.

But somehow, days pass. Almost the whole spring passes. I don't
actually meet anyone else in the club scene or really try to. Maybe
at some level I know that the only way to escape this part of my
life is to escape even that kind of escapism. (I don't of course think
anything nearly this coherent at the time.) Eventually, I tell Ian and
Will they need to move out. I advertise for new housemates. I do
not—I'm so lucky I do not—try to kill myself. Maybe I'm saved by
my own exhaustion. Or E not being truly physically addictive. Or
my friends having faith in me. Or luck. Or something inside me that
knows—though it's invisible in all that loopy dark—that there's still
a future.

During my fifth month of depression, with Ian moved and Will
looking for another place, as it continues to rain, I receive a voicemail that even now seems unreal. Eavan Boland, an Irish poet whose
poetry I've loved for years, says I've been awarded one of the five
Stegner Fellowships in poetry. For the next two years, I'll be paid to
write and go to workshops, which, although I don't know it yet, will
lead to deep friendships with other writers, and then my first book,
and then a tenure-track job in another state. My life is about to turn
upside down more amazingly than I could ever have imagined.

A month later, another beautiful message falls from outer space. Or
at least from the SF Gate dating site. It begins *Ahoy across the digital
soup!* It's from a man named (really) Dylan Champagne. On our first

date, we decide to do something neither of us would ordinarily do, and see a punk polka band. We end up linking arms and doing a wild quasi-jig, laughing, because neither of us knows how to polka.

But generally, Dylan doesn't like dancing. He's a punk musician, indie songwriter, motion graphics artist, and, more recently, composer, and when his brain hears music, he wants to count odd time signatures. But he loves what really matters most to me: art, adventure, someone who listens, a sense of being alive, a sense of humor, the chance to truly (and often very slowly) transform.

At first, we couldn't believe how seriously in love we were falling, since we'd both just ended long-term relationships (his less messy). We were together for ten years, and almost broke up twice, and hiked hundreds of miles on the John Muir trail through the High Sierras and on the Camino de Santiago in Spain, almost beyond our own limits, before we got married on a rocky beach in Idaho five years ago. After the ceremony, we had a Silent Disco because, even at an off-the-grid campground, you can't get married to the earthbound misfit of your dreams without dancing. Thoa and Alisa and other San Francisco friends were there. Even Dylan danced.

I'm honest with my students—who often talk to me about their depressions, confusions, and possible futures—that I still struggle with depression, mostly successfully thanks to yoga, vitamin B, running, good therapy, more recently, antidepressants. Last year, in a prosody class, I described the interlocking patterns of repetition in a poem as being like a DJ introducing one track inside another, and my students looked amused, or surprised. Maybe they don't expect me to think about DJs. Or they never spent years of their life dancing to what's now called EDM.

I didn't explain. It's a long, twisty story, and looking back, it's still hard to see through all the darkness and rushing and stars. Did I escape myself in those years? Did I arrive where I was always headed? Yes.

In the Idaho college town where I never imagined I'd live, and Dylan and I mostly love living, our professor friends throw two annual dance parties. I volunteer to make, or now get asked to make, the playlist. I spend hours before the parties reordering the songs and feel inordinately proud that my Spotify mixes very, very seldom clear the dance floor. More than electronica, I put on dance hits from the 80s, 90s, and 2000s, contemporary pop and hip-hop, and of course "Push It." We all drink beer and cocktails and dance like we've forgotten gravity, though of course it's always there.

In these "post-truth" times, I think a lot about how dangerous escaping reality can be, but I'm also still sure we need to imagine alternatives to our consumerist, world-destructive society, and that art is one way to do this. More than Artaud, I teach Audre Lorde, who writes, "Poetry [art] is not a luxury." It's "the quality of light by which we scrutinize our lives."

Part of that light, in my own life, comes from that fallen chandelier's red fabric globes lit against the desert sky like fire balloons. In the one picture I have, I'm sitting cross-legged beneath it. I don't look like a diva or Victorian time traveler or druggy club girl. I look like the slightly grown-up version of the brown-haired, freckled girl who once stood in line at Disney World.

I look like a younger version of the forty-seven-year-old woman who still sometimes listens to Underworld on her headphones as she walks the leafy streets to a campus. When Karl Hyde chants "Dirty numb angel boy /. . . / And tears boy / And all in your inner space boy," she does a little dance in her own inner space. She closes her eyes for a second and buckles in for the ride.

Perfect Storms

The Jungle Cruise

My mother and I are on a chlorinated river that's somehow simultaneously the Amazon, Congo, and Nile, floating languidly so we don't
run into the boat in front of us and "don't scare the wildlife": the kind
of joke the Disney guide, in his safari hat and over-pocketed explorer
outfit, keeps making. We round a bend. Animatronic hippos surface
their plasticky ears amid bubbles. A small, caricatured "primitive"
man squats under dense vines—scowling and shaking something.
And just as I realize that what he's holding has lank black hair, the
guide calls, "What's that there in the river, a-head?"

Ba-dum-tss. "A head, ahead!"

In my preteens to early twenties—the decade my family most
often drove from Arkansas to Disney World—I never thought the
Jungle Cruise was as funny as my mother's gallows humor or Monty
Python, but it was hard not to smile sometimes. As in all Magic
Kingdom rides, the script was unvarying, but unlike most, it wasn't
prerecorded. It relied as much on a steady stream (haha) of puns as
it did on robotic tigers. Puns turn on voice and timing; the speaker
can't help it: the language begged to fold back on itself. That's why the
joker often says, "Sorry, I couldn't resist."

The Jungle Cruise guides didn't actually even pretend to be sorry. They grinned and started the next one-liner before the groans had subsided. "Tigers are known for their intelligence, but you can't trust them. You never know when they might be a-lyin.'"

When I was growing up, puns were part of my parents' repertoire of wordy, nerdy jokes. My mother particularly loved tricky crossword clues that turned on puns, which *New York Times* Wordplay writer Deb Amlen calls "forehead slappers."

One of the clearest images I have of my mother's last bedroom, in an apartment in Missouri where she died of chronic leukemia when I was twenty-seven, is of blue mechanical pencils by her hospice bed. She'd always used those pencils for puzzles—often the *New York Times* in big paperbacks we'd get her for Christmas—but by then, with her headaches worsening and eyesight failing, she could barely see the boxes. On my last visits, I read clues aloud: "'Small food'?"

"*ORT*."

"*ORT*? How on earth did you know that?"

"Oh, it's used all the time in puzzles."

"Okay: 3 across: 'Current events.' It's five boxes. We've got a *T* already in the first one."

This was 2001, so I was racking my brain for a five-letter soundbite about President Bush or the human genome. Unlike my mother, her mother, and my sisters, I didn't inherit a love of crossword puzzles. When I stare at the little boxes, I feel like I'm in a bear trap, or maybe my mind is the bear trap: the jaws gaping, waiting, waiting for that one specific perfect grizzly.

"Oh," my mother said joyfully after a moment's thought, "*TIDES*!"

"*TIDES*?"

It still took me a minute. *Current* events.

Cow Town

In many of my earliest memories, I'm playing on the floor of my mother's sewing room in Fort Worth as the machine whirs and country music plays. My mother sews most of our clothes, dolls for me, curtains for our many windows. As a piano teacher, she favors records of Liszt and Rachmaninoff, but she's as likely to tune into new and classic country as classical. Although my mother was born in upper New York state, and then raised in Arizona after her father's death in World War II, she's been in Texas for over two decades by the time I'm born. We live in the same house where she raised my half sisters: near the Stockyards, less than a mile from Billy Bob's, a world-famous honky-tonk. Country music is literally in the air, along with our mostly Mexican neighbors' ranchera.

I sing along to Janie Fricke's "He's a Heartache (Looking For a Place To Happen)" when I'm too young to understand what she means (though, if epigenetics is to be believed, with my maternal great-grandmother cheated on and abandoned by the husband of her six children, and my paternal great-grandmother impregnated by a guy passing through Texas, maybe I know exactly, cellularly, the man she means).

My mother grins when Lee Greenwood comes on, singing, "I took a band of gold and made a 24-carat mistake / And turned it into / Fool's gold..."

In the Arkansas Ozarks, where we moved after our Fort Worth house burned when I was ten, we sometimes took out-of-town visitors to the area-famous hoedown theaters: women in swishy satin, petticoated dresses playing fiddles and banjos, and patched-overalled hillbillies stumbling on stage for comic relief, cracking puns and pretending to be drunk on moonshine.

My parents enjoyed the shows, and the performers were skillful—if you haven't heard two people fiddle-duel "Orange Blossom Special," making their fiddles sound like trains, you maybe should—but the shows also stereotyped gender, poverty, and race (if it was mentioned at all in the very white Ozarks). By my teens, I tried to avoid them. As a self-defined alternative teenager in our hippie-artsy town, I was devoted to The Cure and R.E.M. My friends and I drove VW bugs; one had a giant seventies Oldsmobile we called "Boat of Car" after the They Might Be Giants song. We never listened to country.

During my MFA in Florida in my early twenties, when my professor, Padgett Powell, critiqued the characters in my short story for being "on the correct side of the NPR dial," I was offended and confused. Why wouldn't I want them to be?

Although I didn't overtly think I was distancing myself from having grown up in Arkansas and from the rural Texas poverty of my father's family, I didn't write or talk about either. My characters did not wade in cow ponds, as I had as a preteen, or climb over barbed wire into the fields around a rural Arkansas house on a hill called Rocky Top. I didn't tell—have never told until now—about going to those hoedown shows. Or that, as a preteen, before I knew better, I'd dreamed of growing up to be like those women in taffeta dresses glowing under stage lights with their fiddles.

I never told people that my paternal uncles, cousins, and second cousins still lived on one dusty piece of land outside Fort Worth, where my grandfather had grown up with nine siblings in a one-room house (still standing in my childhood). I left out the junker cars, trailers, dogs in handmade fences. I left out that family's sense of humor, akin to my own mother's gallows humor, with even more inexplicable traumas. In one way, my cousins' cheerfully told stories of miscarriages and drunk-driving wrecks and lost jobs and memory loss seemed like some Baptist form of Buddhist acceptance. *This is how the shitstorm of the world is. What are you going to do but ride along in it, hope you don't get swept into the sewer?* But in another way, the stories seemed terrifyingly naïve or resigned.

Like when my cousin Ashley described her brother blacking out beside the semi he'd been hired to drive, and months later just beginning to remember who his wife and son were. "Maybe something in the gas fumes?" Ashley said. "He didn't recognize his own boy, and you know what? Gail found Dave out in the backyard digging this big ol' hole, and she said, 'What are you doin' that for?' And Dave said, 'I'm gonna dig this hole till my daddy's memory comes back.' He must'a thought it was like diggin' to China or something." Ashley laughed in that well-isn't-that-the-darndest way.

It's not a country song, but it could be: *I was trying to dig my way back to you, but now I'm just stuck in this hole.*

Being *on the correct side of the NPR dial* and having read *A People's History of the United States,* I knew that it wasn't my Texas family's or other rural poor people's moral failing or lack of hard work that had left them in these circumstances. I knew to blame our wildly unequal capitalist system. But, exactly because of that, I wanted to rage against the machine that hired uneducated workers to drive semis with toxic fumes. I didn't want stories or music that ended only in knee or forehead slapping.

And when I moved to San Francisco at twenty-six and my mentions of growing up in Texas and Arkansas were frequently met with jokes about inbred cousins and *Deliverance* banjos, I learned to put even more distance between myself and my country past. The liberal Bay Area was better at being liberal about what was familiarly leftist. When people asked, "Where'd you move here from?" I started to say, "Florida." Coasts were acceptable. (And Florida Man jokes hadn't taken off yet.)

In my thirties, when an artist-hipster friend in Oakland asked if I liked "old-timey music," I unhesitatingly said, "No."

Maybe my swirl of real emotions read to her as confusion, because she gushed, "Oh, I think you'd like it if you heard it!" She clearly found fiddles and twangy singing novel: a "past" you could visit, not a place that real people came from.

The Jungle Cruise

My mother was diagnosed with chronic lymphocytic leukemia in 1998, right before I finished grad school in Florida. But by then, she'd already been sick for several years.

It began the fall she turned fifty-nine when she called me at college to say she'd developed sudden, terrible arthritis. One day her elbows would feel so stiff she'd have to rest while hanging clothes. The next day, she'd walk the eighth of a mile to our mailbox on the county road in Arkansas, and her knees would constrict so badly she wasn't sure how she could walk back.

Once she told me, "I thought I was going to have to crawl back." I pictured her like Christina in Andrew Wyeth's *Christina's World*, dragging herself up the driveway's chert. It was a terrifying image, but my mother had raised me to believe that any of us might someday find ourselves in a bleak Wyethean landscape. She'd always tended to suffer, not silently, but while refusing help. She hardly ever went to doctors.

But after six months of her worsening pain and exhaustion, my father insisted. And it turned out that my mother wasn't suddenly aging. She had *migrating arthritis* from Lyme disease.

Despite my father's frequent mowing, our hilltop in Arkansas had areas of high grass and jungly vines and dense brush, as the Ozarks do. And at the lawn's edge was a huge patch of blackberry bushes. My parents used to get up before dawn to pick buckets of warm, dark berries—coming inside, waists ringed with red bites from tiny chiggers, and sometimes small or larger ticks, like new, crawling freckles.

"Do you remember finding a tick embedded in you?" the doctor asked.

My mother would have pulled it out with tweezers if so, crushed it between her fingernails, dropped it in the toilet, taken a shower. This was part of country living. And Lyme disease wasn't yet common in the Ozarks, so we thought of ticks as inconvenient, not potentially life-altering.

My mother was lucky: she recovered. In another year, she was hanging loads of laundry, refinishing furniture, picking blackberries, and making cobblers.

But then, during my first year of grad school, she came down with a flu that wouldn't leave. She'd be in the middle of cooking dinner and have to go nap (she'd never napped). This time, the doctor diagnosed her with mono, though admitted that, past sixty, she was the oldest case on record.

"I've always wanted to be exceptional," she joked.

Then a perfect storm happened. I mean a bad confluence. But also, there was fake jungle thunder.

It was my second year in the University of Florida's MFA. My mother was well enough that my parents came to visit for spring break, and as we often did, we went to the Magic Kingdom. In the afternoon, we were in line for the Jungle Cruise, slowly snaking through an area with extraneous coils of hemp rope and big wooden boxes marked *CARGO*.

Despite the awning and fans, the Jungle Cruise line always seemed hotter than other lines. Maybe it was the power of suggestion that we were headed from Florida's tropics to the real tropics. We were on our way to see "crocodiles" and what I was fully coming to understand were racist caricatures of "jungle people" with their whooping and drumming and shrunken heads. *Heart of Darkness*, with "The horror! The horror!" replaced by "A head, ahead."

My parents, my husband, and I were talking and joking around and standing stickily in that line, listening to the crackling of fake thunder and rain, when my mother, as she later described it, "felt something fall inside."

She didn't tell us. She just climbed into the boat when we finally reached it and grinned along with the guide's jokes, and got sprayed by the robotic elephants, and maybe subtly touched her abdomen. After, she ducked into a bathroom by Tom Sawyer Island to see if she could see anything. She couldn't, but she could feel "a bulge." Still, she didn't say anything. She spent the rest of the afternoon walking in the oppressive Florida steam, taking pictures of topiaries and eating Mouseketeer Bars. Finally, that night, back at the hotel, she said, "I didn't want to alarm you while we were at the park, but something has fallen in my body."

Of course we were alarmed. This sounded serious. "What did it feel like?" we asked.

"Just heaviness, sort of a pulling, but no real pain. I'll just check with the doctor"—a seventeen-hour drive away—"when we get back to Arkansas."

Maybe, after years of Lyme disease and mono, this new "bulge" really didn't seem serious. Or she didn't want to face a new sickness. Or she thought, as she always used to say, she should just "buck up."

This was still the days of early Internet and before cell phones, so we couldn't search symptoms. We didn't imagine her uterus hanging into her vagina. We didn't know a uterus *could* prolapse until days later when the doctor back at Carroll County Hospital in Arkansas told her.

This happens sometimes with age, he said. It'd be a simple surgery. They'd run the pre-op bloodwork.

But when the bloodwork came back, it showed something strange. Her white cell count was so high her body appeared to be fighting a raging infection. Something worse than mono.

This didn't make sense, the doctor said. They'd have to put the surgery off until her body was more stable. They'd run blood tests again in a few days.

But those tests looked no better. So the doctor ran more and different tests. And within a week, my mother was having surgery for a prolapsed uterus with the understanding that it was the least of her worries. She had chronic lymphocytic leukemia (which, in retrospect, she'd probably had for several years underlying, or confused with, the Lyme disease and mono). She would never actually be well again.

The Cow Parade

After I moved to San Francisco in May 2001—which turned out to be only a few months before my mother would die—she started sending me pictures of cow statues. The Cow Parade had come to Kansas City, where my parents were living by then.

Like Fort Worth, Kansas City is a former cow town—with once-thriving stockyards for cattle drives west—though the Cow Parade didn't originate there. The phenomenon started in Switzerland and spread to US cities in the late nineties and early 2000s. The premise is that hundreds of artists receive and then transform the same blank white fiberglass statue (or variations; there were three cow bodies: reared up on back hooves, grazing, and lying down). The artistic gimmick and title almost always revolve around a pun.

There was *Cowlvador Dalí*, with a clock slumping over its back as it grazed. *Charlie Parcow* reared on hind feet on a stack of giant records, his midnight-blue body in an evening jacket, his front hooves poised on the sax's keys. *The Cowardly Lion* (which my Oz-loving father posed by), with its mane like shag carpet dipped in plaster. *Moolyn Monroe*, balancing in heels on her hind hooves, dress swirling up provocowtively.

My mother had just survived a near-death fever the fall before. She was often weak from the leukemia, and nauseated and headachy with what would soon be diagnosed as a brain tumor. Yet, on the days she could, she was determined to see these cows.

I imagined her holding the insert from the *Kansas City Star* with its map of businesses and streets, circling in mechanical pencil—or having my father circle, if her vision wasn't good enough—the most unmissable cows, the way she used to spend hours poring over maps before our weeks-long road trips all over the country and to Canada. I felt embarrassed for her.

And, also, I felt sick with guilt. The summer before, I'd moved from Florida to Kansas City to live near her, maybe, I'd said, for as long as she lived, but then I'd left for California after only six months. At that point, she really did seem like she might live several more years, and as a twenty-seven-year-old still fighting to define myself as *not* my parents, I desperately wanted out of Missouri, where I'd gone to undergrad near Branson's country shows, and which I'd already escaped once.

My mother wasn't sending me the pictures to guilt me about leaving but because she thought they were fun, and that made me feel even guiltier and sadder. I wanted her to use the end of her life for something artier, smarter. But what kind of daughter was I for judging my dying mother? But also, what kind of educated, art-museum-loving mother would like these cows?

I stared at the glossy picture of *Cow-moo-flage*: a grazing cow hidden in plain view beneath a giant yellow beak and comb, like Foghorn Leghorn with angelic wings. It could have been the ur-title for the whole parade: so obviously a cow pretending to not be a cow, like a kid in a Darth Vader mask who keeps taking the mask off to announce, "Look—I'm not me; I'm Darth Vader."

Although I didn't want to hurt my mother by insulting the Cow Parade—and I'm sure I told her on the phone how great the photos were—I was actually relieved to be in San Francisco (where, I didn't realize, the Heart Parade would come soon—you know, *I left my heart in . . .*). I couldn't imagine posing by the cow statues, pretending I thought they were clever. Sure, you could stick the word *cow* into a lot of other words, but why would you want to?

In one of the pictures, my mother was wearing, as she often did, a handmade smocked sundress and Birkenstocks. Her hair, which had had grey streaks just in the bangs for a decade, had gone mostly grey. She was still heavy, as she'd been most of her life, so she looked in one way solidly embodied, but there was also something frail about her. Exhausted. As if she might not be able to stand back up. She was on a red velvet seat, which had been hollowed into the side of a white-and-black-spotted lying-down cow.

On the back of the photo, she'd written, *Cowch.*

The Jungle Cruise

My mother did not ever want to be "trapped in an infirm body." This was what she used to say, had been saying for almost two decades, long before she had any infirmity.

The first time I remember her saying it, we were leaving the high-rise nursing home in Buffalo, New York, where her maternal grandmother was living. I barely remember Grandma Siggins, but there's a picture of her and my mother on the lawn. Grandma, in her nineties, looking faded and wrinkled as the cloth of her flowered housedress, is in a wheelchair.

"It's so terrible," my mother said as we pulled away. "Her mind is just as sharp as ever, but she's trapped in an infirm body." More than losing her mind—as her own mother would to Alzheimer's—my mother feared this. She prized being capable, mobile. If peaches were ripe in Southern Arkansas, we'd drive half the day to the orchard to buy boxes of their sun-warmed velvet that my mother would boil into peach butter or bake into cobblers with homemade biscuit toppings. If the antique store had a scratched oak table, my mother would strip it and refinish it.

If there was a meteor shower, she'd wake me at midnight so we could lie on our backs in the yard on handmade quilts. If my father had two weeks off, she'd spend days planning a road trip, loading the car, shuttling us out in the dark so we could cover the first three hours before the sun even rose, because we had to make tracks: we were driving from Texas all the way to Montana to see Glacier National Park. (Though we did have to stop sometimes to photograph clouds, which she loved to take pictures of—their cirrus wisps and cumulus castling.)

Who would she be if she couldn't do all this? If she weren't ready for anything?

She loved, as I did, those J. Peterman catalogs of the 1990s, with their hand-drawn pictures of clothes accompanied by stories. The best item—but pricey, so neither of us ever bought one—was their simple black travel dress. As the narratives explained, it could be converted, with just the addition of a scarf and heels, into evening wear. With a belt and sturdy sandals, into an outfit for climbing pyramids. With layers, it became the perfect afternoon dress for eating yak cheese in a Siberian yurt. With a wide-brimmed safari sun hat, a dress for pushing through jungle overgrowth.

The dress, and any woman in it, was like a Swiss Army knife. Exactly the kind of capable-for-every-new-circumstance woman who my mother most wanted to be. So, when she was diagnosed with chronic leukemia, it wasn't a surprise or extended family discussion that she refused to consider chemotherapy. She didn't want to live any longer than her body was naturally ready to. Rather than face the effects of treatment, she would go toward the unknown. If she had to, she'd convert her handmade dress into a gown for a hospice bed, or into a shroud for her own death.

Cow Town

In 1952, two decades before I was born, my mother moved to a house near the Fort Worth Stockyards as a newly married seventeen-year-old. One of her neighbors and first close friends was named Brenda. In my mother's favorite story about young Brenda, she and her fiancé, Ken, were so broke that on Valentine's Day, in place of a gift, Brenda bought a cheap roll of satiny ribbon and wrapped it around her naked body. When Ken got home, she walked down their apartment stairs—red-haired (as she was) and wound only in that red ribbon.

This clearly impressed my mother, who had always been shy about her body and valued scrappily seeing and creating beauty where it wasn't obvious.

By the time I knew Brenda, Ken was a doctor, and they lived in a fancy ranch-style house in Arlington. Though Brenda was only in her forties, she had long since given up nakedly flouncing down staircases. She'd been diagnosed with scleroderma a few years after she and my mother met.

For the decades since, day by day, her skin had been gradually suffocating her. As it lost its elasticity, it pulled tight against her jaw; concaved her cheeks; closed her fingers into claws, then fists. It constricted her throat, which looked, like all of her, almost transparent. She was in a wheelchair and could not move her hands to pin up her own red hair, which, piled high, still gave her a sort of china doll beauty. Eventually, her skin would shrink-wrap her lungs and stop her from breathing.

I'm not saying that physical mobility equals quality of life or that my mother ever overtly said she feared becoming like Brenda. But when I think of my mother's decisions about her own death, I see Brenda, dressed up by her helper for our visit—unable to stand on her own. Unable to hold a pen to write (she was a poet) unless a helper stuck it between her fingers.

The Jungle Cruise

When my mother was first diagnosed, she reassured us that chronic leukemia meant she could live for years. She would be well for a while, then less well, then less. But that is not at all what *chronic* means. Or that's not what happened.

For the three years after her diagnosis, she'd have months when she'd feel energetic enough to go for walks or cook elaborate new recipes, as she'd always loved to. She'd do crossword puzzles. She'd travel. But then she'd catch a flu, and her fever would spike so high she'd be in bed, nearly delirious, for weeks. She'd say, "I think this is it. I think I'm really dying this time."

Once, when I was still living in Kansas City, my husband and I rented a car and raced to see her. I sat by her bed, and it's hard to explain how sick she was, except to say that she seemed to be dissolving into water molecules, like a blurry photograph of herself. I cried and cried and looked at the wall above her bed, crowded with family photos all taken by her: glamour black-and-whites of my older sisters and me and a chronicle of Thanksgivings: 1970s headscarves (my sisters) and *Little House on the Prairie* bonnets (guess who) to all of us in 1980s baggy khakis and too-bright T-shirts to my quasi-goth lace leggings as a teen in the nineties.

Because she was self-conscious and tended to hide behind the camera, there was not a single picture of my mother, and yet she was everywhere. She had given birth to all of us, to who we were as a family. She could not be leaving, and I was sure this time she really was.

But then the fever broke. We went out to eat (though she had almost no appetite). We saw *Memento* twice in the theater, because she loved it. We talked in detail about its reverse chronology.

But, a few months later, she was *I'm-going-to-die-this-time-but-don't-worry* sick. And we were back in the same long, winding line we'd never left.

Like amusement park lines do, it kept doubling back on itself, so we'd find ourselves right next to where we were months before, and sometimes we'd get so close to climbing on the boat that I could see the river lapping at my sandals, all the world's crocodiles and alligators beneath that water. Here it was, the ride I couldn't even say the name of: My Mother's Death.

But then the guides would load the boat from some other line. My mother would recover from the fever. She'd get some of her strength back. For days or weeks, we'd loop back away again.

But then she'd feel new pressure in her abdomen. The doctor would explain that her spleen was now "way big." He really said that: like her spleen was a wave in a surfing movie. It sounded funny, but what he meant was horrifying: white cells had filled her spleen. Her organs were starting to fail. She was trapped in an infirm body.

On every side were huge cargo boxes marked *GRIEF*, and I was exhausted with grieving and waiting for more grieving. Sometimes, I wanted out of the line, whatever it took. Even if it meant her dying, because to wind back and forth like this, closer and farther, felt unbearable.

It's no wonder I fled Kansas City. Staying felt like announcing that I was waiting for her to die, and of course all I wanted was not to think of her dying (though of course moving didn't help).

On the day I left Kansas City, my parents came to my apartment, and my father took a picture. In it, my husband and mother and I are standing in the dim lobby. I'm holding a pan of homemade brownies my mother has been well enough to bake, or has forced herself with her limited energy to bake because she loves us. The camera flash shatters against the aluminum foil, but despite the flash, my mother isn't blinking. Her eyes have a hopeless steadiness behind her bifocals. I can't place the expression, but the longer I look at it, the more I feel sick with the knowledge that my mother thinks at that moment she is seeing me for the last time.

She knows, though I don't yet, that the ride I am waiting for is not just her death, but all the years she won't see me living. She will never see the real love of my life, whom I won't meet for five years, after Will and I divorce. She won't see me wondering if I look like her: holding up the picture of her at sixteen beside my own face in the mirror, her brown hair waving toward her shoulders, bow lips, slightly round face, casual but somehow 1950s movie-star glamorous in a gingham shirt.

She won't see my first book get published. She won't see me crying on the floor of apartments for years after she dies—suddenly struck down in the midst of whatever I'm doing by the migrating arthritis of grief.

But even that time she thinks she's seeing me for the last time isn't the real end. She visits San Francisco a month after Will and I move there. We go to Cliff House and take pictures reenacting scenes from *Harold and Maude*. We go in the Camera Obscura; we eat Italian food back in the Lower Haight. But, in the midst of lunch, my mother is struck with a blinding headache. On the Amtrak to Kansas City, she's so dizzy my father has to help her walk down the aisles. When they get home, she falls suddenly forward onto a cedar chest and splits her forehead. My father rushes her to the ER. It turns out she's developed a brain tumor.

I fly back for Labor Day. Again in October for our birthdays. By then, she can barely get out of bed. She apologizes that she won't be able to make me the birthday tiramisu she'd planned. She can't sit up for more than a few minutes, even with the hospice bed helping. She's in a new kind of pain she describes as lightning the whole length of her spine.

I call the hospice nurse, who says, "Give her as much morphine as she wants."

And my mother jokes, as she's been joking, "But what if I get addicted?"

Her classic gallows humor. But the gallows are real now. She must know this, because for the first time, she doesn't refuse the morphine. She lets me open the little bottle, fill the dropper, drop one drop and then another and another into her mouth.

(Moose) Town

If people had made "bucket lists" in the eighties, both my parents would have included *See a moose*. So, on a road trip through eastern

Canada, when I was maybe seven, they were overjoyed to see a billboard advertising a moose farm. We'd be racing to make it before sunset, but what was an eighty-kilometer detour after driving from Texas to Canada? Finally, we'd see moose: mythical, towering antlers, like cows crossed with trees.

Just before sunset, we pulled through the gates and my father hurried to the farmhouse to ask what we owed and where the moose were pastured.

"Oh, I'm so sorry," the woman at the door told him, "but it died yesterday."

I'm not sure if my father said, "What?" or just looked dumbstruck, but the woman rushed to clarify, "It'd been sick a while."

"You only had *one* moose?" my father said. "And it died *yesterday*?"

As soon as we got over sitting in the car feeling stunned and sad and mooseless, this became a family joke. The lengths we had gone to for a dead moose. Its tragicomic timing. When something disappointed us, we used to say, "Oh, it died yesterday."

If my mother could have talked to me the day after her death, I can imagine her joking, "Oh, she died yesterday." Though, in cosmic-joke fashion, it was hard to tell when "yesterday" was. She died in the middle of the night on October 27, the night daylight saving time ended. We had to live an extra hour of our most immediate grief.

She was the one who'd taught me the mnemonic that clocks "fall back" in the fall and "spring forward" in spring, but that year, I didn't need to be reminded that time would always be falling backward toward her alive, and it would never fall back far enough. I could never again reach the moment before my father knocked on the bedroom door, his voice like a record almost scratched beyond playing, and said, "She's gone." And I ran to the guest room, and she was right there in the same bed—not gone, but gone. Her infirm body there, but her mind no longer trapped in it. Her blue mechanical pencils on the windowsill, waiting for a crossword puzzle, like always.

The Jungle Cruise

I've always been afraid of naïveté. I cover my eyes in movies when characters do things that the audience knows will hurt them. I want to rush into the screen and warn them. I want a dress for the safari–river-crossing–mountain-climbing so I'm not humiliated by being unprepared. I want to rush back in time and stop myself with that dropper of morphine.

At the crematorium, when I've momentarily pulled myself together, what makes me hysterically sob again is when the man doing the paperwork asks my mother's date of birth.

"October 13, 1935," I say. And I suddenly, clearly picture a portrait of her as a baby: chubby, ringleted. She's sitting like she's been set down in her white ruffled portrait dress and isn't sure how to move, her doll-like lace-up shoes jutting toward the camera. She's smiling at an out-of-frame parent, and her eyes are big and dark brown, or what I know is dark brown, though the photo is, of course, black and white.

It wasn't possible. That baby, with her little shoes and old-fashioned ruffled socks, could not be the exact same body whose fingernails (look—they're so tiny, so pale in 1936) were already blue-purple by the time, an hour, and the same hour later, men came from the funeral home to carry her down the apartment stairs. They could not be the same body. Life could not deceive me that terribly.

But of course, again and again, it can, it does.

Cow Town

In 2011, exactly a decade after my mother died, I was hired as an assistant professor in Moscow, Idaho. Huge grain silos, rectangular and cylindrical, loom in the gravel lot at one end of Main Street. Now I think they're iconic and charming. When I got here, I sometimes thought that, and I was sometimes scared I was in the middle of nowhere. I was scared that the love of my life, whom I'd met four years earlier, was going to leave me and move back to Oakland. He'd begrudgingly come, and we were not doing well. He did not want to replace the Bay Area punk shows he'd played with watching a band sing, "You say 'one ounce,' I say 'jig.' One ounce. Jig. One ounce. Jig."

He did not love—I didn't know if I loved either—the surrounding wheat and canola and lentil and chickpea fields (none of which I could have identified). It was an hour-and-a-half drive to the nearest bigger city, Spokane. At points, no radio stations came in. At other points, all you could get was Christian talk radio or country. There were multiple country stations: Bull Country, Big Country, Coyote Country. Some played newer country; some played classic; some played a mix.

I didn't really know the difference. Once, on our move, I tuned in to keep myself awake. And later, sometimes, when we were driving to Seattle or Spokane, I'd tune in as a joke. All those *cold river waters* and *cold beers* and *tank top straps* and *girl-you-look-good-in-those-jeans.* Sometimes the songs were a little funny; mostly they were dumb.

But one day, driving to yoga in the midst of a winter depression, I heard a song that I loved despite myself. It started, "She's so complicated / That's the way God made her / Sunshine mixed with / A little hurricane." I wasn't into this yet. I was now a *correct side of the NPR dial* assistant professor of poetry, and the rhymes in the next lines— "T-shirt" and "hurts"—were strained and corny. But then something else happened. Wait for it.

"I never meant to fall like this," Brad Paisley sings. And then he gets where this has all been heading: "But she don't just rain, she pours / That girl right there's the perfect storm."

The pun made me smile, like after riding one of the janky county-fair rides (which I also rediscovered in Idaho) that's trying so hard it has flashing lights that say *FUN!* (with a bulb or five burned out), but you find yourself stepping off dizzily joyous. While I'd been distracted by the cheesy "God" and "T-shirt" lines, a reversal, some sort of linguistic alchemy, had happened. Somehow, via that pun, "perfect storm" ended up meaning both its usual cliched self—a bad confluence—and its inverse: the perfect girl.

I'm not denying the objectification and slight misogyny of that stormy girl. And I'm not saying I'm more likely to listen to Brad Paisley or Blake Shelton than Patti Smith, Rage Against the Machine, or The National. True to form, I'm about to quote an NPR story. In "Puns in Country Music Songs Done Right," Geoff Nunberg says that a lot of people, like I used to, think country music is "a linguistic trailer park." He doesn't agree. He explains that puns are "a fitting device . . . particularly when they're tackling [country's] favorite themes—the fragility of happiness, the loss that's always immanent in love and family. . . ."

I'd extend Nunberg's metaphor and say that if a "linguistic trailer park" is a space where language is up on concrete blocks, unmoving, then puns do the opposite. They're where language moves double-time and transforms.

In "Neon Light," when Blake Shelton sings, "I prayed, prayed, prayed / For a sign, sign, sign. / Now there it is in the window / ... / There's a neon light at the end of the tunnel," doesn't he take the worn-out cliché of the "light at the end of the tunnel" and turn it into an actual bar where people can slap their knees, slap their foreheads, slap each other's shoulders in sloppy commiseration over the love he's lost? Isn't this Word turned into the sad but also sustaining complexity of real World?

I didn't think this all through when I first heard "Perfect Storm." I just knew I looked forward to listening to it. Maybe I'd regressed to the little girl who'd loved Janie Fricke (with her perfect country name) in her purple ruffled shirt and concho belt. Or maybe I'd grown into someone older and sadder and wiser, like my mother, smiling at her sewing machine in Fort Worth, as Lee Greenwood alchemized all his mistakes into "fool's gold."

The Jungle Cruise

From a linguistic standpoint, puns rely on naïveté. You're deceived into accepting, in seemingly good faith, one meaning of a word or line of logic, only to have it double back on itself, or reverse. Like you accept *you're being born into this body to live a beautiful life*, and then realize, *and to die a painful death*. As Nunberg says, our "innocent reading" of a phrase is made "more sad and knowing."

Or, as Josh Osborne says, "Lines that twist around themselves or are almost a pun, those are the cornerstones ... of country music." And so often, the lines of our lives are twistier than we thought—or maybe than we wanted to think.

But it's not that the first meaning is wrong. It's just part of the story.

The Cow Parade

When I first saw those pictures of my mother with the cows, I'd wanted to stop her from leaving them as part of her last record on earth. Had she become that naïve, that old, that desperate?

No, and yes, I think now. What if she loved the Cow Parade not *despite* but precisely *because* the cookie-cutter cows remained so obviously themselves while insisting on being something else?

By the time of the Cow Parade, my mother knew she'd really never again be well enough to spend the day at Silver Dollar City (the old-timey amusement park near Table Rock Lake, where the River Rats played Dixieland jazz she loved) or go to brass shows on the Kansas City Plaza. Lifetime inveterate reader that she was, she couldn't read more than a few pages. She would never watch another movie with Marilyn Monroe, or spend a leisurely afternoon, as we so often did in my childhood, in an art museum. She would never go back to the Fort Worth Stockyards, where she'd spent more than thirty years, or stand on the Arizona cattle pens in her jeans and cowboy boots as a teenager, or help her older brother rope a steer.

She knew, before I did, that this was all truly ending.

But here were *Cowculus, Cowntertop, Jazz Moosik, Moo-lyn Monroe*. Even at its most reduced, couldn't the world still surprise her? Linguist Xiaoli Gan says that puns are multiple meanings "give[n] birth . . . at once," and wasn't it wonderful that so many meanings could be packed into, or born out of, so little space? And wasn't it wonderful that when she was too tired to stand, she could sit, cowlapse even, smiling slightly, on *Cowch*?

The Jungle Cruise

When I was a child, in the early 1980s, when everyone suddenly did aerobics, my mother went through a period of putting on a black leotard and tights and bouncing between the grand and upright pianos singing along to "Wasn't That a Party": "Could have been the whiskey / Might have been the gin / Could have been the three or four six-packs / I don't know / But look at the shape I'm in."

She only drank the occasional Mexican-restaurant margarita or sangria, and I seriously doubt she had ever been hungover, so she wasn't kicking her legs in commiseration. Instead, still quite overweight and embarrassed by her body, she was amusing herself by making herself into a visual pun.

"Just look at the shape I'm in!" Bounce bounce.

It took me decades, until years after she died, to get this joke or learn the Rovers really sing "Look at the mess I'm in." I told you: I'm dense about puns.

I suspect now that my mother felt the same way I do, and probably a lot of people do, about naïveté. To preempt it, she doubled language back before the world could double back on her.

Maybe there aren't enough words to get at the twisty messy neony lightning-struck painful sloppy beautiful fake real jungle river of being human. We have to use the same words over. We have to lay them right on top of each other. We have to look backward and forward at once. We have to admit that we're both in and not-in on life's joke.

Or, as George Strait sings, I'm "Lookin' out my window / Through the pain."

Building Character

Act I

My favorite puppet, Purry Puss, asks loudly, "Didn't someone say we'd be stopping?" He sticks his head between my parents, above the Oldsmobile's center console. His alert triangle ears are so well loved their white cotton lining is unstitching; his eyes are half marbles of scratched green glass. He's been my most talkative stuffed animal since arriving from Pakaluk Puppets three years ago, when I was six. He goes on all our trips with us. He likes pancakes, barely golden, like I do. He speaks in a high, insistent, wheedling voice my parents and I would be too polite to use. He likes being the center of attention. "You're going to look at a bunch of corn?" he asks.

We're driving to the Corn Palace in Mitchell, South Dakota, which is famous—with bulb-shaped domes and corn-cob mosaics—because the billboards say so. "I think it sounds corny," Purry Puss quips, wiggling his thread whiskers on his pink velvet nose. My parents smile.

My dad was an actor in college in the late sixties, and my parents have taken me to black-box theaters to see *The Fantasticks* and *Ain't Misbehavin'* since my early memories. At home in Fort Worth, I invent *Fashion Cruise,* a show in which fabulously dressed characters (played by my imagination; I'm the only child at home) are always falling overboard. We don't have TV, but maybe I've seen *The Love Boat* flickering on a rare visit to a neighbor's? Sometimes my father pretends to be my student and sits in a cramped desk in rows of my stuffed animals. Le Mutt and Minnie Mouse are better students than "David," who asks questions about simple addition. I'm a very good teacher: I patiently write examples on my chalkboard. I do everyone's homework in scented marker, except David's, which he has to do himself.

Or I put on plays in the puppet theater that appeared in 1982, the same Christmas as Purry Puss. Like almost everything in my family, it's homemade: a flowered curtain my mother sewed, two-by-fours my parents hammered into a proscenium arch, painted *Alexandra's Puppet Theater.* My puppets aren't confined to plays, though none of them talks as much as Purry Puss, whom my parents and I all voice. Even in my teens, when he'll live mostly on a bookshelf, Purry Puss will chime in about family decisions. (Though he'd huffily reply if he heard this, "I don't know what all this talk is about *people* speaking for me.")

Technically, none of us really believes Purry Puss speaks for himself, but we don't breach the fourth wall. I don't remember my parents ever answering Purry Puss: "But, Alexandra, what do *you* feel?" If my memory is right, they sometimes even talked just to each other through his voice.

In Terry Gilliam's wonderful, strange movie *The Imaginarium of Doctor Parnassus,* which I'll see decades later, Buddhist monks floating on carpets sustain the story of the universe via meditation/imagination. If they stop telling the story, reality below will crumble. Being raised by my parents feels, in retrospect, like this. We believed so deeply in creativity and stories that to say which stories were true or not might break the spell of all of them. Might send us plummeting from our clouds.

It's not surprising my father's favorite role as an actor was Elwood P. Dowd, a grown man whose best friend is a six-foot-tall, invisible rabbit, Harvey. The play and movie, which I grew up with, walk a thin line between suggesting Harvey is imaginary, so Dowd's family is right to think he's crazy, and suggesting Harvey is there and everyone else is crazy for doubting. If you ask my father if Harvey's real, his eyes will sparkle (bright green, like his grandson, Purry Puss), and he'll say, "What do you mean *real*?"

My father didn't come from a family who believed in invisible rabbits. His twenty-four-year-old father had grown up in a one-room shack with nine siblings. His seventeen-year-old mother was the only child of alcoholics. My grandparents met honkytonking in Fort Worth and divorced in 1949, when my father was a few months old; it was the first of my grandmother's six or seven marriages.

I don't know the number because she didn't. Once, she found old snapshots of herself with a man, and told my father, "I'd forgot 'bout him. Now tha' I see his face, I think we might'a got married 'cause he said he'd take me to Disneyland. You remember his name?"

My father didn't remember this maybe-stepfather, but he did remember that he and his mother went to Disneyland. It was a rare week with his young, wild, unmotherly mother, whom he saw infrequently beginning when he was three, when his mother called a phone number in a newspaper ad for babysitting and told the stranger on the phone that she'd be waitressing from Friday to Sunday and needed someone to watch her toddler. My grandmother dropped off my father at this woman's house with a change of clothes. On Sunday, my grandmother didn't come back. Or Monday. Or Tuesday. Or the next Sunday. Three weeks later, she finally reappeared to get my father.

I don't know what explanation my grandmother offered that day, but I imagine Ruth Hendrick—in her house dress and sensible black Christian pumps—saying, "He can stay any time." This was 1951, and there was no Child Protective Services to report my grandmother to. And Ruth was a good Christian and mother. She and her husband had two children, plus ones they babysat, some of whom, like my father, became their de facto foster children. Through luck (or, Ruth would say, God), my grandmother had abandoned my father with loving people, who packed lunchboxes with bologna sandwiches and had bedtimes.

For the next five years, my father mostly lived with Ruth and her family. His mother would occasionally visit, or more often say she would. My father remembers sitting under the Hendricks' mimosa tree, his heart beating faster with each passing car. Only when the street darkened would he start to cry, though he kept watching for headlights that hardly ever came. He came to love "Aunt Ruthie," as he always called her. For the rest of her life, he sent her Mother's Day cards. But he also longed for his own mother. He knew that he belonged *with* Ruthie's family, not quite *to* it.

"Why didn't you live with your father?" I ask once I realize how strange this all is. His father had remarried and had two more sons and a daughter. He worked construction in Fort Worth, was active in the Masonic Lodge, had been sober since he came home drunk and his new wife threw a frying pan at his head.

"He was busy with his new family," my father says simply.

"Did he know your mother had left you with Aunt Ruthie?"

"Oh, yes," my father says. "He'd send presents there at Christmas."

My father isn't sure why his mother finally took him back when he was in third grade. By then, she'd married Don, a verbally cruel, distant man, whose own children didn't even live with him. I have no memories of Don, though he was married to my grandmother my whole childhood, except the few months they divorced before remarrying.

My grandmother had the slightly lizardy skin of women who live in the desert, which she didn't, but aspired to. She had short greying hair and an impenetrable Texas accent I often didn't understand. She'd occasionally show up unannounced or we'd drive to her house by a Texas lake full of water moccasins, where her incessant yelling at her bulge-eyed chihuahuas matched their manic yipping. She seemed to have a succession of clones of the same two awful dogs for my whole childhood. She usually forgot to offer us anything to eat or drink. Don would stay in his tool shop, avoiding us. In my father's childhood, Don had most often referred to my father and his mother as "Stupid and Stupid."

Maybe it's truest to say that my father, like other 1950s latchkey or foster kids, was raised less by humans than by cartoon wolves (and mice and dogs and rabbits). The first generation to grow up with TV, he became a devoted member of The Mickey Mouse Club and still has memorabilia.

In a famous family photo of my first trip to Disney World, when I was six and my father was thirty-two, he's wearing a button-up shirt my mother had sewn, the fabric printed with tiny Minnie Mouses, and the "real" Minnie is leaning over at a restaurant to kiss him on the cheek. My father is grinning, overjoyed, as Minnie is clearly over-joyed—because that's how her mouth is made.

"Industry has lost credibility with the public, the government has lost credibility, but people still have faith in Mickey Mouse and Donald Duck," Disney ambassador Martin Sklar is quoted in *Vinyl Leaves: Walt Disney World and America*. Or in my father's case, his parents had lost credibility, so my father looked for whoever would offer a sense of belonging. I've heard my father sing the Mickey Mouse Club theme song many times, even in recent years.

Theater in high school was a natural fit. Show tunes were natural. So was, eventually, talking in the voice of his daughter's stuffed animals. If I were him, I'd probably be angry at my parents for life or have spent years in therapy, but my father isn't and didn't. When I ask if there was anything good about living with Don, he says, "No," but then adds, "I always said you couldn't live *with* Don; you had to try to live *around* him."

My father excels at *living around*. He was the listener to my mother's stories, the helper with her endless repainting, wallpapering, cooking. He lived around her judgments, the world's bad news, his parents' continued disinterest. Though he finally did move in with his father and stepmother during college to save money, they never attended any of his plays. By the time I was a child, our visits consisted of my grandfather rocking in his patched vinyl recliner with a

Western on TV and one of two intermittent conversations happening. The first script went:

GRANDFATHER (*tilting head toward spindly sapling out window—sometimes in white bloom, mostly bare branches in dirt yard*): What do ya'll reckon that tree's gonna be?

FATHER (*a journalist who knows nothing about horticulture and has been asked to speculate about this same tree for two springs already*): I don't know. Maybe a plum?

GRANDFATHER: Might be a cherry. I reckon it's still too soon to tell.

(*Silence, rocking, Western*)

The second script went:

FATHER: I'm doing a story on Mexican restaurants, so we've been sampling nachos all over town. (*Or substitute another story; he's been a features and travel journalist for a decade.*)

GRANDFATHER: Is that so? (*Silence, rocking, Western.*) When d'ya reckon you're gonna start your life's work?

> *Spotlight on fake-gold trowel on pedestal behind GRANDFATHER, engraved with his name and Worshipful Master of the Rendon Masonic Lodge. It's beside the lava lamp, in a place of honor. Audience knows "life's work" is code for "Joining the Masonic Lodge." Or maybe audience is confused like DAUGHTER is for years, when she waits for her father to explain, "Being a journalist is my life's work."*

FATHER (*living around this question*): Sure is a pretty day out. Maybe after lunch we'll take a walk down to the creek.

(*Silence, rocking, Western.*)

DAUGHTER looks at boringly mysterious tree out window of boxy cheap-paneled house her grandfather built on the land adjoining the one-room shack (still standing) where he grew up. Three generations

of Teagues have lived on this land (it's named Teague Road not because the family matters, but because there's no one else out here).
She is tied to this road by name yet does not belong here. She has
grown up in a huge, hundred-year-old-house her mother bought in
the 1950s and has been restoring since. She has what her grandfather
and step-grandmother think are fancy tastes (though her family lives
on her father's salary and drives an old green Chevy with one black
door leftover from a wreck). She's grown up going to art museums.
Her favorite drink, in elegantly rounded green glass all the way from
France, is Perrier.

How did her father end up like he is: the first person in his family
to graduate high school, much less college, the only one who learned
to articulate his words, the theater geek and then journalist who married a decade-and-a-half-older, brilliant, domineering woman from
upstate New York, and had this fanciful, fancy daughter?

Maybe he's a plum that grew on a cherry tree. Or maybe his life is
a story he's successfully imagined and written around himself, which
he has to keep writing and performing. Definitely, I knew intuitively
as a child, it was up to my parents and me to make everything: to
keep ourselves above the sad world, above class, above and around
our family's past.

In an article about making puppets for therapy, registered art therapist Lenore Steinhardt writes, "with basic raw materials such as clay,
paper and paint, we must 'touch' everything into existence." Within
puppet therapy, "touching" the world into existence is empowering.
Within life, it's empowering but also exhausting. I used to joke I never
saw my parents sit down at home unless they were reading or eating
or working at a sewing machine, and it's not quite a joke.

My mother sewed matching patterned shirts for my father and me
as well as smocked dresses and bonnets as if I were in *Little House
on the Prairie*. (This was the late seventies, but her version of this
style was still extreme.) She cooked from scratch: whole-wheat pizza
crust, ice cream with egg and honey custard cranked in a canister,
cream-of-potato soup with organic milk from a dairy where we met

the cows. (This was also the seventies health-food craze; we were re-making ourselves bite by bite.) She converted the closet at the top of the stairs into a darkroom for her photography. She cut and soldered stained-glass windows: rainbows and ships to block out our run-down neighborhood.

In our large yard, my parents built me a playground with swings, ladders, landings—like a park (but with no homeless people peeing in the sandbox, no peeling lead paint on the bouncing hippos; though no bouncing hippos either, nor friends).

Sometimes, when I got older, neighbor girls (Mexican-American, like most of the neighborhood besides us) came to play, or I went to their houses, but I wasn't usually allowed to venture beyond our chain-link. Outside were gang-tagged overpasses and broken side-walks. Inside was a secret garden (my father read us that book!), Narnia (he read that too), concrete yet Grecian fountains burbling to drown out hot rods' revving. Inside our house, which my parents were wallpapering back to its antique glory, was another: an exact miniature they'd meticulously glued and decorated for me. A doll-house with my bedroom, our clawfoot tub, our staircase, tiny lace curtains.

Each night, in place of the TV we didn't have, my father read aloud, bringing to life *Great Expectations*, "The Raven," *The Lord of the Rings*, *Alice in Wonderland*, most of the Oz books. When my mother told him that finishing his master's thesis on L. M. Montgomery would take too much time away from me, my father lived around it. He never earned his master's. He read us all of L. M. Montgomery's *Anne of Green Gables* books instead.

By the time I have memories, the *Fort Worth Star-Telegram* had promoted him from school board coverage to features and travel. He helped people see Texas as Oz (his favorite movie): told them where to travel for the best historic inns, which restaurants had the best Tex-Mex nachos, which caves to visit (Natural Bridge with its dinosaur billboards, Sonora with its fairy-tale crystals). He wrote the world into being.

When we went to restaurants he was reviewing, I often felt royal: the owner waving us to the best booth, special cheesecake arriving. But, though my father was all silly antics and patience with me, he'd sometimes snap at strangers. He hated smoking (his parents smoked), and he'd march across restaurants to announce "that smoke is going right in my face," even to people in the smoking section. Or he'd chastise the hostess. I'd cringe at these flares of anger edged with imperiousness. Wasn't it obvious, his tone suggested, we were superior to *this*?

Wasn't everything in my life arranged to suggest superiority and difference? And, though I was spoiled and often happy, didn't I also stand at the fence watching the neighbor sisters, whom for years I knew only slightly, shyly, through the chain-link? But wasn't loneliness just a failure of my imagination? What fairy-tale princess in her magic yard would want to be like those girls?

Yet, once I was a little older and allowed at their houses, I longed so much for just one jar of their trashy (my mother said), artificially dyed (my father said) pickles (so sour my tongue felt electric! not like the grey-green health-food dills sogging in milky brine) that once at Piggly Wiggly, I refused to leave the pickle aisle. Finally, my mother said she was going to leave me. And she did. She drove away, with seven-year-old me still in the store. I'd started to panic, and an older woman had taken me to look for my mother by the time she returned—having made her point. We had standards, and if I fell below them, it was not just the Vlasics, but me, who'd be rejected.

Fairy tales told of even more desperate bargains: to walk on land, the Little Mermaid is willing to give up the entire ocean. But I still felt ashamed that I wasn't good enough for the world my parents had built for me. Without my continual effort and imagination, I was a girl who could spin straw into gold but chose to feed a stupid donkey instead.

Once, I arrived home from a rare afternoon at Roseanna's (the site of adult siblings, cars on blocks, and delicious pickles) and said, "Roseanna gave me potato chips." But when my mother saw orange dust on my hands, she yelled, "Those were Cheetos. You should have known better than to eat that junk," then yelled at me more for lying. I tried to protest that I didn't know: I'd never had potato chips *or* Cheetos. But I "should have known better" about not knowing. I remember her in the doorway, me on the porch with blaring orange palms, unsure I'd be allowed to reenter the castle.

Another time, my father brought me a rare store-bought doll, a Cinderella from New York City. My small fingers kept bungling her shoes' rubber straps, so a neighbor and I decided to cut them (creativity! scissors!), but again, as she often did, my mother got mad and said that I should have known better. Ever after, the doll was a reminder of my failure, her lacey beauty ruined. I wasn't sorry when she burned with our house a few years later.

I'm in my forties before I understand that even if an FAO Schwarz Cinderella was a splurge in a single-income family, a misjudgment with scissors shouldn't feel tantamount to hacking apart the world. I'm shocked when I read about attachment theory and learn that parents should help their children face threats by giving them manageable pieces, like parent birds feeding offspring from their own chewed food. In contrast, parents who never learned to face their own fears may magnify their children's, or react to them unpredictably. I see myself for the first time in a clarifying, frightening mirror when I read that these children may become what's called, in attachment theory, *ambivalently* or *anxiously attached*: perpetually scared the world is capricious, or in my case, prone to disassembly.

What was created could always be destroyed. There was, for instance, the Christmas Eve with the raining dolls.

After my father read us *Little Women*, my mother made me a doll of Amy, the youngest March sister. Each Christmas after, Beth, then Jo, then Meg arrived, and unlike ordinary girls' dolls, my mother had stitched every thread. The Little Women had sculpted cloth faces, embroidered eyes, Victorian dresses, layers of lace petticoats, ankle boots with seed-pearl buttons, tiny gossamer-thin stockings, handbags with drawstrings, caps that tied with velvet bows, silky hair made from wigs. The dolls were works of art: labors of love that must have each taken my mother a year of nights after my bedtime. My mother loved me so much she would make the world for me.

But one Christmas Eve, when I was maybe eight, I pitched a fit over something, and in retaliation, my mother threw the Little Women and all my stuffed animals out my second-floor window. I sobbed and sobbed—imagining their terrified faces pressed into the grass, or staring into the dark night sky alone. Each of them had favorite foods, a voice, a life story. Snoopy's father had tragicomically died face-first into his birthday cake. Le Mutt, the beige stuffed dog from France, said "Ooh la la" about everything. My mother knew how alive they were, and still she left me to sob. How could I be excited for Christmas morning when holding them was all I really wanted?

Without emotional "containers" or a sense of her own stable skin to hold her fears, an ambivalently attached child may adhere to an out-side object: what psychoanalysts David Meltzer and Esther Bick first called "adhesive identification." ("Adhesive identification sounds like mumbo jumbo to me," Purry Puss says, looking out the car window. "Do you think if the Corn Palace caught fire, it'd turn into popcorn?")

At the private school where her parents get her tested for scholar-ships, the ambivalently attached child may fear getting kicked out if she fails to demonstrate the "extraordinary verbal aptitude" that got her admitted. She may fear her thrift-store flats stand out amid her rich classmates' shiny penny loafers (they do; she's ridiculed). She may cry at feeling isolated, but also guilt herself. Isn't pain part of building character? Doesn't her mother say it's good to *build charac-ter*? Doesn't building character explain why her family doesn't have air-conditioning in their house or car—like they're still living in the 1950s Arizona of her mother's teens?

"Some like it hot!" my father sings, à la that musical, tapping the steering wheel.

"What heat?" Purry Puss says from the front passenger's seat.

In this scene, it's 1982, and we're on our way to Galveston: my favor-ite place in Texas. We're in Houston traffic—sweat-stuck, after four hours in the car, the humid air well over one hundred.

We've been making this drive repeatedly because my father is covering the restoration of the Tall Ship *Elissa*. It's a perfect fairy tale: a square-rigged ship built in 1877 in Scotland later had her masts cut and an engine installed to run contraband and was about to be scrapped in Greece when the Galveston Historical Society, looking for a tall ship to showcase in its harbor, rescued her. And now, before our eyes, crews are rebuilding the masts, repairing the hull, sanding the deck. Sometimes, after work, they sing shanties on deck with accordions and guitars. There are women in overalls and sailor hats, unselfconsciously strong: the kind of woman I want to make myself into. There's a captain, funny and charming, with his trimmed beard and braided-band sailor's cap. He's befriended my parents and invited them on the maiden sailing.

Children (even extra-special seven-year-olds) aren't allowed. I have to stay on shore with my twenty-six-year-old half sister Anne, whom our mother has conscripted for babysitting. It's my first whole day alone with Anne, and I'm in awe of the novelty. We wave long after anyone on board can see, then wander souvenir stands, where she buys me a paper fan that accordions into a picture of a blossoming tree—cherry or plum—and curving moon bridge.

On the drive home, I open and close the fan—using it to stir the sweltering, staticky air that sticks to me anyway—and excitedly pump my parents for details. I'm going to grow up to be a sailor, I think, and spend months, maybe years, at sea.

My mother particularly loves ships, and says it was magical: Galveston fading and only water filling their view. Then my parents get to the scary/exciting/strange part: my father climbed the rope ladder to the crow's nest, the little platform on the mast. Way out on the gulf, rocking in the waves, he swayed one hundred feet above the water—sure his sweat-slicked hands would slip.

In the front seat, Purry Puss listens intently. With my mother voicing him, he teases my father: "Why is it called a crow's nest if there are humans in it? Why didn't you climb back down?"

My father didn't climb back down because Captain B was climbing right below him; Captain B had insisted my father see the view. My father is strong, but he types at a desk all day and notoriously fears heights. He thought he was going to plunge to his death, though he tries to joke: "I don't even remember the view, but I think there was sky."

He had to let go with one hand and lean backward to grab the first landing, then do it again, leaning farther, to hoist himself to the crow's nest. Then do it all in reverse to get down.

Why didn't my father just refuse to climb?

At the time, I assume research. We do a lot of things for stories: eat greasy nachos at five restaurants or listen to the owner of a B&B, in only a falling-open bathrobe, give us a drunk tour of each piece of furniture in her antique home.

But, years later, I'll learn that it wasn't research. My father climbed the rigging to prove his love. For the two years we'd been visiting *Elissa*, my mother and Captain B had been more and more brazenly flirting. By the time *Elissa* sailed, my father was scared my mother was going to leave him.

"Mama was flirting with Captain B?" I say.

"Oh, yes," my father says. "I felt like he was challenging me. He was trying to prove I wasn't man enough to climb up with him."

Until my father tells me this, in my forties, I didn't know my mother ever flirted with anyone—only the famous story she used to tell about her own jealousy. When I was a baby, my father got assigned on a travel story with a pretty blonde journalist, and, although he kept insisting he wasn't attracted to her, my mother was jealous. She asked, or told, him not to go. When he said he had to, she pulled the potatoes she was baking from the oven, hurled them on the linoleum, and stomped on them, screaming that he wasn't going anywhere with that "predatory blonde." She told the story for years after as humorous, though it had cautionary edges. My father was ever after careful not to be too friendly with blondes.

My father pauses in his Captain B story, and says, "Maybe he was hoping I'd fall and get out of his way."

"How was the view up there?" Purry Puss cheerfully asks in that long-ago car.

Was my mother teasing my father about his fear? Was she trying to show sympathy? Did she want to hear him recount the lengths he'd go to for her? Did my parents ever talk about her flirting?

Or was *this* the conversation: through a puppet in a scorching car?

I'm writing these stories in my forties when it finally strikes me: as much as endurance, weren't we building character in another sense? The characters we wanted to be, or wished we could be, or needed to be to live around our hurts?

Once, when I had to be less than ten (because our house hadn't burned yet), I got so furious with myself over something that I pried the screen off an upstairs window and climbed onto the shingles. Feeling vividly self-hating, I stared down at the grass and imagined jumping. My memory of this moment blurs with *Picnic at Hanging Rock*: those girls in white late-Victorian dresses on a strange, high rock in Australia. Though this is not how it happens, I've always remembered the girls walking, as if in a trance, to their deaths—stepping one by one into the faded blue of sky.

In reality, *Picnic at Hanging Rock* never explains exactly what happens on that Valentine's Day picnic in 1900, when, against the head mistress's warnings, a few girls slip away through a crevice. One is found unconscious, the rest never found. As Vincent Canby wrote in the *New York Times*, "Such horror is unspeakable not because it is gruesome but because it remains outside the realm of things that can be easily defined or explained in conventional ways."

But what can be "easily defined or explained in conventional ways" in a world of the imagination?

I'd seen *Picnic at Hanging Rock* as a child because my parents always took me with them to a Fort Worth art theater, having promised the owner I'd fall asleep on the linoleum before the adult parts. I sometimes did, though I also remember David Bowie as a naked alien, flickering above me like a bizarre planetarium in *The Man Who Fell to Earth*.

The day I did not jump from the roof, I climbed back inside and went downstairs to find my father. I remember the scene in surreal slow motion, myself sobbing and saying, "You almost lost your little girl today." Even at the time, I knew the wording was strange—as if I were more the omniscient narrator than the scared little girl.

My father hugged me and maybe gave me a glass of orange juice (our family cure-all), but he didn't call a doctor or therapist. I was prone to drama (as, it turns out, ambivalently attached children, and adults, often are.) And maybe I didn't seem serious. Or maybe my father, who despite his childhood says he's never felt suicidal, didn't understand that I could be.

Or maybe all that mattered was the happy ending. I was still with him on our cloud.

◆

A PARTIAL CAST OF FAMILY CHARACTERS

MOTHER: Nearly forty when her final child (me) was born; only a child herself, seventeen, when her first daughter, Beth, was born. Spent her life grieving her father's sudden, violent death on an ammunition ship. After which, her own mother had, like some cruel stepmother in a fairy tale, given away all her dolls and toys without telling her.

MATERNAL GRANDMOTHER: The cruel woman who gave away those dolls. Also, a thirty-one-year-old grieving widow trying to move across the country—all her possessions in the trunk of a car—with three young children.

MATERNAL GREAT-GRANDMOTHER: Mother of five children (my grandmother the youngest). Left by her bigamist husband when she discovered his other family and confronted him. Plunged overnight from middle-class life to working as a domestic.

FATHER: Marries, in his twenties, a more-than-decade-older, domineering divorcee: his first real relationship. When he tries to tell her he's also attracted to men, she tells him he isn't. Wants, more than anything, to give his only child the childhood and love he never had.

PATERNAL GRANDMOTHER: Overtly tells her only son he wasn't wanted. Claims to have had a happy childhood, of which she has no memories. As an adult, working at the Texas Hotel, freakishly meets her biological half sister and learns her own true story, which she never tells any of us.

PATERNAL GREAT-GRANDFATHER: Violent, abusive man off-stage in Tennessee. Travels through Texas and has an affair with a woman who gives birth to my grandmother. Back in Tennessee, beats one of his daughters until she runs away. Then beats his own wife to death. My father will learn this in his sixties from the woman he thought was his mother's friend, who was actually secretly her half sister. (I know it's hard to keep track of the characters.) My father will call to say he has huge family news. I'll think *secret inheritance!* He'll arrive in Idaho to tell me I'm the great-granddaughter of a wife-beating murderer.

PURRY PUSS: Stuffed cat puppet. Charged with cheerful, creative quips in all circumstances.

◆

Act II

In the stories my mother told of her first marriage, she'd been a trapped 1950s housewife with an unloving husband. When he lost his job with Central Airlines and left to work on the other side of the state, she became a single parent for two years: cooking and cleaning and walking everywhere because she had no car and her husband wouldn't let her get a license.

"But Mom used to drive us places in Judy's car, so she must have had a license," my half sister Beth tells me, years after our mother dies. Judy was my sisters' father's niece, about my mother's age. She lived with my mother and half sisters during those years to help pay the mortgage.

In my teens my mother mentioned in passing that she and Judy had once been a couple, and I imagined them dating briefly when my half sisters were teenagers, my mother newly divorced. Most of my parents' friends were gay or lesbian, so I was less surprised to find out my mother was bisexual than that she'd been attracted to Judy, who—when she dropped by our house in her nurse's scrubs or came to Thanksgiving—was nice, but gruff, and tended to view the world darkly. "She's like Eeyore," my parents used to joke behind her back.

"The affair wasn't after Mom and Daddy divorced," Beth tells me. "Anne and I were little, and Daddy was away working in Laredo. Judy had her own bedroom, but she usually slept with Mom. When Daddy moved back in, Mom told him *he* had to sleep in the other room because the bedroom was hers and Judy's now."

"She did?" I ask, trying to rewrite our mother from trapped housewife with no agency to 1950s radical who kicked her husband out of their bedroom for her female lover.

"Yes," Beth says. "And Judy and Mom used to have the most knockdown, drag-out fights. In one, they were fighting in the car, and Mom ran into the house and locked the door, but Judy slashed through the screen with the pointed end of a bottle opener. In another, the argument escalated to Mom grabbing a jump rope, wrapping it around Judy's neck, and tightening it until Judy buckled to the floor, blue-faced. I was hiding under our play table, and all of this happened right there in our playroom beside the table."

Beth continues, "When Mom finally stood up, I said, 'Why didn't you kill her?' That seemed to me like an ordinary question. I thought, *If you hate someone that much, you should just go ahead and kill them. Once you've crossed that line, why stop?* I'm sure I just wanted the fights to stop, but for years after, I really worried there was something sociopathic about me. It scared me that I was the kind of person who could think that."

Our mother tried to strangle Judy with a jump rope in front of child Beth? Beth worried *she* was the sociopathic one? No one, in the first three decades of my life, ever mentioned this?

"What did our mother say?" I ask, reeling.

"She said she didn't want to go to jail and have someone else raise us," Beth says.

When Beth tells me this story, standing in her Arkansas kitchen, I wish I knew how to go back in time and comfort her or stop our mother, though of course, raised by the same mother, I've also spent much of my life not feeling comforted.

In another story Beth tells me around this time, our mother was dating a man named Mark and my sisters were teens. In the version I knew from my mother, she'd spent two decades in Arizona and Texas "missing water that ran under bridges." Although the Trinity River ran through Fort Worth, it was slow and brown, nothing like the Adirondack rivers of her childhood. So when someone told her about the Arkansas Ozarks, and she first drove the eight hours to see water rushing and rippling over stones, she fell in love with it. She used to take my sisters camping there.

"But there wasn't room for all of us in Mark's pickup," Beth tells me. "So Anne and I had to ride in a dim plywood camper. The tailgate closed over the door and locked us in. She'd give us flashlights for reading."

Was the camper an imaginative, scrappy way to take my sisters somewhere magical? Was it slightly abusive? What kind of woman would lock her daughters in a wooden box for eight hours each way, then tell the story as if all that mattered was that she'd found "water that ran under bridges"? How do I fit this with the LOVING MOTHER who would, each year of my life, make ten Thanksgiving pies from scratch—each family member's favorite—carefully latticing over cherries, whipping cocoa powder, eggs, and cream into a custard? Or the woman who stitched me those Little Women dolls not once, but twice?

When our house burned to the ground when I was ten, I lost all my dolls and stuffed animals, except Purry Puss, who was traveling with us. I sobbed and sobbed, but my mother reassured me the others had escaped out windows and were traveling. Probably some would find me in Arkansas.

And it was true: over the next few years, not only Le Mutt and Minnie but also Amy, Beth, Jo, and Meg reappeared, one by one, with their little traveling cases. My mother meticulously remade every petticoat, stocking, skirt, shoe, and eyebrow. She loved me so much she would remake the world for me.

She also had, or built, that kind of character.

"Each child, woman and man should know a limit of containment. Nobody should be asked to hold more," Terese Mailhot writes in her memoir *Heart Berries*. But of course generation after generation, people are asked to hold more than they can. Maybe at best we build fantasies or characters to try to contain the uncontainable—what keeps spilling anyway.

Beth says our mother had mellowed by the time I was born—though mellowed is, of course, relative. When I was a teenager, furious over something, I screamed I was going to kill myself, and my mother grabbed our largest kitchen knife and chased me up to my bedroom, shouting, "Oh yeah, well if you really want to, I'll help you! Watch me help you!"

I remember that blade inches from my neck.

Was she trying to out-melodrama my melodrama to show me it was ridiculous? Did she want to terrify me by reflecting my own threat back at me? Was she in a perimenopausal rage (as I'm coming to consider in my late forties)? Could she have really hurt me?

We talked about none of this. An hour later, we sat down to pasta with homemade tomato sauce with onions and garlic probably chopped with that same knife.

FATHER (*humming "Bella Notte" from* Lady and the Tramp): This looks scrumptious.

DAUGHTER (*unfolding a handmade cloth napkin from the swan into which she'd folded it; she's been teaching herself napkin origami. She has washed her face with cold water, but it's still puffy from crying. Everyone lives around this*): It smells delicious.

MOTHER: There's tiramisu in the oven. (*It's a joke: tiramisu isn't baked, but she's really made one.*)

Food was love in my family, and we never *de-symbolized* any object:

the term in puppet therapy for the step at the end of a session when the patient says, "This is just a puppet now. It's no longer x [the character or situation it was enacting]." It's dropping the curtain on the play: redefining the line between fantasy and reality.

But for fantasy to retain its power, it can't be questioned or de-symbolized. No wonder, as Kurt Andersen explains in *Fantasyland,* his brilliant book on the longstanding American affair with unreality, that Disney staff, by company policy, aren't allowed to say they *play* characters—e.g., "I'm Minnie Mouse this week." Instead, the person playing Minnie has to say something like "I'm *helping* Minnie this week," as if Minnie, in her polka-dotted selfhood, just needs a personal assistant to powder her big black nose. As if, when the park closes, Minnie goes home as Minnie, still smiling.

After our house burned when I was ten, we began the ritual of going to Disney World—although we didn't discuss the connection between our loss and these trips. Every year or two, we'd drive seventeen hours from Arkansas. While Disney may seem like the antithesis of making everything from scratch, it's also the mecca of imagination. At Epcot, a whole character—the purple dragon Figment (a toy version of which has lived for three decades on my father's desk)—is its embodiment. On the Journey Into Imagination ride, Figment sings, with almost aggressive cheer, a nasally showtune about turning dreams into reality via imagination.

In their famous origin story, my imaginative parents had met because of their shared love of language. My mother: a thirty-four-year-old, divorced high-school dropout. My father: twenty-one. The setting: a community college English classroom in Fort Worth.

The professor had asked my mother, the star student, to hand back essays. And then she saw the impossible: a higher grade than hers. "Who *is* this Raymond Teague?" she asked bossily.

And a handsome, green-eyed man in the back row raised his hand. "I am," he said, his first line in the play that became my life.

In that play, my parents laughed over silly, wordy inside jokes, studied French together, made each other scrapbooks—my mother annotating newspaper articles with funny comments, my father writing her poems. My mother loved my father so much she'd make a new family (she'd later say she had "a dependent child at home for thirty-six years," Anne having graduated high school the year I was born). My father loved my mother so much, he'd live around stomped baked potatoes; he'd climb a ship's rigging.

But my junior year of college, I was on the phone with my mother, confiding that my husband and I had been fighting. Maybe I even admitted he'd punched me.

My mother said, "Relationships are hard," and I said, "Well, yours and Daddy's isn't."

And then she told me something had happened when I was in high school, something that had made her feel betrayed and devastated. She and my father were still having trouble; she said she was thinking about leaving him.

How was this possible? How could my parents have failed to play their starring roles with each other? I was crying, and my mother was crying, and then I remembered we were supposed to leave for Disney World in a few days. "Obviously, we can't go to Florida for spring break," I said.

"Of course we can," my mother said. "We'll just go and have fun."

What I remember most vividly from that trip—my parents and my husband and I: two adult couples on the verge of separating—was sitting in the new MGM Studios blacklight play of *The Little Mermaid*, clapping as yellow eel puppets snaked through purple coral. As Ariel sang about longing for land, I longed to be like that living actress with her magical, glowing, sparkling tail. When would I finally become both the woman and the fantasy creature I was supposed to be?

Thanks to blacklights and Disney magic, I temporarily forgot that in the original story, reality is nothing like the Little Mermaid has imagined it: each step she takes on land feels like being sliced by knives, the prince doesn't love her, and in the end, she throws herself off a ship.

Whatever she's dreamed of slips away, turns into nightmare.

For as long as I can remember, I've dreamed darkly: less often monsters or the people I love dying than elaborate failures my mind keeps reconfiguring: *I need to turn on a lamp to read something vital, but the lamp has no bulb. For hours, I search through mazelike streets, in and out of empty stores, to finally find the one box of bulbs. I know I'm terribly late, and hurry to the cash register, but of course, I have no purse. I search through more mazes for someone to loan me money; I buy the bulbs. I return to the lamp. But it's not a lamp. Why did I ever think it was? It's an overhead light too tall for me to reach. I go looking for a ladder but can't find one; I search instead for a pay phone; I need to call someone to explain why I'm so late, but I don't know their number. I dial every combination. But the phone isn't a phone; it's an avocado. My fingers squish into its soft green fruit.*

I know an avocado phone sounds funny, but in the dream, it's the world disassembling again and again in my hands.

Waking after these nights, everything inside and outside me feels gaping, untrustworthy. As former mental health nurse Nathan Filer writes in *The Heartland,* people "overestimate the likelihood of something happening if it comes readily to mind. . . . influenced by how recently a memory, opinion or worry was formed, as well as how unusual or emotionally charged it is. It's why nobody wants to go swimming in the sea after they've just watched *Jaws.* . . ."

By my twenties, I tried to block out all dreams: sleeping less, smoking pot before bed. But dreams still leaked through, and I'd spend all day feeling gauzed, anxious, depressed—my mind, in the midst of the worst depressions, like one of those dreams saying, *you need to go for a walk,* but then, *you can't go for a walk because your coat is too tight because you've gained weight so you need to go for a walk, but you can't because it's also raining, so you can't walk anywhere, although you have to walk.*

Although I've never again stood on a roof, I've gone through months-long periods of feeling suicidal three times as an adult and have had trouble finding therapists who don't assume that my "extraordinary verbal aptitude" means I'm well. If I can say *you almost lost your little girl today,* I must know how to stop climbing out of windows.

Once, in my thirties, desperate after a therapist told me to do cognitive behavioral worksheets and check back in two weeks, and, oh, also, I might be bipolar (I'm not; she was a terrible therapist), I call a hospital crisis line. The woman asks my name. Then—surely against all protocol—she says, "Oh, Professor Teague, I was in your class a couple of years ago but had to drop because my schedule changed."

I am, in that moment, holding a smashed avocado I only thought was a phone. I have failed to get the world right. I have failed to avoid humiliation. I've revealed that inside the polka-dotted mouse suit of PROFESSIONAL, OVERPREPARED TEACHER is this desperate, crying woman.

Though even the best therapist I've seen couldn't magically fix me, Dr. Bruce did teach me about Parts Therapy (or Integrated Family Systems), which is based on the idea that the mind or Self is divided into multiple parts or subpersonalities. As in a family, each subpersonality is part of the larger unit and can complexly interact in ways we can learn to change.

Each week for a year in my thirties, Dr. Bruce guided me to close my eyes and imagine how different parts of me looked and felt, and what age they were. I had to learn to talk and listen to each one. I was, not surprisingly, good at this.

The hurt little girl who felt lonely and left out.

The angry teenager who just wanted to be heard.

The young woman in an abusive relationship, desperate to be a Disney mermaid.

The girl and woman who should always know better and perform better.

The woman who decided not to have children partly because she didn't know if she had the right kind of character or could make a world for them.

The teacher who worries so much about her students that she

dreams all summer about classes in which her notes blow away from her or the photocopying wipes off onto her hands.

I learned to try to validate what motivated each of these parts so they wouldn't all demand attention at once. I had to ask myself—or that part of me—what it wanted. Yellow-dyed pickles! a poetry prize! reassurance! I had to distinguish these parts from a core self that exists more stably beyond this.

Does my core self live *inside* these other parts, or does it live more mindfully around them? I have no idea really. Maybe they're the same thing to a point?

My mother didn't ever leave my father. As she was dying of leukemia a decade later, she told both him and me that their relationship was by far the happiest of her life. In her journal, she wrote that he took the best care of her she could imagine, and *He'll never need to worry if he did enough. He did.*

When I finally face reading her journals, I expect them to be critical of my father and sisters and me, but she cheerfully notes phone calls, progress on house projects, movies, meals she's cooking. Reading them, I wonder if she was at core less critical than she seemed—if at some deep level she felt the cheer and dark humor she channeled into Purry Puss—or if, in this account she knows will outlast her, she is also building character.

She's been dead twenty years now, almost half my life, so of course I'll never know.

My father still sings show tunes. When he visits Wales while I'm writing this, we miss our bus and have to walk in the rain. "We're singing in the rain, just singing in the rain," he sings slightly off key. Sometimes I want to snap at him to pay more attention to the real world. But this is his real world.

A few years after my mother died, he met and married a former journalist, who used to be an actual puppeteer. Her home office is stuffed with wood-faced Balinese puppets, duck puppets with squat yellow bodies, drapey-armed monkeys. She loves my father's boyish exuberance. She calls him "the chairman of the optimism committee."

When he came out to her, she accepted it. He retired early to live with her, though he works part time as an interfaith wedding officiant. Although we weren't religious when I was growing up, he started trying out different New Age paths when I was in college. *A Course in Miracles. The Game of Life.* Unity. Christian Science. Eventually, convinced all paths led to the same place, he did a correspondence course to become an interfaith minister. He flew to New York for the ordination and ended up chanting through the streets, including Broadway, with a group of Hare Krishnas. He joked he'd finally sung and danced on Broadway.

The couples my father marries rave about how well he writes their stories. He gives everyone the best lines. He calls his blue silk suit and priestly robes his "costumes." Maybe weddings are the perfect place to not distinguish play from life. Maybe, in these rituals, he's found, like his father, his "life's work."

A few years ago, for my father's seventieth birthday, my husband and I went to India with him. It was my father's sixth time. Our first. My father thought I was too frightened of stepping over bodies in Tiruvannamalai's hectic, trash-fire-lit streets, buses driving at us in every lane, stray dogs rushing from alleys. He said these were all "the great cosmic dance." When we passed a dusty parking lot where people were blessing a truck by chanting to the sacred volcano, my father sang along, "Arunachala Arunachala, shanti shanti shanti shanti Arunachala."

It made me happy to see my father so happy—like he somehow belonged in this dusty, distant town—though I cringed at moments of cultural appropriation and couldn't understand why the guru he follows was considered enlightened for letting rats nibble his toes as he meditated. Maybe I'm just not enlightened, but shouldn't there be limits to living around?

But I loved the temples with gods carved on top of gods who are also human. As our guide explained, Shiva's first wife, Sati, died and was dismembered to make the Himalayas, then reincarnated as Parvati, Shiva's second wife. Vishnu is also Rama is also Krishna. All this tangle, maybe one clearer way to tell the tumultuous story of family and loving and being.

It's true my father was raised by Mickey Mouse and a stranger who also became a mother. It's true my mother loved me and chased me with a knife. It's true I grew up lower middle class in a run-down neighborhood of Fort Worth and that I was raised in a floating castle.

It's true, even now, it's hard to explain all this without replicating the fantasies. Creating characters and a story to show you how I learned to create characters and a story.

And the self-proclaimed star of this play? Most of the time, Purry Puss lives in an antique hope chest my parents gave me when I left for college, but for my year's sabbatical when I began writing this, I moved him to a plastic storage bin so he'd be safe from dust and mice in our shed. I set him beside my husband's stuffed monkey, Zip, who is as old as Purry Puss, but never had a voice, as far as my husband can remember.

"No voice!?" Purry Puss says.

Or I say.

Stage fades to black, then small spotlight on plastic storage bin. Forty-something-year-old woman—me—is arranging it. Even though the room will be dark for a year, and Purry Puss's eyes are just half marbles that someone sewed to polyester fur, then—because two parents loved a little girl in Texas—mailed in the eighties in a box marked Pakaluk Puppets, I set him facing out, like he's looking out the window on a road trip. I carefully smooth his whiskers.

20,000 Leagues Under the Sea

The deadest of all the dead people in our family was my mother's father. He died on an ammunition ship in 1944 when she was nine. He continued to die for the next fifty-eight years that she lived: each time water drained from our clawfoot tub, suctioning through ancient pipes of our house, where my half sisters were raised before me, where I was raised in rooms our mother had restored and hung with old-fashioned wallpaper.

He died each time our bodies sank into that tub's prow-like curves. In the teakettle's smokelike plume of steam. In the match gritting the box to light the gas stove's pilot.

He died in the fireworks that exploded each Fourth of July into dandelions tall as Fort Worth buildings, as we watched, decades in his future, from the neighborhood's highest hill, the North Side Cemetery.

My grandfather was not buried in that cemetery and had never been to Texas. He was from far upstate New York, almost the Canadian border. He and my grandmother had met in the late 1920s as teens at a camp—a place I imagine as rowboat-specked lakes and trees with huge shelf mushrooms like the ones in the Adirondacks, where years later my mother taught me to carve names and hearts.

My grandfather died as we dug *Sylvia* and *Alexandra* into those mushrooms' soft white flesh. He died as we walked the pine-needled trails by the dock where he'd taught my mother to swim. She'd had to wear a scratchy wool bathing suit because, as he said, the Adirondacks got "nine months of winter and three months of late in the fall." That last summer before he died, she had swum all the way across Lake Titus and back to his open arms.

After he sank into the South Pacific, my mother was too terrified to submerge her head. When, at fifteen, her mother sent her to Catholic boarding school, my mother tried to refuse to swim. But the nuns insisted. Small, stooped orcas, safe from sinking, they stood on the tile and made her try again and again to dive. As if fear could be taught away by pressing your body into an arrow and closing your eyes. As if it were a small thing, fear—not oceanic and branching.

My grandfather died and none of us were ever again safe.

As if in proof, one of the few times my mother tried to trust water—an inner-tube trip in Texas when I was eight and she was in her forties—we both almost drowned. A small waterfall's rapids flipped us, and when we sank, an undertow pressed us down. I remember the frantic but also slow-motion brown-gold churning. No up, no down. Or not that I could see, although my mother later said she'd kept trying to push me from her toward what she hoped was the surface. And each time, I'd fought my way back to wrap my arms around her neck and shoulders, my only landmark.

We learned later that if you're caught in an undertow, you have to *not* try to surface; you have to swim with the current or let it carry you. And despite our flailing, this must have finally happened. What I remember is the river suddenly eye level: the glorious line where churning silenced to air, how dry everything seemed: the green-yellow grass on shore, even the mud, the silvery glare of light on the water. My father waving desperately, hip-deep near shore, his tube beached beside him.

Later, my mother said that he'd stood panicked while we almost drowned, although having seen him overcome his phobia of heights to save a stranger's sunhat on the edge of the Grand Canyon, and knowing his love for us, I can't imagine this. I suspect time slowed for us underwater, and that by the time he realized we'd vanished, he couldn't find us before we surfaced downstream.

What is most true of that memory is that my mother felt abandoned in the water and, believing we were beyond rescue, still fought for rescue. She was never one to give in to undertows; she pushed again and again toward a surface without believing she'd surface.

Unlike some friends' mothers, who, I would later learn, sat entire days in bathrobes in Barcaloungers, too immobilized by depression to make their children sandwiches, my mother packed her grief into mason jars with stiff crowns of dill from our garden, coriander beads, salt, vinegar, and cucumber. She mixed homemade batter for three-tier cakes; made ten Thanksgiving pies, each family member's favorite, plus extras—rolling-pinning perfect circles, latticing crust across blackberries she'd picked at 5 a.m. before the morning heat. She scrubbed the porcelain of the existential void. And when our house in Fort Worth and her two decades of work on it burned to the ground, she sanded the floors of a new old farmhouse in Arkansas. She was the most industrious fatalist.

That nothing she did mattered didn't change her responsibility to do it. That none of us usually seemed be drowning did not change the fact that we were.

She had learned this philosophy not from Nietzsche or Sartre, but from her Victorian-proper grandmother, Martha Jane Berry. *Nana Berry,* as my mother always called her, lived, even in the 1930s of my mother's childhood, by codes of the late 1800s middle-class propriety into which she'd been born. Because unpinned hair was for girls and floozies, Nana never wore her thick auburn hair down. Because grown women didn't cry in public, Nana held herself together even when her nine-year-old, Carol, chased a ball from their yard and was killed by a car. She raised the rest of her children, including Floyd, my mother's beloved father, like roses trellised around this loss.

In October 1935, my mother was born in one of the bedrooms

of the house next door to Nana's. The family attended the Malone Baptist Church, where my mother's father played piano. On Sunday evenings, he'd read aloud: my mother curled on the floor with her older brother, Derek, and her younger sister, Martha Jane (Nana's namesake), laughing at the voices he'd create for characters in the funny pages.

Even in the midst of the Great Depression, when my mother's family split the house with renters and barely had money for milk, my mother was raised in a world made bright with voices, a world solid and old as Nana's meticulously dusted dark wood furniture. My mother's parents were in love in a still-young way captured in one candid photo I have of them: my grandmother in a 1940s long, straight skirt, legs crossed and heels lifted from the ground, sitting in my grandfather's lap at a kitchen table, her head leaned back against his shoulder, both of them laughing unselfconsciously.

But in early 1944, my grandfather was drafted into the Navy. A few months later, he came home on leave. For a few deceptively normal days, he hugged my mother and Derek and Martha Jane and read to them. As an early Christmas present, he gave my grandmother a rectangular beveled mirror and asked her to smile each time she looked in it, and to imagine—as if it were a magic window across the world— he could see her.

Each day, he sent her a love letter, often also with messages for the children—letters that arrived weeks after they were dated; letters that continued to arrive after the telegram about the ship's explosion as if, beyond all ordinary maps, my grandfather continued living, unharmed, sitting on deck on break in the sun, writing in small cursive on thin airmail paper.

A few months after the telegram, my grandmother gave away most of my mother's and her siblings' toys. She wrapped a quilt around the mirror, which she could no longer stand to look at, and loaded it and a few possessions in the trunk of the car. Then she drove her children across the country to central Arizona. A doctor had told her that dry desert air was necessary to cure Derek's asthma. And one of her older brothers lived on a ranch nearby. But for my nine-year-old mother, neither fact explained the dense New York woods and lakes and ice skates and Nana Berry and her father and the only home she'd ever known sandblasted away.

In the one-room school in Congress Junction, Arizona, sand gritted between the boards. In the rented house, cockroaches skittered the cupboards. In every direction, the desert stretched as far as she could see: the sand restless and raked with shadows so long they seemed detached from any actual objects. The desert stretched until it joined the white-gold sand beaches of Manus Island, a place she hadn't even seen a picture of, but which her father had named, where his ship had been anchored.

My grandfather died outside Congress Junction, Arizona. He died in its desert sand, which had blown from the tropical beaches of Manus Island, Papua New Guinea.

He died in the deep desert washes where my mother wandered alone in the afternoons, looking for mica, listening anxiously for the scuffle and snort of packs of javelinas, and beyond that and the occasional wind-chime of cactus rattling, her father's voice. He was out here somewhere. He could not have really abandoned them. It was impossible he would not come walking home to her—calling "Honey," as he'd always called her, as if it were her name, scooping her up against the stiff blue wool of his Navy peacoat he'd worn that time on leave.

Sometimes, she swore she could see him walking toward her. Some evenings when the heat's shimmer cleared and the light grew stark, he was a shadow in that coat: his crooked smile and hawkish nose and wire-rimmed spectacles distant but clear, like something seen through a telescope.

But he never came any closer. She could never run fast enough to reach him.

Each night, my mother said her prayers, adding a bargain: "Dear God, I'll pray every night of my life to thank you if you'll just bring my father back." Sometimes, she whispered this into the puckered shell her father had mailed her from the South Pacific, which was, because it had to be, the brown-and-white speckled ear of God Himself.

She prayed every night, but God didn't keep His half of the bargain. And, because it was impossible her father no longer existed, my mother knew it was God who did not exist.

In 1947, the fall she turned twelve, as her new half sister was being born, my mother was sent—or maybe asked to go—back to New York to live with Nana. In the house where her father had been raised, and Nana had now lived through the deaths of two of her children, my mother learned how to polish a silver service: circling the soft cloth on its scalloped tray. She helped Nana set the table: spoons, knives, and salad forks in their proper places, even when dinner was only the two of them and Grandad Berry.

Half a century later, when a man I was dating said, "*Nana Berry* sounds like an ice cream flavor," I didn't even get the joke at first. Although *nana* derives from baby talk for *nanny*, it has always sounded to me like the only proper way to say *grandmother*.

It is what my nephews called my mother.

It is not what I learned to call my mother's mother: a woman who would abandon New York for Arizona, marry an alcoholic, and then divorce him and marry the Texaco station owner with a leering teenage son. A woman, who in contrast to my grandfather's vividness and laughter and Nana's Victorian propriety, was both too absent and too overbearing in my mother's life.

Nana is a woman who sweeps the sidewalk even as the ghost of her daughter chases a hard rubber ball again and again into the street. A woman who scrubs the bathtub even as a ship keeps sinking in it.

When my almost-thirteen-year-old mother returned to Arizona, the desert was still there. In a different house, spiders crawled her bedroom, really just a screened porch with a cot. Reaching for what she thought was a hair rubber band once at twilight, she picked up a tarantula.

With her stepfather drinking and her still-grieving mother immobilized by postpartum depression (although no one knew to call it that then), my mother whisked gravy as Nana had, careful not to burn the butter, smoothing and smoothing the flour so it didn't clump. In the grotty kitchen, with cupboards painted the glaring red of red velvet cake, which had just been invented, and would soon become a 1950s craze, she taught herself to make Nana's angel food. Even as a teenager, she refused artificial dye and mixes; she spackled buttercream frosting over the cracks as the world kept cracking.

In the late 1800s, in *The Gay Science*, Friedrich Nietzsche posited the concept of Eternal Return as a question:

> What, if some day or night a demon were to steal into your
> loneliest loneliness and say to you: 'This life as you now
> live it and have lived it, you will have to live once more and
> innumerable times more; and there will be nothing new
> in it, but every pain . . . will have to return to you, all in the
> same succession and sequence—even this spider and this
> moonlight between the trees, and even this moment and I
> myself.'

In a world without God, and without inherent meaning granted to any of our actions, Nietzsche offered this as a hypothetical, a test. Are you at peace enough with your life's choices and their consequences that you're willing to relive them? (Though in later versions, he would argue that in the finite configurations of occurrences in infinite time, we have no choice but to relive them).

An inveterate reader, with a master's degree by the time I was born, my mother surely read Nietzsche, though I don't remember her mentioning him. But I do know I was raised to believe—and recognized with skin-prickling clarity the first time I read—that *every pain will have to return to you.*

In my mother's ontology, this was not a choice, nor future inevitability. It occurred in a single lifetime. This tarantula. This moonlight on the desert. These lost Adirondack trees.

My grandfather, Floyd "Bill" Ford Berry, Carpenter's Mate Second Class, died on Friday November 10, 1944, aboard USS *Mount Hood*, an ammunition ship named for a volcano.

Since September, when *Mount Hood* arrived at Seeadler Harbor, Manus Island, Papua New Guinea, the crew had been gearing up for the Philippine Offensive—loading and unloading ammunition. Naval regulations said that ammunition ships were supposed to be berthed at least eleven hundred feet from adjacent ships and facilities whenever possible, but *Mount Hood* was anchored in a busy part of the harbor, near hundreds of other ships. As the declassified report says, "speed of transferring ammunition was ever of prime necessity."

On November 10, *Mount Hood* held approximately thirty-nine hundred tons of ammunition. At 8:30 a.m., eighteen crew members left for shore, at least some to the post office.

About twenty minutes later, the ship exploded. It wasn't struck by enemy fire. The explosion came from carelessness, an avoidable accident.

According to the official report by the commander of the naval base, USS *Mount Hood* had "a relatively inexperienced crew. There was a lack of leadership among the officers, and lack of discipline among the crew. This condition was reflected in rough and careless handling of ammunition and lack of enforcing prohibition of smoking in boats alongside."

A Navy investigation, including interviews with the eighteen crewmen on shore, revealed "boosters and detonators stowed contrary to regulation; lack of signage; pyrotechnics and napalm gel incendiaries stowed under hazardous conditions; damaged ammunition that should have been destroyed or disposed of by dumping in deep water; infrequent fire drills." The report concludes, "the most likely force to have caused the explosion was a load of ammunition set off by dropping into, or striking the hatch of, number three or four hold."

The first explosion shot flames and smoke as high as the masts. Seconds later, a larger explosion, triggered by the first, blasted a trough in the ocean floor more than one hundred yards long and forty feet deep. Smoke plumed seven thousand feet, obscuring the sky in all directions for five hundred yards. As a torpedoman aboard USS *Rainier* remembers, "the column of smoke rose straight up, and 'mushroomed' at the top . . . a complete preview of how the A-bomb looked a year later." According to the Navy's report, "When [the smoke] had lifted from the waters, a few minutes later, only small pieces of debris were to be seen. The ship had disappeared."

Although, in my adult life, Manus Island is sometimes in the news as the site of Australia's offshore refugee detention centers, and, during World War II, it held the largest Southwest Pacific air and naval base, with as many as four hundred ships, in my imagination, inherited from my mother's, the island is a wasteland of sand. Uninhabited. Windswept. Everything, with *Mount Hood* and its 249 crewmen, *blown to bits.*

If there is anything on that sand, it is a single cross engraved *Father* or *Floyd* or *Bill,* which was the name everyone but Nana called him.

Is it iron? Wood?

If there is a cross at all, there must be rows of crosses. In addition to all the men on *Mount Hood,* the explosion killed hundreds on ships nearby, with hundreds more injured by shrapnel.

Yet, even if there is a cross, Manus Island is not my grandfather's real grave. He is, as the Navy Incident Chart says, *Missing.* (Though beside this, on the copy I find scanned online, is, more honestly and bluntly, handwritten and underlined, the word *Dead.*)

If my grandfather is buried anywhere, it is at the bottom of the sea—in *Davy Jones's locker,* a term I learned as a child, long before I ever had my own school locker. He is with all the other sailors and shipwrecks taken by Davy Jones, the sailors' devil.

And to be buried at sea is to be both not buried and buried everywhere.

I first remember learning about the water cycle in preschool at the Fort Worth Museum of Science and History. In the chart connected by arrows, laminated so even the paper looked glossily wet, oceans evaporated into rain that fell into lakes that rose as fog and fell again into rivers that pumped into water towers that spilled from our faucets that passed through our bodies that evaporated from ponds that fell as rain into oceans. Water was finite in quantity, yet infinitely cycling.

I remember my mother demonstrating this too once on our stove: a day when summer storms kept us in from the yard and garden. She boiled water in a saucepan and held the lid a foot above to show the beads condensing on the concave metal, ready to fall.

My grandfather died in a saucepan in Texas. He died in firehose spray as our one-hundred-year-old house burned to the ground a few years later. He died in the water-moccasined lakes of the Arkansas Ozarks where we moved. I was ten, grieving the loss of my stuffed animals, so my mother told me that when the fire started, my Snoopy and Le Mutt and teddy bears had climbed out our second-floor windows and down the crepe myrtle to safety. My mother was good at inventing alternate stories, which for fictional characters, like my "living" stuffed animals, were usually comforting. But for those of us in real lives, the Eternal Return allowed no real alternatives.

In one story my mother told again and again, on the morning of November 10, 1944, my grandfather could have been—and only narrowly wasn't—at the optometrist's. In one of his daily letters, he'd written that he was straining to do repairs in the dim light below deck. He thought he needed a new prescription. He'd scheduled an appointment for the eleventh.

But what if that appointment had been one day earlier? What if he'd been the nineteenth man on shore leave? When the ship exploded, he would have been reading the eye chart, second-guessing himself in that charming, simple way the living can afford to—*E V P. Is that a P?*

He would be the one to tell the story for years after: the unplaceable-at-first thunder, the building trembling like it was made of a child's blocks. By the time he scrambled outside, the sky had been blotted out with black. This was not a problem with his eyes.

In this alternate future, my grandfather must have PTSD, but we don't discuss this. He is alive. What are the odds? He's lucky in a way that makes his whole family lucky.

My mother thinks about his luck each time she gets her eyes checked. Like everyone but me in the family, she wears glasses, bifocals by the time I'm a child, though I'm never a child, never born in this story. The family does not move to Arizona, where my mother does not meet the man who becomes my sisters' father, does not move to Texas with him, later meet my Texan father.

Even in this story, my grandfather's death evaporates only so far into imagination before condensing. The desire to imagine him safe in the optometrist's chair exists only because he was not. The days on the calendar, like the fact of his death, like the letters on the eye chart some other service man must have been reading, remain *all in the same succession and sequence.*

In another story my mother told, when the government extended the Selective Training and Service Act of 1940 after Pearl Harbor to make all men between twenty-two and forty-four liable for military service, only unmarried men were initially drafted. Next, married men without children. Then men with only one child. Then two.

My grandparents discussed the odds: surely the draft wouldn't reach fathers of three before the war ended. But by early 1944, almost ten million men had been drafted, and the "draft deferment for dependency" had been repealed or kept counting higher. It didn't matter that my grandfather needed to support his children or love them or listen to *The Shadow* on the radio, or once, in the midst of the Depression, bring home a box of kittens he'd found behind the sawmill (to my grandmother's consternation and my mother and her siblings' joy). Although his children should have saved him, they didn't.

Being a conscientious objector did not save him. He'd considered registering but felt too guilty since his brother was already serving. His sense of duty did not save him.

Luck did not save him. One account of the World War II draft describes a giant fishbowl filled with capsules of numbers, each matching a name. Like a great, wooden metaphor for the hand of history, the capsules were stirred with a beam taken from Philadelphia's Independence Hall. A capsule was pulled. Another capsule. My grandfather died because his number was placed, was pulled. He was chosen.

But my family did not feel he was chosen the way some people mean it: chosen by God, for heroism. Because his death saved no one, because his death was avoidable, it could and should have been so many other ways.

My grandfather died in a fishbowl full of random numbers.

He died because he left Virginia in July on a ship that would make it ten thousand nautical miles, but less than five months.

Or, he died because the ship was cursed. Not only did all the men aboard die, but the one crewman subbing on a nearby ship was also killed by shrapnel. My mother always said he was a cook. I imagine him in an incongruous white apron, stirring a huge pot on deck, as chunks of iron rain on him, and the *Mindanao*'s hull is cratered with explosions.

Before the cook realizes that everyone on *Mount Hood* is dying, he is also dead.

My cousin Natasha, Derek's daughter, says she's read that the eighteen men on shore all died of various causes within a year. I haven't found this corroborated. And, like every alternate story, whether the ship was somehow cursed changes nothing for my family.

Because my mother's lifetime of survivor's guilt was not enough to bring her father back; because he never got to choose if he would live his life again; because he never finished his life—we lived it for him. Or at least we lived his death *once more and innumerable times more*. We lived everything that could have been to stop the pain but wasn't.

A working-class father during the Great Depression, my grandfather had taken whatever jobs he could. He'd squatted at the end of bowling lanes as a pin setter. He'd worked at a sawmill. Done construction. He liked construction, and when he was drafted, he asked to serve in the Naval Construction Battalion (CBs, or, heterographically, *Seabees*). Even in the midst of wartime "theaters of operations," being a Seabee was relatively safer than the alternatives.

I was on an airport inter-terminal train last year when one older man noticed another's ballcap. "You were a Seabee, too?" he asked, pointing at the insignia of a cartoony bee flying with a drill aimed like a gun, a wrench and hammer clasped in two of its other legs. The men exchanged names, where they'd been stationed. Swept up in eavesdropping, as I was climbing off, I called, "My grandfather was a Seabee, too!"

The doors had swooshed closed and I was rolling my suitcase toward Terminal C before I realized I'd lied. My Seabee grandfather is just a fantasy: what my grandfather wanted and my mother imagined could have saved him. It's a story I've heard so many times alongside the real story they've become inseparable. In the end, like every alternate version of my grandfather's story, it is not a real escape from the pain but another way to visit it.

Nietzsche writes, *every pain and every joy . . . will have to return to you*. But if the pain is strong enough—and in my mother's case, the childhood shock deep enough—the joy becomes the negative space around it.

If you are my mother, you become a loner: even after you've given up hope of your father's return, you go for long walks in the desert, waiting for him. You read Victorian adventure: *Around the World in Eighty Days. Twenty Thousand Leagues Under the Sea.*

Decades later, never having seen a therapist, never having been diagnosed with PTSD, you follow your grandmother's recipes, your own, meticulously written-out on cards in thick binders. You bake layered orange chiffon cake for your youngest daughter's birthday, German chocolate for your husband. Nothing from a box, never tacky red velvet. You sew handmade clothes, wallpaper your thirteen-room house, construct an elaborate playground. You are capable in ways that could involve repairing a ship if there were a ship to repair.

Your readiness is part vigilance, part vigil.

In 1981, when your second husband, a journalist, is assigned to fly to Florida to write about the Magic Kingdom's ten-year-anniversary celebrations, you decide to take your seven-year-old daughter, Alexandra, out of school for a week so you both can join him.

Despite disliking what is tacky and prepackaged, you have always loved to travel. And you discover, at forty-six, from the moment you pass through the portal of Cinderella's blue-turreted castle to Main Street USA that you love the Magic Kingdom. Here is a past you can enter identically again and again. Walt Disney's childhood Main Street has been reconstructed as its better self: the buildings made subtly taller or shorter to enhance the sense of distance but also coziness.

A little theater shows *Steamboat Willie*, Mickey Mouse's first starring role, in which Walt Disney himself, like your father with the funny pages, did all the voices. On loop, at any time of day, Mickey cranks a goat's tail as a phonograph to play "Turkey in the Straw"; he runs from Captain Pete on the steamboat; the soundtrack blares the skittering jazz music of just before your childhood.

In Fantasyland, under black lights, you glide with Peter Pan and Wendy over dark cityscapes, Big Ben, ticking clocks inside alligators. These books you were raised with, these books you've read again and again and loved, have been constructed as spaces you can enter.

While my mother was most excited for the rides based on books, I begged to stand in line again and again to ride the Haunted Mansion. Raised in a high-ceilinged, chandeliered Victorian house, I was thrilled less by the mansion's strangeness than the sense I was peeking into what was usually hidden inside the ordinary world. In rooms with filigreed wallpaper and tables draped with lace and set with proper china and candles, ghosts waltzed, their invisibility thrown off like fur stoles. The manic and cheerfully spooky music seemed to always have been playing somewhere beyond what living ears could hear.

Back at the Contemporary Resort, I told my parents I'd only been scared "when that skeleton kept trying to lift the grand piano's lid but was trapped inside."

"The piano?" my parents asked. And then they realized and laughed. "That's not a piano, honey; it's a coffin."

This was only months after my mother's graduate-school mentor and best friend, Joan, had died of cancer; a few years after my Texaco-station-running Arizona step-grandfather had died of lung cancer; soon after my great-aunt Norma's husband and my paternal step-grandfather had died in New York and Texas; shortly before my father's sister would be diagnosed with a brain tumor. In my child mind, these deaths all swirled like water toward the central drain of my grandfather's. It made sense, like another simple science project. We were a family in which people kept dying.

I didn't realize this was unusual until years later when I learned that many of my older friends still had not even lost grandparents.

We were a family in which people died, but we did not go to funerals. Or, if my parents went, they didn't take me. I'd think they were sparing me, but I remember hospital visits: Joan, who had always been serious and intimidating, reduced from her blue teaching blazers to a hospital gown.

But I don't remember funerals. Had I actually never seen a coffin? Or did I just not think of the dead as lying in them? Being, as they were, everywhere: in the folds of our picnic blankets spread on their graves as we watched fireworks. In the little embossed leather purse Joan had given me, barely restrained by its clasp. Inside our grand and upright pianos where my mother taught her students. In every body of water.

We rode the Haunted Mansion again on a road trip a few years later; again and again the summer I was thirteen and my parents worked in Orlando; on spring breaks; on a trip to visit my future graduate school in Gainesville. We swirled ourselves dizzy on the Alice in Wonderland Mad Tea Party and climbed the Swiss Family Robinson's banyan treehouse.

But my mother's favorite of all, based on another book that she loved, was 20,000 Leagues Under the Sea.

Each trip, at least once, we'd wait in line by that too-blue lagoon and climb down the metal stairs of a submarine to take our seats facing the portholes, which were always fingerprint-smudgy.

Even as a child, I knew those submarines didn't really descend more than a few feet. From the line, it was easy to see this. Of course my mother knew this. But also, as we watched the bubbles drifting up, perfectly round against round porthole windows, and craned to see the fish and mermaids slipping past, it felt as if we were really going somewhere.

"Deep" underwater was a place streaked with sunken beams of light, where giant fish flicked against the hull and sea turtles flippered by, the "amphibious descendants of the dinosaur." We glided over treasure chests spilling jewels, the water as clear-blue as aquamarines themselves.

"The *Nautilus* can dive safely below the violence of ocean storms," Captain Nemo reassured us. "Surface vessels are not so fortunate." Beneath us were shipwrecks, strewn, visible as the Haunted Mansion's ghosts. This was fantasy, of course it was. But also, weren't we really on those faux-velvet fold-down seats? Wasn't this our real lives continuing?

Once, late in her life, my grandmother admitted to my mother that nothing after my grandfather's death had ever seemed fully real. That is, the more than forty years during which she kept living without him, moved to Arizona, remarried, had another child, divorced, remarried, did crossword puzzles, wrote letters to my mother complaining about the price of lettuce, developed Alzheimer's. All of this was simultaneously her only real life and a strange fiction written around her: beginning the day she held the telegram with his name (which was not the name she or anyone but Nana called him) and *Missing* (which didn't ever really mean missing).

Of course my mother and I understood when Captain Nemo said that we "probe depths seldom seen by man." We had come to do this, hadn't we? *Once more and innumerable times more.*

More bubbles sped outside the window, as above, through strangely tropical water, the glaciers glowed, and above that: the aurora borealis, rare and predictably spectacular. The voice of Captain Nemo was ordering us further: to "maximum depth" to avoid a storm at the polar ice cap. Disembodied, fatherly, busy with controls somewhere invisible, Captain Nemo was calm and commanding as God if we'd believed in God. He was piloting us into a "realm of eternal darkness."

In Jules Verne's original, Captain Nemo is also fleeing from grief. He's traveling twenty thousand leagues, not deep, as the English title suggests, but around the world—under the multiple *mers*, or seas, of the original French, cycling through the world's oceans because his family has been murdered on land.

He's a complex and not always sympathetic figure, his name a translation of "no man" from *The Odyssey*. But here, he was only a voice, a narrator. When he told us we were nearing the civilization of Atlantis, "lost thousands of generations ago," we didn't question.

"The eternal hourglass of existence is turned upside down again and again, and you with it, speck of dust!" Nietzsche says.

"There are limits beyond which man and his puny efforts cannot survive. We have almost exceeded those limits," Captain Nemo says.

But where are the limits if the hourglass of existence turns over infinitely? If *every pain and every pleasure, every friend and every enemy, every hope and every error, every blade of grass and every ray of sunshine* cycle back through our individual lives, and then through generations? One generation's wars and hurts carried, as epigenetics suggests now, into the very cells of the next. The water in this Disney lagoon, once rain in a saucepan, once the South Pacific off Manus Island, once the lake where a father held his arms open to catch his daughter swimming toward him.

20,000 Leagues Under the Sea closed in 1996, the year I began graduate school two hours north. The official reason for closure was problems with ADA compliance, although fans—who still discuss it lovingly on websites—say that the Walt Disney Corporation claimed the ride was also becoming less popular, too dated. This wasn't true, these fans argue: it was running at capacity. People still loved the fake squid and sci-fi nostalgia. The real problem was that Disney didn't want to "deal with the upkeep." It was expensive to pay real divers to clean the lagoon, since the water was, despite its chlorine, dredged from tropical reservoirs. There were chemical-damaged engines to repair, chlorine corrosion, leaks that frequently flooded the staff lockers in the nearby subterranean tunnels.

After closing it temporarily in 1994, then briefly reopening it, Disney shuttered the ride for good—carting off some submarines to junkyards and two to the real sea floor off a Disney-owned Caribbean island where tourists could rent scuba gear and dive to see them.

On a website, beneath the header *In Memoriam. . . "The Best Liquid Space Journey Ever,"* one fan writes, "They scuttled our dreams just to save a few million dollars. What a bunch of bastards."

If my mother were still alive, if she ran an amusement park, she would not have given up so easily. She would have *dealt with the upkeep*. She would have scrubbed every submarine porthole and filter and bolt. She would have bristle-brushed the walls of the lagoon and the fins on the fish, the same way at least once yearly, she soaped the uselessly beautiful prisms on our dining room chandelier, standing on a chair for hours to unhook them, then scrubbing at the sink with a soft brush and Ivory liquid, then balancing hours again to rehook them.

The same way, the day before she died of chronic leukemia, when she could barely see or sit up, she called from her hospice bed to dictate to me, in real time, each step of my birthday tiramisu—apologizing repeatedly that she couldn't come to the kitchen and make it herself.

After a lifetime of baked cakes, she had fallen in love in her early fifties with tiramisu: its delicate coffee-and-liqueur-infused whipped cream and mascarpone and ladyfingers layered and chilled. She'd tried recipe after recipe, borrowing from each, ordering it at restaurants, analyzing, until she knew exactly how long to soak the ladyfingers in coffee (which she otherwise did not keep in the house, or brew, or drink); how to make the whipped cream into clouds, bitter and sweet with vanilla and Kahlua (which she did not otherwise buy or drink because she did not like anything interfering with her keeping up the world as it should be, and never would be).

I have not been to Disney World since she died. From what the fan pages say, after the lagoon's water was drained and the submarines hauled off, the sunken concrete basin, still painted blue, became a photo spot where you could pose with the Little Mermaid, Ariel. Now the depression has all been filled in, leveled and topiaried into a Winnie the Pooh playground.

The sites say you wouldn't even know there had been water.

But of course we would. There's the giant squid coming into view with its candy pink tentacles wrapping and warping toward us, and Captain Nemo calling, "Surface, surface, surface."

He means to save us, though we can't stay up forever.

Soon he'll be calling again, "Steady as you go. Stand by to dive."

White Rabbit, White Rabbit

February 3, 2019, two years and ten months after my nephew Gabriel died, I received a letter from him. When I first saw it in my inbox, I couldn't believe I was seeing it.

I had to be imagining it. Just the night before, I'd read my husband a draft of an essay I'd written about Gabriel's death, and then we'd had a conversation about whether I thought I could communicate with Gabriel's ghost.

In the essay, I'd described carrying Gabriel's casket into my sister's house. The casket was impossibly heavy, like everything about those days. After my sisters, Gabriel's father, Gabriel's uncle, and I finally lifted the casket onto sawhorses in the dining room, we tried to eat dinner beside it, the way people try to do ordinary things when they're grieving so much they have no idea what food is.

When I went to bed later in a drafty upstairs room of that huge Victorian house where Gabriel had grown up, all I could think about was him downstairs—cold and pumped full of embalming fluid despite my sister's and his father's instructions not to embalm him. Gabriel, or Gabe, my youngest nephew, dressed in a strangely formal suit and shiny shoes. I sobbed and sobbed, and must have finally fallen asleep, because I woke—in the darkness—with a strange incantatory rhyme chanting in my head. *One two three, a jar of pillowed me.*

I've never heard a ghost, and it wasn't Gabriel's voice. But, still, I couldn't help feeling it was a conversation with him or about him: embalmed and swaddled in a suit inside that casket that his father, Michael, had made and his mother, my sister Anne, had lined with fabric. *A jar of pillowed me.*

The rhyme haunted me the next morning, but I didn't tell my sisters. It felt tangential to our huge shared grief. But Anne told us she'd woken in the middle of the night to a rock plunking against her window. She'd run downstairs, thinking it was her older son, Nathan, arrived from Santa Fe without his key. But when she got to the door, no one was there.

"Strange," my sister Beth and I said, or "wow," or something that meant we knew the sound of the rock could just be Anne's grief-distraught mind. But also, we'd all read *Wuthering Heights* and were in a rural Victorian house with a dead body. And, more than anything, we *wanted* Gabriel to speak: to reassure us he was alright, when what we could see of him was definitely not alright, dead from a self-inflicted gunshot wound days before his twenty-sixth birthday.

My sisters and I were raised by our mother, and my nephews were raised by my sisters, to believe in a legible world. As Gabriel's favorite poem, "The Ecclesiast," by John Ashbery says, "Ever since childhood there / Has been this special meaning to everything."

I didn't know this was Gabriel's favorite poem until Anne asked me to read it at the funeral, but its beautiful strangeness, and those lines, make sense to me. We believe in a world in which, like in a novel, you can make meaning if you pay attention to pieces interacting. A world in which synchronicities, or what Carl Jung called "meaningful coincidences," matter.

As a writer, I'm a seeker of meaning and patterns. All humans, to some extent, are. As Michael Shermer, publisher of *Skeptic* magazine, writes, "We look for and find patterns in our world and in our lives. . . . Such is the stuff of which myth, religion, history and science are made

. . . [T]he essential tension (as Thomas Kuhn called it) pits skepticism against credulity as we try to decide which patterns should be rejected and which should be embraced."

This is, of course, the *essential tension*. Everyone I know has stories of experiences too meaningful, unlikely, and aligned to be mere coincidence. The purple flower that appears on the sidewalk on the ninth day of praying the novena; the wedding ring that vanishes from a drawer and then reappears on the same day a beloved grandmother dies.

Hadn't Gabriel's father, Michael, turned down this road when he was looking for property because this ancient, drafty Victorian house *was supposed to be* in our family? Wasn't it proof that Michael said, "I love your house," and the caretaker answered, "It's for sale"?

But scientific studies repeatedly prove that supposed synchronicity can be explained by statistical chance or by confirmation or hindsight bias: seeing what we're expecting to see. As an article in *Psychology Today* says, "The human tendency to believe that everything happens for a reason (and it's all about me) is quite pervasive . . . and it is amplified in mental illness."

On the phone with me the year before he died, struggling with what was probably bipolar disorder with delusional, grandiose tendencies, Gabriel moved seamlessly from Machiavelli's theories to Flannery O'Connor's words that a life with no faith had "no meaning." Was his mind attaching too much special meaning to everything? Or was he struggling to find meaning at all?

People use the term "a meaningful life" as if *meaningful* is like *long* or *adventurous*, but it's not so easily quantifiable. For O'Connor, a Catholic, God granted meaning, but for my atheist family, how do we know when our search for meaning has made life meaningful? How do we—how does anyone—know what really is synchronous and what we're reading into?

I didn't discuss any of this in that essay about Gabriel's death, and Dylan asked what I was saying about *a jar of pillowed me* and the rock. *Did* I believe Gabriel was communicating? "Maybe you need a whole essay about your family ghosts, and whether you think you're in communication with them," he suggested.

"Maybe," I said skeptically. I'd already written another essay questioning my mother's self-proclaimed psychic abilities. I was trying to look rationally at fantasies I'd been raised with. Though sometimes when I was struggling with the essays, it was also true that I'd think about something that had happened when I was getting our house ready to leave on sabbatical. I was moving a magnetic poetry set that had been in a drawer under phone books, and when I set it in the cabinet, only two words were facing out: *ghost flow.*

I hadn't mentioned this to Dylan because it felt private, by which maybe I mean I'd invested those words with a charm I was scared of breaking. I'm sure a mathematician could tell me the odds of only *ghost flow,* in that order, being visible in a box of three hundred words, but I was, for the first time in my life, writing family essays, and I loved the idea that my family ghosts—particularly Gabriel and my mother—were helping me. That some flow existed between them and my words.

Still, that night after reading Dylan the essay, I went to sleep with no intention of writing about synchronicities or ghosts. I got up the next morning and spent an ordinary few hours reading. And then I checked email. I had one message. It said *Letter from Gabriel.*

◆

Special meaning? Synchronicity? Confirmation bias? *Ghost flow?*

◆

Here are the facts: the letter was attached to an email from my father, who explained that my stepmother had found it while looking for something in a keepsake box. She didn't remember receiving it, but it was clearly a thank you for a book called *Second Nature* that she'd sent to Gabriel.

The fact is that Gabriel's letter is really to my stepmother, not me; it did not just arrive; it has been in a box since 2013; it is about a book I haven't read.

But there are other facts. I was on sabbatical in Wales, and given the time difference, my stepmother found the letter very close to, if not at, the time Dylan and I were first having the conversation about Gabriel's ghost. My stepmother is organized, yet she'd found the letter in a box of photos for her own daughter. She had no idea why it was in there. And then, without even knowing I was working on essays about Gabriel, my father emailed the letter immediately, rather than waiting to call me, as he usually does with news.

No other letter from Gabriel has appeared in the now more than six years since he died.

All of this is strange enough. But then there is what the letter says:

> Thank you so much for the copy of "Second Nature." I just finished it on Saturday. It was a very pleasant respite from the everyday world, and it seemed to have an overhanging lesson between the lines as well. I thought it was: everyone who gains love, loses it as well, and usually under tragic circumstances. This brings up the question, is love real? Or is it just like the concept of ghosts, something many people talk about and very few have seen? . . .

◆

What am I supposed to think, through my tears, as I read this?

"But the new dimension of truth had only recently / Burst in on us." (John Ashbery, "The Ecclesiast")

◆

Dear darling nephew Gabriel: What if love is like ghosts? What if ghosts are just another way of describing our ongoing love for the dead? Does that make them more or less real?

And also, how, how are you possibly writing to me?

◆

In the years before he died, Gabriel took the white rabbit as his personal totem. Not just the animal (though he'd always loved rabbits), but the special meanings attached to rabbits. The druggy, down-the-rabbit-hole, Jefferson Airplane rabbit. The original pocket-watch-checking white rabbit of *Alice in Wonderland*: that rabbit you follow to your true self, into the depths of the Jungian uncon-scious. The white rabbit: that messenger between worlds.

For Lewis Carroll, following the rabbit to Wonderland is a "curious dream" from which Alice wakes. This is also how it's portrayed in the 1951 *Alice in Wonderland,* and an earlier Disney movie: a 1923 black-and-white short called *Alice's Wonderland.*

Disney himself costars with a blonde ringleted little girl in *Alice's Wonderland,* which was made as a promo to establish (or reestablish) him as world's greatest animator after a studio stole the rights to his most popular character, Oswald the Lucky Rabbit. *Alice's Wonderland* isn't particularly well known, but Disney did become famous soon after by creating an animated mouse using many of Oswald the Lucky Rabbit's characteristics.

Alice's Wonderland opens with Disney drawing in his studio when Alice appears for a visit. Before her eyes, his drawings become ani-mated. Mice twist corkscrew tails; cats get into a boxing match, play saxophones, and jitterbug. *What Alice saw would make any little girl's heart flutter,* one intertitle says. Wonderland is the world of the imag-ination and creativity: a place we can enter at will. A place that inter-acts peaceably with the real world, at least at first.

But then the imaginative world becomes all-consuming. Disney is so powerful that the living Alice finds herself riding a cartoon train. She sits in a howdah on a parading elephant. Cartoon li-ons chew through their cage and chase her. By the end, she has to jump from a cartoon cliff to wake. This seems an apt metaphor for a mind so caught in its own imagination that it arrives at the logic of suicide. Though in *Alice in Wonderland, The Wizard of Oz,* and countless other stories, waking is salvation. When the imagination becomes too much, you can return to a world that obeys ordinary, unmagical rules.

But dreams exist inside us, in our own minds, which are still there when we wake. Though most movies don't point this out.

◆

The version of *Alice in Wonderland* that seems truest to me is Czech director Jan Svankmajer's 1988 movie *Alice*. I don't know if Gabriel ever saw it, but I imagine he must have. The movie is uncanny because, even though most of the action is obviously constructed via stop-motion animation, Alice is again played by a human. In one of the opening scenes, she's in a messy quasi-Victorian parlor, throwing rocks into a cup of tea. Across the room sits a glass display case holding a taxidermy white rabbit. Unlike Walter Potter's popular Victorian-era tableaux—dead bunnies chalking school sums on slates or stiff kittens getting married—that made taxidermy cute, Svankmajer makes the gristle visceral.

After the rabbit wakes, or is brought back to life, by those rocks clattering in the china cup, he tries to move, but he can't lift his feet, which are nailed to the tableau's grass. We watch him use his giant incisors to rip and then spit the large nails out—gashing a hole in his chest in the process. Then this zombie rabbit flips open a drawer in the grass and pulls out lace-trimmed gloves, a red-velvet tailcoat, and a top hat. He dresses himself for his role in his famous story.

With Svankmajer's jerky stop-motion and the off-kilter mixture of live action and animation, the scene seems constructed, tenuous. The gentleman rabbit isn't a cute fantasy but part of this world that's been killed and brought back to life. There's no clean line where logical world ends and rabbit hole opens to the fantastical.

When the rabbit picks up the giant pair of scissors in his tableau and uses them to smash the glass case, he steps out alive into a real parlor with the living Alice and into a fairy tale.

And then, from the sawdust spilling from his chest as he moves— from his wounded body rather than a waistcoat pocket—he pulls the famous watch. It's as if time and the story have been sewn up inside him, and to reach them, he must disassemble himself.

In "Broken Knobs and Glass Eyes," Jacob Bews writes, "the white rabbit's eyes threaten to pop out of their sockets, the caterpillar's dentures are held tenuously by the frayed edges of a hole, and the skeletal animals which aid the rabbit have limbs clearly taken from other animals. . . ." Bews calls Svankmajer's technique "collages in the open" because Svankmajer "makes no effort to hide the seams." Though Bews says this technique suggests "the viewer, and the dreamer could wake at any instant," I see the constructedness as suggesting much messier lines between reality/dream/fantasy/real.

Bews goes on to describe the style: "Just imagine, if, instead of farmhands in makeup and costumes in *The Wizard of Oz,* Dorothy skipped across the yellow brick road with a set of kitchen utensils with glass eyes. . . ."

Or imagine you're trying to explain, in rational language, what it means that your dead nephew has seemingly communicated with you hours after you discussed whether you believed his ghost could communicate with you.

What can I do but make a "collage in the open" of the strange, mismatched pieces of logic and emotion?

What can I do but reach into the sawdust in my chest where grief and time are kept?

◆

When Gabriel was alive, he and I never talked about whether we believed in ghosts or an afterlife, though Nathan told me just before Gabriel's funeral that Gabriel had said he believed we continue somehow or somewhere, and that he would be better off there.

And later in his letter, Gabriel writes, "love is made out to be something more than a feeling, something that can overcome all obstacles, and that's ALL obstacles . . ."

Does that include the obstacle of death?

Isn't his letter proof of that?

But if the universe can split open to send love across time and death, what else is it capable of? Or maybe I know and fear that answer: it is also capable of making my youngest nephew lose touch with reality and kill himself.

◆

When I was in junior high, my best friend Leslie and I sat in her walk-in closet, amid racks of disembodied clothes, and floated our fingertips above a Ouija planchette. We wanted to test the limits of this world. We were scared it was all there was, and scared it wasn't. And we feared and hoped that we wouldn't be able to control whatever we could summon—which is a pretty good explanation of how it feels to be thirteen.

The odds of meeting a ghost were in our favor. We lived in Eureka Springs, a notoriously haunted town. Even our home ec teacher often talked in class about an older man in a bowler hat who lived in her upstairs guest room as he had a century before. His name was Hank, and she presented him as being as real as our sewing machines.

"Are there any spirits here with us?" Leslie asked in the candlelight. And then the planchette began to drift. Y E S

We breathed in, held our breath again. "Who are you?"

ROBERT ZAMINOV

There he was, it was: too-solid letters, yet insubstantial—floating into the closet on some otherworldly wind. "Who are you?" Leslie asked, her voice soft, awed.

A SHIP CAPTAIN

The Ozarks were a two days' drive from the nearest ocean, so clearly, Robert Zaminov had crossed the country for a reason. We had to ask. And then, slowly, but clearly, too clearly, he told us: I WAS MURDERED. Our arms goose bumping, we looked at each other with a panicked, silent alphabet of "Should we say we have to go? Can you lie to a ghost? Do we keep talking to him? Is he angry?"

I'm sure we told him we were sorry he'd been killed. I know we quickly stopped the conversation, both of us so scared that we shoved the board under coats on her shelf, and never again touched it. In one sense this was the "it's just a dream" trope: we closed the Ouija board in its box and the fantasy world was gone; we were back in an ordinary closet.

But we were also frightened. For years if friends mentioned Ouija, Leslie and I would try to warn them, but would only be brave enough to do so elliptically. If ghosts could come when we asked, couldn't they come when we didn't? What if all the years we lay on her carpet drinking root beer, and eventually her parents' stolen wine, were like the quiet lake beneath the dam, and upriver, just behind the closet door, darker waters waited to flood us?

Even after I grew up enough to learn that Ouija board planchettes move because people are secretly or subconsciously directing them, I had a healthy fear of summoning the dead. I didn't logically believe it was possible, but I wasn't going to play around. For a year after my grandmother died, Thomas Hardy's line "Woman much missed, how you call to me, call to me" replayed in my head, but I didn't actually hear her call. While she and my mother claimed to have seen ghosts, I lacked this vision. Small synchronicities happened, but nothing that suggested the world had gaping holes to other worlds, or that my mind did.

But in October 2001, days after I turned twenty-seven, I sat crying beside my mother's hospice bed and asked her to promise to send me a sign after death. For some reason, I remember picturing a feather, though I didn't say this, and she and I didn't have a special connection to feathers. Maybe, despite not being raised religious, I still associated the otherworldly with sky.

By then, after decades of atheism, my mother had been attending a Unity church and had come to believe life was a "mystery train" that we're riding. Not a train animated by a benevolent God like Disney, but more like Shakespeare's "There are more things in heaven and earth, Horatio, than are dreamt of in your philosophy." She had faith that there was much more than she could know, and that she could, as the Unity saying went, "let go and let God" (which in the Unity theology means letting the power of universal energy or love).

Maybe the truest faith is not asking for answers or signs. But I wanted signs. I asked anyway.

"Yes," my mother said. "I will if I can."

In the note she left me when she died—her almost-blind, sloppy cursive sentences overlapping the lines on paper torn from one of the steno pads she used as journals—she wrote, "What I cannot now tell you, you will just have to know." She meant how precious I was and how much she loved me. If her note is to believed, she did not expect to tell me anything more.

A few days after she died, I flew back to San Francisco. At work at City College, the admin assistant asked, "Did you get your mother all squared away?" as if she were a stack of paper for the photocopier that always jammed. This was how most of the world treated me. Square it away, move on.

I went numbly, surreally through days that were mostly painfully ordinary, devoid of signs except the obvious signs that I was slightly insane with grief. I began to walk across the city to stand in an aquarium store with two stories of tanks that seemed on the verge of crashing through the rickety wood floors. With its unseasonal tropical heat and churning, that store felt alive in a way no place else did. Maybe womblike, though I didn't consciously think this. I had trouble thinking. I drank too much at the Irish bar next door and played darts. Other days, I walked to my second job: MacroVU, a small publishing office owned by Robert E. Horn, a researcher in cognitive and behavioral science, who was mapping concepts for a Stanford think tank.

Bob would take concepts such as the Turing Test and artificial intelligence and map out possible directions that the logic and thinking could lead. We two assistants, who worked in a spare room in his Pacific Heights apartment, would fill the bubbles on these maps with propositions and assumptions and warrants and claims and conclusions he'd developed. Then we'd proofread the linking chains of logic and combine files to make what would become large fold-out logic maps.

According to Bob's research, information could be divided into seven types: procedures (instructions or sets of steps); processes (series of events, or how things work); principles (statements to guide behavior); concepts (classes that share a set of attributes); structures (descriptions of components, or things with parts or boundaries); classification (chunks sorted into classes); facts (empirical information, or statements assumed to be true). The whole system seems both intuitive and overcomplicated, which is how trying to make sense of the world often feels. As Bob writes on his website, "we are integrated human beings who always have aspects of both thinking and feeling in our ongoing human being-ness. We cannot avoid emotion and cognition as always deeply intertwingled." (*Intertwingled* is a computing term, which means to interconnect or interrelate in a deep or complex way—because neither *intertwined* or *intermingled* gets at this complexity enough alone, apparently.)

It strikes me now that even as I was meticulously mapping human thought, I was mapping how unmappable it is. Does rabbit lead to love, which leads to nephew, which leads to computer screen, which leads to. . . ? Where does the page even end?

At the time, I didn't fully understand that Bob was famous for inventing Information Mapping. I just knew that he paid me, and his other assistant, the stylish, beautiful, half-Spanish Yolanda, to type text: a fairly mindless job. And he often told me I was too smart to work at City College, which I appreciated (I wanted to be smart and writing the poetry I'd gone to grad school for) and resented (it seemed elitist to assume students at City College didn't deserve smart teachers).

One day, a few months after my mother died, I was at his office, just starting work. I Control-C'ed some text about artificial intelligence. I moved the cursor to the next bubble and hit Control-V. A simple copy-paste. But what appeared in the bubble was *Angelina Ballerina*.

If Robert Zaminov was a ship captain, Leslie and I had only his word to go on. But I knew exactly who Angelina Ballerina was. She was a small white stuffed rabbit. She'd been on a chair by my mother's hospice bed the day she died.

My family didn't usually send Easter gifts, but the spring of 1998, shortly after her diagnosis with chronic leukemia, my mother became dangerously sick with a flu. I was teaching in Miami and couldn't afford to send myself, so I sent a care package. In my family's style of narrative and backstories, I wrote a card explaining that the enclosed rabbit, wearing a yellow vinyl rain slicker and hat (as I'd found him in a grocery store floral section), had come from South America, where he'd been gathering rare medicinal herbs to care for her.

My mother loved him and named him Pablocito, after Neruda.

Two years later, I sent a second white stuffed rabbit, though I had no idea until decades later that *rabbit, rabbit, or white rabbits, white rabbits* is an expression to ward off bad luck and death.

The only rabbit Pablocito's size I could find was wearing a lavender leotard and tutu. My mother named her *Angelina* and invented the backstory that she'd just given up her touring career as a ballerina. So Angelina and Pablocito would be more comfortable, my mother sewed them both small, loose flannel nightgowns, miniatures of the ones she wore.

Seeing the words *Angelina Ballerina* on that computer screen felt like Wonderland had fallen into Pacific Heights. Somehow my mother was spelling out her ongoing existence and love in a chain of logic and letters and light. She had sent not the feather I'd randomly pictured but what she knew I would recognize as meaningful to the two of us.

◆

"We are together at last, though far apart." (John Ashbery, "The Ecclesiast")

◆

Was *Angelina Ballerina* there to show me the world was animated by forces beyond me? Was my mother saying that she was watching me (which I'd admittedly asked for, though her gaze was not always benevolent even in life, and I'd already started to realize the occasional comfort of believing she could *not* see me up at midnight smoking pot and watching VH1 when I should have been grading)?

If she was somewhere, did this mean I would also someday be somewhere and didn't need to fear death as I'd grown up doing?

Or was I just animating ordinary fact with wishful thinking? One false premise or assumption can skew the whole chain—as Lewis Carroll the logician well knew, and the information maps I worked on proved. Illogic, which can easily be driven by emotions such as grief and longing, can develop its own convincing systems that start to look like logic.

Here are the facts (statements assumed to be true): at least a time or two each year, I'm typing too quickly and fail to really hit Control C, therefore Control V-ing something I've already copied earlier, from an email, for instance, into a Word file. I usually think nothing of this and just delete the text.

In addition to my mother's rabbit, Angelina Ballerina is a mouse in a series of children's books. Bob Horn was in his seventies, with an adult daughter and grandchild. He also used the office computers. It's entirely possible he was copying the title of the book to a list of gifts for his grandchild, and I just picked up the "ghost" of this.

Though I looked up *Angelina Ballerina* that day and discovered the children's book, I didn't ask him. If I hadn't wanted to make Robert Zaminov real, the truth is, I didn't want to make my mother's message unreal. I understand this may be lying to myself: that seeing those words as a sign could be confirmation bias.

I also think of a story my mother used to tell. In it, a man is stuck on his roof in a flood and keeps calling to God to rescue him. Another man comes by in a rowboat and offers to save him, but the man on the roof says, "No, I'm waiting for God." And then a helicopter flies over and offers to rescue him, and the man says, "No, I'm waiting for God." And finally the flood waters rise to his neck, and he cries to God again: "Why did you abandon me?" And God calls back, "What do you mean? I sent a rowboat and a helicopter."

Above all, my mother had faith in pragmatism. Even if there wasn't a God, sometimes the world would offer me ways to save myself, or the signs I'd been asking for, and I had better take them while I could.

I understand it's maybe wish fulfillment to believe that *Angelina Ballerina* was a message from her, and it's a far more equivocal sign than *Hello, Alexandra, this is your mother!* But I can imagine myself explaining, "Logically, my boss, who seldom talked about his family, was copying the name of my mother's stuffed rabbit between files right before I got to work," as my mother calls down, "But I sent . . ."

I didn't tell many people about *Angelina Ballerina*, but I held it close to me, lighter than a feather, mere pixels, but potent. Over the years as I wrote about my mother and her death, I loved believing she had once written back to me. Maybe only two words. But it mattered that language connected us, as in many ways—inveterate storyteller she was—it always had.

◆

Italian philosopher Franco Berardi distinguishes between what he calls *connection*, which is the prescribed meaning-making a computer enacts via code or existing syntax, and *conjunction*, which is human interaction in which there are unpredictable variables that cannot be accounted for. Berardi says code "contains, in itself, the future deployment of the coded object": input certain data with other data and receive something contained already within them. But in conjunction, humans create "the meaning of what we exchange." Berardi says our lives need less code and more conjunction to create meaningful selves and societies.

When humans see meaning in synchronicity, is this meaning *coded* somehow into the event, or is it *conjunctive*?

Contemporary neuroscientists would say it's code: our brains searching for pattern and meaning based on existing patterns and meaning and knowledge—or what's known as "predictive processing." As Lars Muckli, professor of neuroscience in Glasgow, explains, "The main purpose of the brain, as we understand it today, is basically a prediction machine that is optimizing its own predictions of the environment it is navigating."

People who believe in God and/or in systems of arcane signs and prophecies (as increasing numbers of people online seem to) would also see code, but with a mystical source.

Carl Jung, who coined the term *synchronicity* for *meaningful coincidences*, would, I think, say human meaning-making is conjunction. Jung writes, "Synchronicity therefore means the simultaneous occurrence of a certain psychic state with one or more external events which appear as meaningful parallels to the momentary subjective state."

Einstein's theories of relativity and quantum physics helped inspire Jung's theory, and Einstein, in turn, called some theories supporting synchronicity "by no means absurd." Of course, if I want to believe in synchronicities, this gives me comfort.

Jung's studies, and those that he read about, led him to argue that synchronicities exist outside ordinary causal relations and the effects of time and space. They exist when our mind is in touch with its unconscious and archetypes and interacting with them in real time. In Jung's thinking, the unconscious is the home of our true selves, and also of madness, which he did not necessarily distinguish from our true selves. It was from experiences during his lengthy mental breakdown that Jung developed much of his own philosophy.

Though Jung differed from Schopenhauer's understanding of causality, he quoted him to explain synchronicity as "a subjective connection which exists only in relation to the individual who experiences it, and which is thus subjective as his own dreams." Jung didn't believe that the subjective, reflexive nature of synchronicities made them less real. Where but from the combination of our subjective perceptions and prior experiences and current experiences (and in Jung's view, our unconscious, or archetypal reality) are we ever making meaning?

(I know: this way lie alternate realities and completely subjective experiences and signs of mental illness.)

(But also, this way lie the stories by which we make meaning of our lives.)

◆

Angelina Ballerina, Angelina Ballerina.

◆

In Svankmajer's *Alice,* sometimes we see Alice's lips in close-up. During the opening credits, we watch her lips say, "Alice thought to herself, now you will see a film made for children. Perhaps." Later, we watch her lips speaking the other characters' lines—e.g., "'Oh dear, how late it's getting,' sighed the white rabbit." Alice is actress and narrator and maybe ventriloquist.

To get to Wonderland, she does not climb through a neat hole in the grass, but instead pushes herself through an old-fashioned school desk—past sharp pencils and protractors.

How am I ever not the girl who is living her life for the first time, yet also telling its story? The girl scraping herself as she climbs down the rabbit hole of her own desk?

◆

Four years after *Angelina Ballerina*, I was, as often, at Ritual Coffee in San Francisco, trying to grade one more essay before they closed. I was the last customer, and the staff had started to clean and had turned off the radio for a record, or vice versa. The song that came on—"Sylvia's Mother"—is about a man calling to talk to Sylvia and being told by her mother that Sylvia can't come to the phone because she's trying to start over; the song ends with the singer saying he just wants to say goodbye. I'd never heard this song before, though there aren't many songs about Sylvia, and Sylvia is my mother's name.

Obviously, this song is about *Sylvia's mother*, not Sylvia *as* a mother. But it's also a song about trying to call Sylvia, and in the years after my mother's death, the image that most often recurred to me, and most broke my heart with its hope within despair, was that I would be able to pick up a phone and call her. That a phone line still existed somewhere that could connect us.

In this recurring fantasy, she was just at a number I didn't know yet. Once I found it, the phone would ring in some house, and she would hurry to dry her hands on the dish towel hanging on the stove as it always was, and pick up the cordless phone, with a little flour stuck to the side of her hand from kneading bread, and say, "Hello, sweetie."

Oh, I just want to tell you goodbye.

Did I mention that this day was October 13, which would have been my mother's seventieth birthday?

In the decade and a half since, I've never again heard that song played in public. Internet research told me it was written by Shel Silverstein and recorded by Dr. Hook & the Medicine Show in 1972, the year my parents married, though I don't remember my parents ever referring to it. In these slightly twisty, overlapping details, it's hard not to hear my mother's sense of humor, timing, love of music, and all of our years of phone calls as I lived across the country, and all the years after her death when I dreamed that she'd call me. If I were to write a song for her to send me as a sign she was still there—and maybe that she was moving on to somewhere else—this would be it. Which of course cycles back to the fact that this could be only *my* narrative I'm stringing together. Or as literary theorist Barbara Johnson says we do with all texts, I could be rereading the text even as I read it for the first time.

◆

Alexandra thought to herself, now you will hear some more facts about my family and white rabbits: Gabriel was only eleven when my mother died. He and I never discussed the stuffed white rabbits I sent her. I don't know if he knew about them. She didn't live long enough to see the business cards he made for the company he wanted to start called White Rabbit, Inc., nor his arm tattoos of his own white rabbit symbol and Brer Rabbit.

As far as I know, neither of them knew the expression *rabbit rabbit*, or *white rabbits*, which for centuries has been repeated in England— often on the first day of the month—as a spell against evil and to ward off death. It's likely this expression grew out of Celtic mythology, in which rabbits were seen as animals that could communicate with the underworld and spirits.

I didn't learn this until I was writing these essays.

On New Years Eve 2020, I finished a major revision of this essay. Less than an hour later, I checked Facebook. The first thing I saw was a post by Meow Wolf, the immersive, surrealist art space in Santa Fe where Nathan had taken me the year after Gabriel died. Among the installations is a huge, glowing-eyed white rabbit statue that you can walk inside of.

"Did Gabriel ever," I'd started to ask, but Nathan had just shaken his head and quickly left the room. Later he said, "I wanted him to see it. He would have loved it."

That night, New Year's Eve, in Idaho, with a new draft of this essay on my computer, Meow Wolf was streaming a video titled "Live from the House of Eternal Return." And when I clicked the link, a girl wearing a half-shirt of a white rabbit—not with a rabbit on it, but the half shirt actually shaped like a rabbit's head and floppy ears—was talking to the camera.

◆

Watch my lips: I'm telling you the story of my lips telling you a story. But also, this is all true.

◆

The year before Gabriel died, another series of experiences opened vast rabbit holes in my understanding of time and synchronicities.

It started early in the summer of 2015, when I got lost on a drive with two friends to the Wallowa Mountains in Oregon. What should have been a three-hour drive became seven. My friends and I reached Lake Wallowa at nearly sunset. On a curve on the narrow two-lane road, a mother deer ran in front of me. She was followed by a fawn, which bolted just in time past my front bumper. But then came a second fawn. I tried to brake, but there were cars close behind me, in front of me, no shoulder.

As a lifelong vegetarian, I have never knowingly killed more than a bug in my life.

My friends tried to comfort me, but I was inconsolable. I tried to call my partner, Dylan, but my phone didn't have reception, so I had to go into a motel bar, where I made a long-distance call to his cell, crying so hysterically he could hardly hear me.

Dylan and I had been talking about getting married, and a few weeks after I killed the fawn, he proposed to me on a camping trip at our favorite Idaho lake. Shortly after, we went back to the Wallowas. We ended up doing the same hike I'd done with my friends. We spent the first night, sleeping without a tent, in a field midway up the ascent. We were just waking in our sleeping bags in the grass in the morning dew when a doe walked up. As a deer has never done in our thousands of miles of hiking trips, it stood a few feet from us and looked at us for a long time, seemingly unafraid and interested only in us. I'm sure there are odds that explain it, but also, there is how it felt: the conjunction of us, that doe, the field, and the fawn I'd killed.

Two weeks later, by the lake where Dylan had proposed to me, another deer appeared at our campsite. This time, it was a buck. It came even closer. In all our visits to that lake, we've seen only a few other deer far off in the woods. But this young buck walked inches from our tent, close enough to touch, and looked in our eyes.

We started calling this "the summer of the deer."

When I was growing up in the Ozarks, deer were ubiquitous, as they are in much of the West. I never gave them much thought. But once, when I was in my early thirties, a wise older woman at a California hot springs asked if I wanted to know my spirit animal, then pulled a deer from a deck of spirit cards. I admitted that I don't think of myself as deerlike—gentle, yes, but also far more fiery, like my astrological scorpion—but she said that deer are noble and quietly powerful: it was a very good animal to have.

At the end of "the summer of the deer," Dylan and I flew to Baja on a rare family trip to meet up with his mother, sister, niece, and a family friend, Jim, who lives there. The first night at dinner, we toasted our engagement. The next morning, Dylan, his sister, his niece, and I crammed ourselves into the seatbeltless back seat of Jim's very old jeep; Dylan's mom sat in the front. We had a half-day drive ahead of us, part of it on rutted rural roads, to reach Jim's house, and he was driving fast. The highway rose steeply, winding—cliffs to one side, rocky desert sprawling to the other. Dylan isn't usually a nervous passenger, but he gripped the safety handle.

When Dylan asked to stop to pee, Jim said he'd pull over. Before any of us knew what was happening, we heard a sickening crashing; the jeep was spinning toward the cliff side of the road.

When we came to a bumpy stop—on a wide gravel pull-out—I remember sharp, thin desert light. The stunned space of trauma when an ordinary day rips open to reveal another day inside it.

Dylan's mom said, "We're all fine, right? We're fine."

And Dylan softly said, "I don't know if I am."

He'd hit his head hard against the window as a car—which had been passing at sixty just as Jim turned—crashed into us.

Dylan climbed out, a little unsteady, and I stood next to him, in case he got dizzy. But before I could hold him up, he fell backward. His head hit the pavement, and his eyes rolled back. On a desert highway in Mexico, the love of my life, my partner of ten years, my new fiancé, was going in and out of consciousness. I screamed and screamed and screamed for him to come back to me.

Dylan remembers hearing my voice and his mother's. He remembers drifting, returning.

When we got him settled in the back of the jeep, he kept drifting away again, then saying over and over that he loved us all. It was hours, or what felt like hours, before the ambulance arrived from Constitution, the nearest town.

How can I explain that time?

There was sawdust pouring from my chest.

In the hospital, with its sagging ceiling tiles, Dylan stayed conscious, but without a CT scanner, all the doctors could do was x-ray and monitor him. We stood by his bed. We held his hand.

Later, he told us that he remembered feeling anxious in the jeep, and gripping the safety handle, because he felt clearly that something bad was about to happen.

And earlier that morning, in the shower, he'd thought out of nowhere: *I'm in a culture where people believe in guardian angels. If I have a guardian angel, I wonder what it would look like.* Though his mother's birth family is Mexican Catholic, she was adopted at age one by an Anglo Catholic family, and then abandoned religion in her teens and didn't raise Dylan or his sister religious. He didn't remember ever thinking about guardian angels before.

When Dylan told us about the guardian angel, his sister got a strange expression. Then she said that when she'd ridden in the police car from the hospital to the station to give the accident report, a tape was playing ABBA's "I Have a Dream" with its refrain about believing in angels.

Of course we all got goosebumps as she said this.

What was happening? Synchronicity? The Mexican police just really liking ABBA? Confirmation bias? Angels?

The next day, we drove hours to the nearest hospital that could do a CT scan—on highways frighteningly dotted with roadside memorials, or *descansos*. We were, of course, scared the scan would show brain damage, but the doctor said Dylan had no internal injuries. Despite two concussions, he had "un cerebro perfecto."

After Dylan and I got home to Idaho, carrying a large manila folder of his brain scans, I had an appointment with a therapist I'd been seeing. She was technically retired and did therapy sessions from her apartment where she often told digressive stories that uncannily anticipated what I'd come to ask her. I'd already talked to her about the summer of the deer, but I wasn't thinking of it now.

When I described the wreck—how shaken I still was and how grateful that Dylan was alive and fine—she answered: "Some people believe that a spirit animal will sacrifice itself to save a loved one's life. That fawn must have died to save Dylan."

When she says this, time begins spinning. It wraps around itself. If what's she's saying is true, who or what could have known two months before the wreck that Dylan would need to be saved? Wouldn't that mean that our whole lives were laid out, fated?

Or did the deer appear because I would know, in retrospect, how to read them and feel safe?

Or are we reading into them entirely? As one article on confirmation bias by Benjamin Radford says, "a person dying when a flock of birds is present is an event; a person not dying when a flock of birds is present is a non-event, and therefore not something anyone pays attention to."

In "I Have a Dream," ABBA sings about believing in angels, then says, "I have a Dream, a fantasy / To help me through, reality." Does it count as believing in angels if you know it's a fantasy?

Or does it count as agnostic if guardian angels find you anyway?

(Later, doing genealogy on his Mexican family, Dylan will learn that some of his ancestors were from Sonora and likely Yaqui. The deer is one of the Yaqui's two sacred animals. One article says, "the deer comes to the Yaqui people and they sacrifice him to the Gods, in return they perform a dance and ritual in his honor and thank him for giving himself for their well being.")

A joke I saw once: "You may not believe in unicorns, but they believe in you."

Sub in angels. Send in angels. Send in deer.

But how did they arrive? What conjunctions? What code? And who has written it?

What logic map unfolds with arrows between *guardian angel, spirit animal, deer, love, car, head, concussion*? What directions do the arrows go?

Is something in the universe calling "I sent a deer!" as I ask question after question?

◆

Because there is of course another question underneath these questions. If I believe a deer died to save Dylan, then why was there no deer—no rabbit, no anything—any of us could have hit to save Gabriel?

◆

John Ashbery, "The Ecclesiast": "There was a key to everything in that oak forest. / But a sad one."

My mother's name, Sylvia, means *spirit of the forest*. Near the end of her life, she believed she could talk to an oak tree. That it could hear her. That she could hear it.

There are so many rabbit holes in this forest I could go down.

◆

The day before my mother died, October 26, 2001, a movie premiered that became a cult classic and favorite of my sister Anne and my nephews. I first saw it a few years later at their house, crowded into armchairs and the couch, with the pellet stove creating one spot of radiance the chill could congregate around, which is what heating a high-ceilinged, poorly insulated Victorian house feels like. And also what being in a family sometimes feels like: a knot of heat that is both too intense up close and too dissipated a few steps away.

In the movie, a teenager named Donnie is visited by a tall, creepy rabbit. While Donnie is outside following the rabbit, a plane engine falls into his bedroom. Donnie wakes on a golf course to discover his own near-death. Seeking control in his spiraling life and mind, Donnie believes the giant terrifying talking rabbit, Frank, is his only friend. Hasn't Frank saved his life? Isn't Frank warning him of a coming apocalypse? Shouldn't Donnie follow Frank's advice to flood the school?

It's unclear if Frank is a boy from the future in a Halloween costume, a hallucination, or a prophetic vision. It's unclear if Donnie should trust Frank.

Maybe, Donnie reasons, he needs to follow Frank's advice until, like following bread crumbs in a darkly too-real fairy tale, he can figure out how to turn back time and undo everything he's done: how to be in his bed when the engine plummets—so his own death spares everyone else who will die instead if time plays out in its original sequence.

Though forums argue and dissect and argue more about meanings and time-travel logistics, at one level, *Donnie Darko* is the story of a mentally ill teen who doesn't know how to live in his own hallucination-filled mind, and reverse engineers the plot so he'll die.

When I first watched it, in maybe 2004, Gabriel and Nathan were teenagers, precociously smart and arty, the perfect audience. When Donnie asks why the rabbit is wearing a rabbit suit, the rabbit asks, "Why are you wearing that human suit?"

Then, besides my mother, we were all still in our human suits, in minds we recognized. I still imagined that time worked in ordinary ways. My nephews would grow up. I'd gradually become happier, recover from the grief of my mother's death. Some of which has happened.

Then, we thought the movie was uncanny for the same reason everyone else did: it had originally been slated for release the week of September 11, 2001. What were the odds that a movie about time travel and a plane crash would be slated for that moment?

But what my family would not have believed, if someone could have appeared from the future to tell us, was that we were watching a version of our own lives. In less than ten years, Nathan would find Gabriel in a flooded apartment where he'd left the shower running for days. Evicted, living in a trailer, unable to hold a job long, and refusing medication, Gabriel would believe he was going to start an angora clothing business called White Rabbit, Inc.

And finally, he would believe he would be better off, and we all would be, without his life.

♦

Of course, Gabriel, your dying won't spare us any pain. We will live what feels like all of it: time moving forward to your death, time stopped by your death, time going on in our lives, time looping back in grief, our minds looping back to try to make meaning, make meaning.

And sometimes we receive letters. Or at least once, in Cardiff, Wales, I received a ten-sentence letter that ends:

> *Because love is made out to be something more than a feeling, something that can overcome all obstacles, and that's ALL obstacles, and make gods of men. (and Goddesses of women, also). In this story, that didn't seem to happen . . . or did it? In its own unique way? I suppose it just depends on how you look at it. Many things are like that.*
>
> *Love,*
> > *Gabe*

The Panharmonicon

On a cold September night in 2017, I'm in Santa Fe, New Mexico, extremely drunk with my youngest surviving nephew. Earlier, we met for dinner and what I thought would be one margarita, and now it's almost dawn and I've followed him on a tour of bars (at some of which he used to be a doorman or DJ)—from a basement with punk playbills and Sharpie-inked graffiti to an outdoor plaza bar with the city's best Manhattans and tipsy dregs of a Pride party just visible inside velvet curtains to a narrow, Western-style, pool-tabled, wood-planked, too-new-to-be-true dive where we pause our Manhattans to drink IPAs, carelessly and fast, to this two-story dance club with its crowded main floor and small upstairs room ricocheting hard house.

On a white leather couch in a very loud chill-out room, we're drinking Manhattans. It's true the drinks have been fast; it's true I've lost track. But they haven't been careless. As we've moved past pool tables' jostle, down narrow adobe alleys, Nathan talking to doormen, saying just one more here, we've been desperately trying to outrun ourselves or locate ourselves. This is hard to do if you exist between times—if you are, as Nathan said earlier at that plaza bar, a "feral Victorian."

He said it offhandedly: "You know what our family is? Feral Victorians." And I wasn't sure whether to laugh or cry, because I'd never heard us named so clearly. But perfectly naming a contradiction doesn't resolve its contradiction.

At thirty and forty-three, Nathan and I are closer in age than I am to his mother or my other sister. Time has always been confusing in our family—not just ages, but what century we're living in. Even in the 1980s and 1990s, my nephews and I were raised beneath the lacey shadow of Victorian propriety, which my mother had inherited from her grandmother. We knew "nice girls" didn't get their ears pierced until thirteen (if ever); we lived in nineteenth-century houses with silver services and fluted cream pitchers; we spoke in expressions from old novels, like "stand on ceremony." Like my mother's great aunts, who carried tiered layer cakes up New York mountains on picnics—not on cake plates that fit in wicker baskets, but on pedestaled glass—we were creative, elegant, extravagant.

But we were also impractical and often poor: those great aunts scrimped butter for frosting; they felt claustrophobic in their own kitchens. When my sisters were young, our mother sold her thick auburn hair to a wig maker to buy the silver service. In my childhood and my nephews', we lived in old houses on a brambly Arkansas hilltop and a New Mexico ghost town. There was something wild about us—a green stain of mildew growing up the proper velvet.

We were descendants of people who'd flown to the moon. Not the real moon. The one at the 1901 Pan-American Exposition in Buffalo, when my great-grandparents were teenagers. On A Trip to the Moon, people climbed onto a great, red plane with flapping wings and rose "high" above a diorama of Niagara Falls through fan-blown clouds. After the ornithopter landed, people watched insect-eyed aliens dance or bought bags of moon cheese. Then, instead of flying back (Luna only flew up!), they slid down a slide. The Earth was a plane ride away and also a quick slide-slip. Never mind the contradictions. Look at them tucking their long skirts and petticoats as they whoosh back to Earth.

It wasn't entirely strange almost a century later when Nathan's younger brother, Gabriel, started reading aloud old hardcovers in a cemetery, or, in his twenties, handing out business cards for White Rabbit, Inc.—like the Victorian calling cards I think we'd all imagined having. And though Gabriel was struggling with delusions by the time he announced he was going to raise angora rabbits and knit their fur into shawls he'd sell in catalogues, this was also scrappy and old-fashioned like the shoebox dioramas my mother, the family matriarch, taught us all to make: paper cities pasted in the far end, so when you look through the hole, the scene becomes the world.

In the six months since I last saw him, Nathan has become serious in a boxed-in way that could just seem like the strong, silent type if I didn't know better. Right now he's asking me for advice: should he invite his girlfriend when he moves across the world for grad school? It's an ordinary question about the future. But he's also looking into a diorama of the past. Even talking about Cyprus, I can tell that he's seeing all the times here in Santa Fe he raced to try to save his younger brother. Gabriel, who loved writing stories. Gabriel, who designed his own personal symbol: an ouroboros, with snake scales that look like old-fashioned floral wallpaper and a head made of overlaid triangles, like Yeats' gyres spiraling history in two directions. Gabriel who, here in Santa Fe, a year and a half ago, alone in his room, shot himself.

Seeing Nathan tonight, for only the second time since the funeral, I can tell his grief has become differently loud with time. What began as one deafening noise now blares and bangs against everything. Maybe this is why we've come to this club—to try to find a space even a fraction as loud as what's inside us. Maybe we're getting so drunk because it's the easier kind of noisy not-knowing.

What can I say about suicide? It's like a sentence made entirely of ellipses that are also sentence-stopping periods. It is ending after ending after ending that also trails off forever.

Like the fortune I got once from one of the old Victorian carnival machines at the Musée Méchanique in San Francisco, back when I was Nathan's age and stayed up all night to come to clubs like this. The fortune was "written" by the mechanical hand of a turbaned fortune teller in a glass box. On the front, in red ink, the heavy card-stock card says, *The 'Magic Ray' reads you like a book: The 'Mystic' Pen sends you the message.* And on the back, in black cursive: *You are determined and settled in all your plans and undertakings, and while you are assuming in some respects, you are intuitional, sensitive, and idealistic. You have executive ability and practical perseverance* . . .

I still carry the card in my wallet because those ellipses strike me as the truest kind of fortune. They suggest a self or future that might go equally in any direction: that might solidly continue what's been said, or might undercut it entirely, or might happen so inexplicably no words are possible. Even when *The 'Magic Ray' reads you like a book,* there are so many words about yourself, and the people you love, that you'll never know. Or you'll never get the chance to know . . .

In our family, very much has always been told through stories—some beautiful, and some terrible—and very little has ever been directly explained or named.

Nathan and Gabriel and I grew up in houses with bookshelves of mass-market, made-to-look-elegant hardcover books with fake gilt lettering. The kind my mother bought from catalogues and book sales in the 1950s. The kind that seemed solid and respectable until you actually opened them. We all read *Raintree County,* my mother's all-time favorite book: Ross Lockridge Jr's one-thousand-page attempt at the great American novel, about a nineteenth-century Indiana man who framed his life with literature and legends. A lyrical, dreamy, sprawling story about a man caught inside stories, by an author who promptly killed himself.

We read Dickens and Steinbeck. We read *Nicholas and Alexandra,* about the Romanov czar and czarina, which my mother had noticed in her library in her third month of pregnancy and named me for—as if I were doomed Russian royalty. (Though we had no royal relatives, nor—I'll realize as I get older and read friends' relatives' obituaries—even relatives famous enough for a half page of praise.)

We read Emerson and Thoreau and Alcott and "The Highwayman" about the inn-keeper's "black-eyed daughter, Bess," who shoots herself to warn her lover, the highwayman, that a trap awaits him. We were somehow both on the side of propriety and the law, and chafing our wrists against it. We lived in the magic kingdom of our feral Victorianism. We did not read books that diagnosed us. There were not words for mental illness amid all those heavy gilt letters and sweet dust-smelling pages.

Yes, we all knew that my mother had had shock treatments in her twenties after a breakdown and a doctor had said she "felt too much." But "feeling too much" is not a real diagnosis. Or not of this century. It's a reason to take to a fainting couch, though my mother was never one for lying down. She believed in making elaborate clothes, and stained glass, and food. Once, she baked several batches of homemade Christmas cookies but then, in the midst of feeling too much—i.e., fighting with me about something—she scraped them all off the baking sheets into the trash while screaming, "Christmas is cancelled." Though by the next morning, it was elaborately on as always.

How terrible to want to shut down feeling. We believed in feeling!

We all knew my grandmother once said that everything after my grandfather's death—i.e., the next sixty years—never "seemed real." But we did not label this PTSD despite the suddenness of his death and the terrible intensity and freakishness of the ammunition ship explosion.

Not until Gabriel's first breakdown did a doctor use words like *bipolar* or *delusions*. Not until Gabriel and me did anyone see a therapist. Not until my forties did I consider that any of this might be generational trauma. We lived with something more inexplicable and ancient than a diagnosis: like Edgar Allen Poe's tell-tale heart that I feared pulsing beneath the floorboards of my childhood bedroom, where a real black ink stain—maybe a century old—still splotched it like blood.

Would it have helped if someone had spoken more clearly sooner?

Earlier, in the basement bar, I finally asked Nathan something I'd never asked anyone: "Wasn't there mental illness on your father's side? An uncle or grandmother who was bipolar?"

I remembered hearing that. I'd sometimes repeated it to myself in the five years as Gabriel's delusions got worse and finally as we buried him in that cemetery where he used to read Flannery O'Connor aloud to the emptiness and Victorian ghosts.

Maybe at some level, I knew I'd misremembered, and feared what Nathan would say.

Then he said it: "No, I think that's from your side. I think Gabe was bipolar like Nana was."

Nana is what my nephews called my mother.

This night in Santa Fe, I'm forty-three. I was raised by my mother, feared my mother, grieved my mother as she was dying, rebelled against my mother, grieved my mother after she died, hated my mother, loved my mother, loved Gabriel, grieved Gabriel, am grieving Gabriel, and this is the first time anyone has ever said my mother was bipolar.

Was she? What does it mean if she was? Are these ellipses at the start of the sentence of my life I need to try to find the words for? Are these the ellipses that carried on at the end of Gabriel's?

Right now, through the thumping music, Nathan is shouting more questions: "Does our family even have any models for good relationships? What about you and Dylan?"

And I'm shouting back, "We talked really openly right when we started dating about what we both needed in terms of time for our own art projects."

But what I want to shout is, "How will we ever understand ourselves at all? What if everything we thought was beautiful was also dangerous? How is my mother still dead? How is Gabriel still dead? How are you and I still living?"

But even if I said all this, it is too loud in this club to hear me. Or it is too loud inside us.

Decades before The Magic Ray at the Musée Méchanique in San Francisco, I used to go to another Victorian carnival museum in Eureka Springs, Arkansas, where my parents and I had moved when I was eleven, shortly before Nathan was born. Eureka Springs is

Victorian and strange—perfect for our family—and among its many strange places was Miles Musical Museum: a carpeted, sprawling building crammed with nineteenth-century mechanical instruments.

Each year at some point the teachers would take our class because it was vaguely educational, and my friends and I would wander the mildew-smelling rooms, complaining they were boring. This was the late eighties, before steampunk and retro-futurism were cool.

Old Mr. Miles died less than a decade later and the museum closed, but it felt like it might be closed, or open only in the past, even when we went to it. I remember it being surreal and loud and slightly frightening. It held miniature carnival scenes sprawled across tables: tattered big tops, tin lions and acrobats, bobsleds gliding manic loops around small, mechanized hillsides. It held player pianos, reed and monkey organs, music boxes, calliopes, hurdy-gurdies, a musical chapel, a panharmonicon. Loud, tinny music blared from everywhere and nowhere.

In my memory, the panharmonicon, a band-in-a-smudgy-glass-box, took up half a room. It had player-piano-style music rolls with sharp brass teeth that looked like they could scrape off dead skin in a pedicure or remove lint from a carpet. It had tubas piled on clarinets on trumpets on organ pipes on drums on who knew what. An odd-angled, tubular, bulbous, belling hall of mirrors in which some instruments collapsed into one sleek black line of reflection and others multiplied: oversized and slouching as Dali's famous clock.

And all the moving parts moved—when you dropped a nickel in—with a manic energy that seemed to be trying to play every song ever written at once: all the music of the past and present and future colliding. The music was so overwhelming, so triumphantly discordant, that you couldn't tell if parts were broken, or if this was how it was supposed to sound at all, in fact.

As a sign maybe explained, Johann Nepomuk Maelzel, a contemporary of Beethoven, had invented the panharmonicon in 1805. In the Victorian era, it grew popular as the related *orchestrion* or *componium*, and in the almost two centuries since, it neither went away nor further evolved. Unlike early cell phones (still in the future in my teens) with buttons so large they look like jokes, or the room-sized computers my parents had written love notes on during college, punching words in the (now) far outdated paper cards, the panharmonicon wasn't the bigger, slower version of a future that knew how to shrink it. It had not directly turned into anything. It just was. Feral and Victorian and enduring. Inexplicable and magical and dented.

And maybe it's most accurate to say that Nathan and Gabriel and I were raised inside a panharmonicon or we carry the panharmonicon of our family inside us—with all those gears that broke time, or the gears that made the music of time.

Inside the panharmonicon tonight, I'm the most blazingly drunk I've been in years. I'm five feet five inches and Nathan is six feet two inches and, though I should and do know better, I've been matching him drink for drink—even now, the rye rising through two thin black straws in little puffs like the reverse of the exhalations I learned in sixth grade, the one year I played the flute.

When Nathan shouts, "Do you really think I can be an artist?" I shout, "Yes, of course," though I've thought till now he was still interested in journalism. But I love him and believe he's brilliant and talented and can study design if he wants to.

I'm the slightly older wiser aunt, and maybe I should be sober. Maybe I should be more practical. But how? At best, I am a sentence that reads: *have executive ability and practical perseverance . . .*

"Did you say the design program's in Cyprus?" I shout, and Nathan shouts, "Yes, Cyprus." I don't know the exact distance, but I know Cyprus is very far away: an island no one in our family has been to. How will he afford this? Who knows! Somewhere there are families where people start ordinary careers, live in subdivisions. We study on mythical islands; we design our own symbols and worlds.

From the beginning, the panharmonicon was advertised as making the sounds of over two hundred musical instruments but also cannons and guns. More than a century before John Cage, the panharmonicon had complicated the distinction between noise and music.

In the 1830s, after Ralph Waldo Emerson heard one in Boston, he wrote about its cacophony and range in his journal as a metaphor for his ideal oratory or literature:

> *Here,* everything is admissible, philosophy, ethics, divinity, criticism, poetry, humor, anecdote, mimicry,—ventriloquism almost,—all the breadth and versatility of the most liberal conversation, and of the highest, lowest, personal, and local topics—all are permitted, and all may be combined in one speech. It is a panharmonicon combining every note on the longest gamut, from the explosion of cannon to the tinkle of a guitar.

Emerson's idea is beautiful: truth not as a single instrument, but as all possible tones and variety. For a single speech, this sounds wonderful. But for a life? How can every note be heard if they're all playing at once? Or how can anyone survive this?

I have, so far as I know, the only body-length angora scarf that Gabriel ever made for White Rabbit, Inc. He sent it to me for a birthday. It's knitted of very soft yarn, maybe truly angora—I definitely called it *angora* when I thanked him. It's made of alternating dark plum, evergreen, and sage swatches, each more than a foot wide and several feet long, sewed clumsily. The thick thread is raised like stitches in bunched skin. It's another prototype for something no one would buy: another past-future that has only stayed itself.

Like so much in our family, it's also strangely beautiful, even magical. It looks as if it has been chewed on by wolves; as if you could wear it on moon ride. I can sit on the couch in the Idaho winter with my feet in its bottom, the other end looped around me like an infinity symbol. It keeps me very warm.

At my most wishful, fantastical moments, I imagine if my mother had still been alive, she would have known the right things to say to Gabriel, and he would not have died. I know mental illness isn't resolved that easily. It may have been her very genes he inherited. But one of her many talents was making you feel as if there were always more pages in the book, more music you hadn't heard yet. In addition to being an inveterate reader, she was a piano teacher, the only one in our family to really play an instrument. She also had a master's in economics, and taught us to be fiscally responsible, scrappy, able to make the most of whatever we're given.

If she could see us in this Santa Fe club, she'd be appalled that Nathan and I are drunk, which is trashy and improper, like using a cake mix. But I think she'd be glad we're together, however ferally.

It's nearly dawn when Nathan and I finally leave the club and walk the dark adobe streets to my motel, where we hug goodbye in the parking lot. The hug is partly reassuring Nathan, partly holding me up.

Hours later, with a terrible hangover, I get on a plane back to Idaho. For several years, I don't see Nathan—who goes to Cyprus and decides he doesn't like the design program, then briefly studies Arabic in Egypt, then does construction in Berlin, then comes home to New Mexico to become certified in wind-turbine installation, then ends up doing construction on movie sets back in Santa Fe.

We email, and when I tell him I'm writing essays about our family of "feral Victorians," he says he doesn't remember saying that: "Maybe I said something like 'prairie intellectuals'?" But I'm positive I heard it. Or maybe I needed to hear it. I needed some way to start to describe us.

I'm always afraid that when I try to tell our story, I'm only adding to the noise or I'm hearing too little. So much still confuses me. There are ghosts in the gears, and grief, and rabbit fur—clumped and muffling in the brass like strange, feral nests. There are ellipses that are also music notes that are also ink blots that are also heartbeats that are also gunshots, or a single gunshot, echoing. I'm still often unsure what mallet is striking what, if there's even a mallet, who's pressing the piano keys, who—if anyone—has the tools to repair the intricate, skewed mechanics.

But I'm sure of the love that plays despite everything. Sometimes it sounds like something else. Sometimes it holds so many sounds, it hurts to hear it.

Acknowledgments

"Perfect Storms" appeared in *The Common* in Fall 2022

"Tea Cups" appeared in *River Teeth* in Spring 2022

"20,000 Leagues Under the Sea" appeared in *Willow Springs* in Spring 2021 and was listed as Notable in *Best American Essays 2022*

I'm deeply grateful to my sister Beth—conversations with you helped lead me to this project and your early encouragement helped keep me going. And to Molly McCully Brown for first telling me to walk to the edge of the field; I would never have begun this book or seen where it needed to go without your insights and friendship across three countries. To Jen Sullivan Brych for your wild drawings and always spot-on, generous feedback that helped each essay find its center. To Annie Lampman, always, for telling me the right things, including "send it out." To Gabe Fried and Civitella Ranieri for the incredible gift of a month-long residency in a real castle, and the other fellows who inspired me through hours of dinners, waterfall swims, and runs: particularly Texu, Nina, Alexis, Jennifer, Sky, Alejandro, and Darragh. Extra thanks to Rachel Donadio for vulnerable, crucial talks. To Polly Buckingham, editor of *Willow Springs*, for key encouragement; Melissa Febos for an inspiring craft talk; Kate Lebo for her insights; Brian Blanchfield for an early reading of "Tea Cups"; Kim Barnes for telling me it just takes good sentences; Donna Graybill and Abigail Ulman for helping when I was wandering lost. To University of Idaho for a year-long sabbatical. Uncommon Ground for the space chair and good coffee, Richard Gwyn for the library access and writing community, and Camilla Brueton and Alice Lovett for company in Cardiff. To Jodie Nicotra who ran me through miles of doubts and helped me see several essays more clearly.

And my other Idaho and Washington friends, colleagues, and students, who create the most supportive, inspiring community to write and grow in—especially Joy Passanante, Stacy Isenbarger, Michael McGriff, Tara MacDonald, Erin James, Jennifer Ladino, Jennifer Sherman, Ryanne Pilgeram, Ben James, DJ Lee, Robert Wrigley, CMarie Fuhrman, Stacy Boe Miller, Rochelle Smith, Leah Hampton, Jess Arndt, Joely Fitch, Brian Malone, Becky Fradkin, Gianna Stoddard, Cameron Martin, Steven Pfau, Laur Freymiller, Afton Montgomery, Cady Favazzo, Trixie Zwolfer, Jourdan Imani Keith, Kristen Millares Young, Sayantani Dasgupta, Laura Read, and Maya Zeller. To the editors of *River Teeth* and *The Common* for wonderful edits and encouragement. To Cris Harris and Kathryn Nuernberger for insightful, generous feedback. To the incredible editors at Oregon State University Press: Kim Hogeland for first believing in this project, Tom Booth for facilitating the cover (and David Drummond for envisioning my story as amazing art), and Micki Reaman and Marty Brown for all the careful edits and conversations. I could not have landed in better hands. To the rest of my California/Wales/New Mexico friends and family, especially Alisa, Thoa, Tree, Magdalena, Rosalynd, Logan, Michael, Natasha, and Bonnie. To my father, Raymond, my sister Anne, and my nephew Nathan for your conversations and trust; I'm so lucky you're my family. And to everyone else who appears here—under your real name, or otherwise. I hope you can tell that this was written with love and from my own fallible memory, my own emotional truths and reckonings. Always, always to Dylan Champagne for listening to every page, and loving me. And finally, to and because of my family ghosts, particularly Floyd "Bill" Berry, Sylvia Teague, and Gabriel Scott New.

Notes on Sources

Throughout these essays, Stephen M. Fjellman's *Vinyl Leaves: Walt Disney World and America* (Abingdon: Routledge, 1992), Kurt Andersen's *Fantasyland: How America Went Haywire* (New York: Random House, 2017), and Nathan Filer's *The Heartland: Finding and Losing Schizophrenia* (London: Faber and Faber, 2019) provided crucial perspective. I'm also indebted to the following sources, which I quoted from and/or consulted.

Tea Cups
Joan Didon, "Why I Write," *The New York Times Magazine* (Dec. 5, 1976); Michel Foucault, *Discipline and Punish: The Birth of the Prison*, trans. A. Sheridan, (New York: Vintage Books, 1977, original work published 1975); *The Catholic Encyclopedia: An International Work of Reference on the Constitution, Doctrine, Discipline, and History of the Catholic Church*, edited by Charles G. Herbermann et al., (published in 15 volumes between 1907 and 1912); Seth L. Schein, "The Cassandra Scene in Aeschylus' 'Agamemnon,'" *Greece & Rome* 29, no. 1 (1982); "Georgiana Houghton: Spirit Drawings," *The Courtauld*, www.courtauld.ac.uk; Georgiana Houghton, quoted in Allison Meier, "Georgiana Houghton Visualized a World Beyond Death," *Nightingale: The Journal of the Data Visualization Society* via *Medium*, (2019); William Butler Yeats, "Leda and the Swan" in *The Cat and*

the Moon and Certain Poems (Dublin: Cuala Press, 1924); Lewis
Carroll, "VII. A Mad Tea-Party" in Alice's Adventures in Wonderland
& Through the Looking-Glass (originally published in 1865 and 1871);
Walt Whitman, "Song of Myself" in Leaves of Grass (originally pub-
lished 1855).

Wings
Milan Kundera, The Unbearable Lightness of Being (New York:
Harper Collins, 1988); Hans Magnus Enzensberger, "A Theory of
Tourism," New German Critique, no. 68 (1996, first published as
Hans Magnus Enzensberger, "Vergebliche Brandung der Ferne: Eine
Theorie des Tourismus" Merkur 126 (1958); Roger Scruton, "The
Strangely Enduring Power of Kitsch," BBC News, www.bbc.com;
Frank Stanford, quoted in Ben Ehrenreich, "The Long Goodbye,"
Poetry Foundation, Jan. 18, 2008; Stephen Spence, "Pure Hoax: The
Norman Baker Story," The 1886 Crescent Hotel and Spa (originally
published 2007, www.crescent-hotel.com); Dean MacCannell,
The Tourist: A New Theory of the Leisure Class (Berkeley and Los
Angeles: University of California Press, 1999, originally published
1976); Alan Parker, director, Pink Floyd—The Wall, (London:
United International Pictures, 1982); Elizabeth Bishop, "Over 2,000
Illustrations and a Complete Concordance" in The Complete Poems
1927-1979 (New York: Farrar, Straus and Giroux, 1983).

Frontierland
Ralph Waldo Emerson, The Topical Notebooks of Ralph Waldo
Emerson (Columbia: University of Missouri Press, 1992); "Abraham
Lincoln's Hall of Presidents Speeches," This Day in Disney History,
www.thisdayindisneyhistory.com; Abraham Lincoln, "Lyceum
Address," Speech, Springfield, IL, Jan. 27, 1838, Abraham Lincoln
Online, www.abrahamlincolnonline.org.; "Billy the Kid's Life
and Death," The New York Times, Jul. 31, 1881; "Magic Kingdom—
Frontierland," Disney Information, www.wdwinfo.com; Michelle
Krowl, "Hearing Abraham Lincoln's Voice," Library of Congress
Blogs. Jan. 3, 2018; Horace White, "The Lincoln and Douglas
Debate," Lecture presented before the Chicago Historical Society,

Chicago, IL, Feb. 17, 1914; "Why Do We Say 'White Rabbits' on First of the Month?" ITVX, May 1, 2015, www.itv.com; Danielle M. Novick, Holly A. Schwartz, and Ellen Frank, "Suicide Attempts in Bipolar I and Bipolar II Disorder: A Review and Meta-Analysis of the Evidence," *Bipolar Disorders* 12, no. 1 (2010); Flannery O'Connor, "The River," *The Sewanee Review* 61, no. 3 (1953).

Space Mountain

Bob Sehlinger and Len Testa, "18 Classic Disney World Attractions," Frommer's, www.frommers.com; Horizons, "Space Mountain Com Chat," Magic Music, Jan. 1, 2009; Subtle, "Red, White, & Blonde," *A New White*, Lex Records, 2004; Yi-Fu Tuan, *Escapism* (Baltimore: Johns Hopkins University Press, 2000); Antonin Artaud, *The Theater and its Double*, translated by Mary Caroline Richards (New York City: Grove Press, 1994, originally published 1938); Frode Stenseng, "Two Dimensions of Escapism: Self-Expansion and Self-Suppression," *Psychology & Health* 23 (2008); Brittany Tackett, "The History of MDMA (Ecstasy)," American Addiction Centers, www.recovery.org; Jerrold S. Meyer, "3,4-methylenedioxymethamphetamine (MDMA): Current Perspectives," *Substance Abuse and Rehabilitation* 4, (2013); Neva Chonin, "The Beat Goes On/ S.F.'s dance scene survived the blows," SFGATE, Mar. 10, 2002; Rosanna Scimeca, "Cleavage in Space," 2003, www.rosannascimeca.com; "MDMA (Ecstasy/Molly) DrugFacts," National Institute on Drug Abuse, Jun. 15, 2020, www.nida.nih.gov; 13 & God, "Soft Atlas" on *13 & God* (Anticon and Alien Transistor, 2005); Audre Lorde, "Poetry Is Not a Luxury" in *Sister Outsider: Essays and Speeches* (Feasterville-Trevose: Crossing Press, 1984); Underworld, "Cowgirl," on *Dubnobasswithmyheadman*, Junior Boy's Own, 1994; Underworld, "Born Slippy," on *Trainspotting*, Capitol Records, 1996.

Perfect Storms

"Jungle Cruise Jokes," *Talk Disney*, www.talkdisney.com; Deb Amlen, "How to Solve The New York Times Crossword," *The New York Times*, www.nytimes.com; Lee Greenwood, "Fool's Gold," on *You've Got a Good Love Comin'*, vinyl, MCA, 1984; Thomas J. Craughwell,

Cow Parade Kansas City (New York: Workman Publishing, 2001); Brad Paisley, "Perfect Storm," by Brad Paisley and Lee Thomas Miller, on *Moonshine in the Trunk*, digital album, Arista Nashville, 2014; Geoff Nunberg, "Puns in Country Music Done Right," NPR, Sep. 3, 2010, www.npr.org; Blake Shelton, "Neon Light," by Andrew Dorff, Mark Irwin, and Josh Kear, on *Bringing Back the Sunshine*, digital album, Warner Bros. Nashville, recorded 2014; Josh Osborne, quoted in Tom Roland, "What In the Word? Bent Phrasing Is On the Rebound In Country Music," *Billboard*, Feb. 21, 2018, www. billboard.com; Xiaoli Gan, "A Study of the Humor Aspect of English Puns: Views from the Relevance Theory," *Theory and Practice in Language Studies* 5, no. 6 (2015); Rovers, "Wasn't That a Party," on *The Rovers*, vinyl, Attic, 1980; George Strait, "Looking Out My Window Through the Pain," by John Schweers, on *George Strait*, compact disc, MCA Nashville, recorded 2000.

Building Character
Leonare Steinhardt, "Creating the Autonomous Image Through Puppet Theatre and Art Therapy," *The Arts in Psychotherapy* 21, no. 3 (1994); Joyce Catlett, "Anxious Attachment: Understanding Insecure Anxious Attachment," *PsychAlive*, psychalive.org; Alexa Plit, "The Attachment Story Completion Test: Analysing the Emergent Themes and Object Relations of a South African Protocol," Thesis, 2013, core.ac.uk; William A. Ward, "Elissa," *Texas State Historical Association*. Jan. 1, 1995, tshaonline.org; Vincent Canby, "Screen: Australian Hawthorne Romance: From Down Under," *The New York Times*, Feb. 23, 1979; Terese Mailhot, *Heart Berries* (Berkeley: Counterpoint, 2018); Let Dillen, Mariska Siongers, Denis Helskens, and Leni Verhofstadt-Denève, "When Puppets Speak: Dialectical Psychodrama within Developmental Child Psychotherapy," *Journal of Constructivist Psychology* 22, no. 1 (2009).

20,000 Leagues Under the Sea
Friedrich Nietzsche, *The Gay Science* (Germany, 1882); Armed Services Explosives Safety Board, The Explosion of the U.S.S.

Mount Hood, Summary and Analysis of Navy Board of Investigation Official Report, 1951; "USS Mount Hood and crew lost in massive explosion," World War II Today; Dennis Donovan, "75 Years Ago Today; USS Mount Hood disintegrates in massive explosion—432 dead," Democratic Underground, Nov. 19, 2019, www.democraticunderground.com; Patrick Clancey, transcriber, "Selected documents relating to the loss of USS Mount Hood, " Dec. 14, 1944–Aug. 15, 1945, www.ibiblio.org; Michael W. Pockock, "Daily Event for November 10, 2007," *Maritime Quest*, 2007, www.maritimequest.com; "Service Member CM2 FLOYD F BERRY," DPAA, www.dpaa-mil.sites; Carl Zebrowski, "Your Number's Up!," *America in WWII*, Dec. 2007, www.americainwwii.com; "20,000 Leagues Under the Sea," Walt Dated World, www.waltdatedworld.com; Savannah Sanders, "Attraction Archaeology: 20,000 Leagues Under the Sea—Submarine Voyage," Touringplans, Oct. 26, 2019, www.touringplans.com; "In Memoriam: 'The Best Liquid Space Journey Ever,'" 20,000 Leagues Under the Sea—the Ride, www.20kride.com.

White Rabbit, White Rabbit
John Ashbery, "The Ecclesiast" in *Rivers and Mountains* (New York: Holt, Rhinehart and Winston, 1966, used by permission of George Borchardt, Inc.); Michael Shermer, "We Are the World," *Los Angeles Times*, Feb. 6, 2000; Ralph Lewis, "Why We Should Not Be Impressed by Eerie Coincidences," *Psychology Today*, Oct. 27, 2018; Walt Disney, director, *Alice's Wonderland* (Laugh-O-Gram Studio, 1923); Drew Taylor, "The Incredible True Story of Disney's Oswald the Lucky Rabbit," Sept. 5, 2020, www.collider.com; Jan Svankmajer, director, *Alice* (London: British Film Institute, 1988, 2011, DVD); Kate Carter, "The Curious World of Walter Potter—in Pictures," *The Guardian*, Sep. 13, 2013; Jacob Bews, "Broken Knobs and Glass Eyes: Jan Svankmajer's ALICE," *Luma Quarterly* 4, no. 14 (2018); Thomas Hardy, "The Voice," in *Satires of Circumstance*, 1914; Robert Horn, Bobhorn.us, www.bobhorn.us; Iva Cheung, "Introduction to Information Mapping," Nov. 9, 2012, www.ivacheung.com; Namahn, "Information MappingTM," www.mti-ca.com; Franco Berardi, *Breathing: Chaos and Poetry* (Los Angeles: Semiotext(e),

2018); Lars Muckli, quoted in Kevin Casey, "Theory of Predictive Brain as Important as Evolution—Prof. Lars Muckli," *Horizon*, May 29, 2018, www.ec.europa.eu; Carl Jung, *The Collected Works of C. G. Jung: Revised and Expanded Complete Digital Edition*, Gerhard Adler, translator, and R.F.C. Hull, editor (Princeton: Princeton University Press, 2023, originally published 1952); Albert Einstein, quoted in Bertrand D. Beltman, "Seriality vs Synchronicity: Kammerer vs Jung," *Psychology Today*, Mar. 25, 2017; Barbara Johnson, *The Critical Difference* (Baltimore: John Hopkins University Press, 1985); Radford, Benjamin, "Synchronicity: Definition & Meaning," *Live Science*, Feb. 4, 2014, www.livescience.com; ABBA, "I Have a Dream," on *Voulez-Vous*, vinyl, recorded March 1978–March 1979, Atlantic; "Inside The Flower World Of The Yaqui Deer Dance," Sinchi Foundation, Apr. 28, 2018, www.sinchi-foundation.com; Richard Kelly, dir., *Donnie Darko* (Pandora Cinema and Newmarket Films, 2001).

The Panharmonicon
John Coulthart, "A Trip to the Moon, 1901," Feuilleton, Aug. 17, 2013, www.johncoulthart.com; "A Trip to the Moon!" Coney—A Trip to Luna Park, www.coneybook.com; "Trip to the Moon!" Pan-American Exposition, Apr. 15, 2011, www.buffalopanamexpo. blogspot.com; Ralph Waldo Emerson, quoted in Roger Thompson, *Emerson and the History of Rhetoric* (Carbondale: Southern Illinois University Press, 2017).